READER'S DIGEST

GREAT BIOGRAPHIES

IN LARGE TYPE

CONTENTS

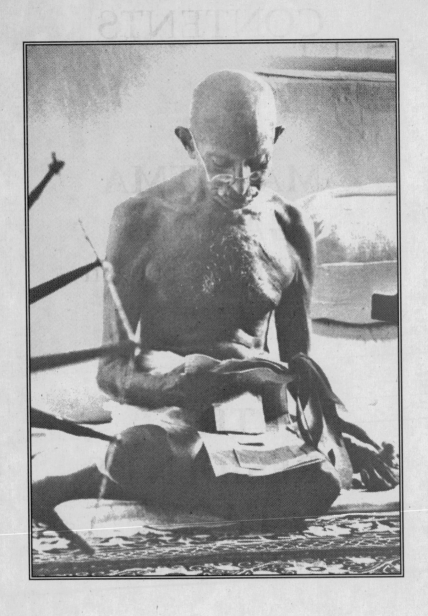

MAHATMA GANDHI

Vincent Sheean

As a little boy, he was too shy to speak to schoolmates. As a young lawyer, he was too shy to speak in court. Yet with a personal magnetism unequaled in this century, Mahatma Gandhi spoke for the world's downtrodden and, in so doing, changed the course of history.

What was the source of this amazing power over people? In part, it was Gandhi's great personal goodness; in part, an utter devotion to truth. Yet his life defies simple analysis, and in this biography the Mahatma is portrayed in all his loving and lusty, eccentric and dedicated, vigor.

I
Before the Battle

GANDHI's existence from the beginning of the present century was subjected to a more rigorous public attention than any other known to us. Everything he said and did was recorded and made public immediately. When he was unable to sleep, millions did not sleep; when he fasted, millions fasted; his slow gentle words were cut into wax and disseminated by radio to half a continent several times a day. He had the unparalleled misfortune to become a public saint in the twentieth century, canonized alive in the glare of flashlights and the relentless gaze of cameras. Only the most resolute attention to his immediate tasks, toilsome and endless, enabled him to ignore the world's fantasies and keep on going. He had to cultivate, with immense difficulty, a patience that was not originally in his nature, so as to endure the environment of his greatness. "The woes of Mahatmas," he said wryly, "are known to Mahatmas alone."

Yet the myth arose and was a true myth, changing the behavior of whole populations, altering the course of history and the fate of empire. Every fact in the case is known and yet their sum amounts to an unknown. We cannot satisfactorily explain the phenomenon of Gandhi. There is truth in a phrase Lord Halifax once used in talking of Gandhi to me: "He was a good little man." The kindly viceroy understood his antagonist.

Goodness might be, of course, the key. My own guess is that the Mahatma thought it was. The only claim he ever made for himself was to have lived the greater part of his life (almost fifty years) in the most literal effort to obey the teachings of the great Hindu poem *Bhagavad-Gita,* and of the Sermon on the Mount. This was essentially an ethical preoccupation, not metaphysical. He wanted to be good, to live the good life.

Goodness, just the same, cannot explain the power of the Gandhi myth. An identity of opposites haunts his entire story: his personality commanded even when he least desired to command; it is just when he was most humble that he was most powerful; and it was by his death that he achieved the ultimate purpose of his life. His death was, indeed, a singular fulfillment, coming at a time when he felt his own people drifting away from him, summoning them and all the world besides to one moment of salutary awe.

To what, then, are we to assign the phenomenon, to what shall we attribute the magic?

We come at last to the mystical explanation as the only one that fits the case. Though Gandhi was a very practical man who never discussed mysteries if he could help it, there is no doubt in my mind that the essence of his effective being, effective, that is, upon mankind, was and always will be a mystery.

MOHANDAS Karamchand Gandhi, the future Mahatma, was born on October 2, 1869, in Porbandar, a very small princely state in the west of India, above Bombay. He was the youngest son of Karamchand Gandhi, known as Kaba, who was prime minister of Porbandar, as his grandfather had been before him. Kaba Gandhi was also prime minister at various times of

Rajkot and Vankaner; but as these also were small states, the family never accumulated much wealth.

Kaba Gandhi was, by his son's recollection, an extremely able man in the practical sense, dealing with all the intricate clan questions and disputes that arose in his jurisdiction. He was also a great templegoer and reader of the *Bhagavad-Gita*. His family belonged to the merchant caste (bania) and to the Vaishnava side of the Hindu religion. The Vaishnava worship Vishnu, and various doctrines of sin, redemption, and divine grace have arisen among them. These ideas are not found in the other great school of Hinduism, which worships chiefly Shiva.

In Porbandar there were many members of the Jaina sect, who refuse to take any life under any circumstances. Jains were lifelong friends of the Gandhi family, and there is no doubt that all the Gandhis felt the influence of Jaina beliefs. Even so, Gandhi claimed to be an orthodox Hindu throughout his life, and although many of his interpretations disturbed the pundits, his claim to orthodoxy was never seriously contested.

His parents were devout indeed, and he always attributed the steadfastness of his behavior, in such matters as vows and disciplines, to the power of childhood examples. Most of all his mother and his nurse, pious Hindu women, exerted this power and were never forgotten. His mother, in obedience to some vow, sometimes fasted when the sun did not shine. The children used to watch anxiously on cloudy days for the first ray of sunshine, so as to run shouting to her that she could now eat.

But on the whole the boy was not remarkable; according to his own testimony, at any rate, he showed no great aptitude for study. He was extremely shy through his early years and used to run to and from school to avoid talking to anybody. One episode of his childhood seems to have made a great impression: it was a performance he saw by a traveling dramatic company of the play *Harishchandra*, based on a great story in the *Mahabharata* epic. It narrates the sufferings and ordeals of a king of old who sacrificed everything for the truth. Only a few days before his

death, Gandhi told me this story at considerable length. As a child he used to act
out *Harishchandra* to himself, he said,
"times without number." The idea of the
truth as supreme good was thus early
implanted, and was to become, in time, a
central idea governing almost every region
of his thought.

He was married, by family arrangement,
at the age of thirteen. His delight in his
bride, Kasturba, was extreme, and in later
years he regarded this premature sensual-
ity with sorrow and shame. In his maturity
he regarded child marriage as one of
the great evils of India. At that time
arranged matches between children pre-
viously unknown to each other were universal, and it has often been remarked that
happy marriages were usually the result. It
was so with Gandhi; although his conscience in later years troubled him, he
found Kasturba the solace of his life so
long as she lived.

The boy Gandhi was lustful, possessive,
and, as he tells us, unreasonably jealous.
The customs of the period allowed him to
meet Kasturba only at night during the
half year that she spent in the Gandhi

household; the other half year she spent with her parents. He wanted to teach her everything he knew, since she was illiterate, but "lustful love," as he calls it in his autobiography, gave him no time to do so, and Kasturba remained without instruction beyond simple letters in the local language, Gujarati.

He, of course, continued into high school, regardless of his marriage. He had his difficulties with study, but after his fourteenth year seems to have made much better progress, actually winning a prize or two. In his own account of these years he makes much of a regrettable episode involving an older boy who was addicted to eating meat and drinking wine in secret. The older boy, much stronger than Gandhi, held that India's troubles would be solved if the Hindus ate meat. He used to quote:

> *Behold the mighty Englishman:*
> *He rules the Indian small,*
> *Because being a meat eater,*
> *He is five cubits tall.*

Young Gandhi resolved to try meat eating. On the first occasion the two boys repaired to a lonely spot by the river and attacked a piece of goat's meat. It made Gandhi sick, and that night he had nightmares of a goat kicking in his stomach. Later on, Gandhi actually learned to like meat, but he finally gave it up because it led him into telling lies to his parents.

The same older friend also took young Gandhi to a brothel, but there his shyness protected him. He was never in his life unfaithful to Kasturba.

These misdemeanors culminated in a fling at cigarette smoking, for which Gandhi pilfered some coppers from home and also a chip of gold off his elder brother's armband. This time Gandhi's conscience revolted. He wrote out a confession for his father with a request to be punished and a pledge never to steal again. His father's tears remained in his memory ever afterward.

Such boyish misdeeds may seem slight in Western eyes. They had enormous importance in a pious Vaishnava family. The eating of flesh was regarded by the family with abhorrence. The cigarette smoking was not in itself important, but to steal coppers and tell lies in order to smoke was very bad.

The final sin, which he calls "my double shame," occurred when Kaba Gandhi died. Young Gandhi had been attending his father in his illness. One night he went from his father's sickbed to his own bedroom and woke Kasturba up. She was then pregnant, and his very keen remorse was partly due to this. While he was with Kasturba a servant knocked on the door to tell him that his father was dead. The child that was born to Kasturba lived only three or four days. Gandhi's sorrow over the whole episode was deep and remained with him for many years.

HINDU students seldom went overseas in the 1880's. To do so meant, as a rule, expulsion from one's caste, for association with foreigners, eating foreign food, and enduring various contaminations were unavoidable on such journeys. This is all thoroughly out-of-date now, and seems as remote to a modern Indian as the Middle Ages to us, but it was still the state of opinion in Gandhi's youth. Hindus who went abroad and came back to be barristers, doctors, or merchants were looked upon as contaminated and as lost to their own religion.

When Gandhi was young the shadow of an untouchable falling across any part of the body of a caste Hindu was a contamination and required of that Hindu a process of ceremonial purification. A caste Hindu could accept milk from an untouchable, but not water. Even among the untouchables one subdivision could perform one task but not another.

Gandhi was not afraid of any of this. When his family's old friend and adviser Mavji Dave, a Brahmin, advised study in England, the young Gandhi leaped at the prospect. His first idea was that he might study medicine, but the Brahmin adviser was against it. He wanted Gandhi to be a prime minister, like his father, uncle, and grandfather, and for this position a knowledge of the law was most important. As he was eighteen and still continuing his studies (whereas his brothers had forsaken them), Mavji Dave thought the youngest son should go to England and study law.

So he did. His devout mother dreaded what she had heard of women, wine, and meat eating in foreign lands. When she had the firm vow of her son to abstain from any of these habits, she reluctantly consented. The vows were never violated.

But on his arrival in Bombay he ran into more caste difficulties because of his decision to go overseas and was, in fact, solemnly read out of his own caste. He accepted this and remained outcaste to the end, though later as a "holy man" he was exempt from all caste rules. He never again observed any of the caste rules, such as wearing the "sacred thread," a symbolical cord, or the various ritualistic shavings.

He was only eighteen, a shy and eager Hindu boy with ears stuck out almost at right angles from his head, when he sailed from Bombay on September 4, 1888. He had new European clothing, and the necktie, which was to become a pleasure in London, was then a torture. He was acutely conscious of his short jacket and trousers. Shoes were unpleasant. But he was equipped for the great journey and alive with anxiety to learn.

All instruction in India above the first four classes of elementary school was conducted in English. Thus Gandhi had an acquaintance with English, but only as a school language. On the ship he had difficulty understanding what anybody, even the stewards, said to him. He was afraid of violating his vows against wine, women, and meat and consequently ate all his meals in his cabin, chiefly from food he had brought with him. He knew nothing of the knife or fork, and was too shy to speak to any fellow passenger. Moreover, he had saved his best clothing, which was white flannels, for his landing at Southampton (having worn black all the way to England) and consequently landed in the grisly English autumn weather most unsuitably dressed. He wept at night for a long time, strange and alone, uncertain of every step, fearful of violating his vows unwittingly or of committing some other Indian sin in an English climate.

The first problem was, of course, food. He could not eat the sodden substances that constituted the English idea of vegetables. He has recorded that in the early weeks he almost starved. His Indian student friends—who had found a boarding-house for him—thought him foolish in his insistence upon his vegetarian vow. But from one boardinghouse to another he took his weary way, never getting his fill, until one day he hit upon a vegetarian restaurant. He found in that restaurant a book called *A Plea for Vegetarianism*. He read it over and over and it converted him from being a vegetarian by religion and tradition into a vegetarian convinced of the rightness of his cause. As was to happen later in his long life, he had found something to support him in what he already believed. He had found "authority."

The vegetarian battle occupied a good deal of his time in London. His Indian friends thought it embarrassing of him to insist on food contrary to the surrounding customs. He tried, in his tenderhearted way, to make it up to them by being conformable to other English customs: he bought evening clothes, took dancing lessons, tried to learn the violin, and made in general an attempt to "play the English gentleman," as he said. After several months he surrendered all that, suddenly and completely, to devote himself to his studies for the bar.

The photographs of Gandhi taken at

19

this age are extremely funny—the little Hindu boy with ears at right angles, the piercing eyes and meager face, the stiff high collar and pomaded hair. He was probably conscious even then of how funny the whole enterprise was. Indeed, laughter, of a gentle and innocent kind, usually at his own expense, was a necessity to him.

His three years in England were fruitful in many ways. After his first agonies were over he learned how to enjoy life and work on English terms. Vegetarianism was a help in unexpected ways: he joined the Vegetarian Society, became a member of its executive committee, and had his first experience in organization, though shyness made him unable to speak at meetings. With the vegetarians he formed friendships, just as he did among the students.

Meanwhile he studied. Admission to the bar was easy enough: the examinations were simple, and the "call to the bar" was automatic if the student had "kept terms" (twelve of them), equivalent to about three years. Gandhi therefore made up his mind to work in addition for the London matriculation examination, and spent a whole year on it, studying, among other subjects, Latin. The unnecessary hard work, useful in many respects later on, was characteristic of Gandhi even at that age.

Also it was in England that he read for the first time both the *Bhagavad-Gita* and the New Testament of the Bible.

It seems a little odd that Gandhi should not have known the *Gita* in either Sanskrit or his native Gujarati, for it must have been familiar to his father in both languages. He read it first with two English friends in the English metrical translation of Sir Edwin Arnold *(The Song Celestial)*. He found in the *Gita* a kind of crystallization of his characteristic beliefs, those upon which his own life struggle was based. He was only twenty at the time, but already his own effort was directed toward the suppression of desire, appetite, and "attachment." The *Gita* reinforced his nature and gradually became the law of his life.

The New Testament, in particular the Sermon on the Mount, had a similar effect, less powerful perhaps because it was Christian rather than Hindu; but during the years to come it was to entwine itself into all of Gandhi's thought.

These discoveries were not followed by any great preoccupation with religious thought, for by this time the young man was actively studying for the bar. Most students in those days hardly bothered to read the textbooks. Instead they studied, and mostly in the last few weeks, notes on previous examinations. Gandhi determined to read everything; and for Roman law he elected to read Justinian in Latin. Much of what he was to do in South Africa in the years to come was to depend on the knowledge he then acquired of Roman law, on which Dutch law was based. He remembered himself as a very limited and shy young man, yet he was actually better prepared for the bar examination than most of his English fellow students. He passed his examinations, was called to the bar on June 10, 1891, enrolled in the High Court on the 11th, and sailed for India the next day.

IN INDIA for the next two years Gandhi was, by his own account, a failure. On his first day home he learned that his mother had died, which was a blow even worse than his father's death.

And, of course, his knowledge of English and Roman law, however thorough, did not make up for a total ignorance of Indian law. He had to start an entire new set of studies, meanwhile establishing himself as a barrister. In the very first case he obtained in Bombay, Gandhi found himself unable to utter a word. He got up to cross-examine a witness and, facing the court, came near to fainting. He sat down and told his client's agent that he would have to give up the case, that another barrister should be engaged. It was his first and last appearance as a barrister in India.

Bombay, with high prices and living standards, was not for a barrister who was too shy to speak in court. Gandhi went home to Rajkot to earn a living by making out briefs for other lawyers, drafting applications, and the like. This period of his life was not happy. The habit of giving commissions here and there, and of using influence, intrigue, and petty politics in carrying out the business of the law, was repugnant to him, so that he was more than ready when a chance came to leave it all.

The chance came from South Africa, where a considerable number of Indians were established in business and a larger number had been brought in as contract labor. There a Moslem Indian firm called Daba Abdullah and Co. had a claim for some forty thousand pounds which had been dragging through the courts for years. The proposal was that young Gandhi should go to South Africa for a year to advise on the conduct of this lawsuit, as well as on other matters. He would receive expenses and one hundred and five pounds in cash.

It was not the most brilliant offer in the world, but Gandhi was making no headway in India. The idea of going to South Africa, of which he knew nothing, appealed to him, even though he would have to leave his family. Obviously Gandhi, then twenty-four, could have had no idea that South Africa would in the next period of his existence alter everything for him, form his destiny in a new direction, and return him to India, eventually, as a national hero and a "Mahatma."

Discovery in South Africa

THE South Africa to which Gandhi went in 1893 consisted of four units: Natal, the Orange Free State, the Transvaal, and the Cape Colony. Only the last bore a distinctly English imprint. At that time the Orange Free State and the Transvaal were Boer republics, with Dutch (in the African version) as their official language. Natal, with a very mixed population, had been annexed to the British crown in 1843, but except for Durban, its chief city, it had no great number of English settlers.

The restless spirits of many adventurers were abroad, and it was a brawling time. The great men of the period included Paul Kruger in the Transvaal (president) and Cecil Rhodes in the Cape (prime minister). Men of sense were all aware that someday the destiny of the region would demand its union for the simplest economic reasons, yet racial and linguistic antipathies were still so powerful that reason could scarcely be heard.

The Boers hated the English with a passion; they felt that all South Africa was theirs and that the English were arrogant interlopers. Now bitterly entrenched in the Transvaal and the Orange Free State, they were herdsmen and farmers, a race of Dutch cowboys landlocked in their domain and resentful of any intruder. An explosion was inevitable because the discovery of gold and diamonds some years before had brought a flood of greedy men into the Boer republics from all over the earth. These *uitlanders,* as the Boers called them, were hated and discriminated against by every means possible and had no votes or voices in government. Indeed the whole of South Africa in 1893 seethed with hatreds and resentments which made it anything but an abode of peace, even for the Europeans. Small wonder, then, that non-Europeans lived in terror.

The South African nomenclature in regard to races was as follows: "European" meant any person of the white race; "native" meant an African; "colored" meant a person of mixed race; "Asiatic" meant a person whose racial origins could be traced to Asia—in practice this meant Indians. Any and all of these four divisions might be native to the country, but the divisions still remained fixed. When Gandhi went there, large numbers of the "European" and "Asiatic" persons were relative newcomers, and the "colored" (mixed) population, later so important, was then much smaller.

As an intelligent and educated young man Gandhi must have been aware of the struggles between Europeans, or of the Europeans against the natives of the country. But these affected him very little. Gandhi behaved like a specific instrument of a specific purpose from the beginning to the end of his life. In Africa he lived for the Indians and thought only of the Indians. The wild struggle of the others concerned him only as it affected the lives of his own people.

Of the plight of his own people in Africa he knew nothing at all when he sailed from Bombay. It took six weeks to get to Durban, with stops at various ports. The ship was crowded, and Gandhi could get a berth only in the captain's cabin, by that officer's kindness. The captain taught him chess, and the fellow passengers were friendly. It was not until he got off the ship at Durban, to be met by Abdullah Sheth, his new employer, that he noticed a difference in the manner of Europeans toward Indians.

Abdullah Sheth, a rich but illiterate Mohammedan merchant, was at first uncertain how to deal with Gandhi. Nobody like Gandhi—that is, no educated Indian barrister wearing English clothes—had ever appeared in Natal before. The Indian merchants in South Africa were prosperous, but had made their own way in a new country by cunning and acumen; they cared little for "hygiene and sanitation"; they knew hardly any English; they accepted a great many disabilities and indignities from the European overlords. Indians were known among the Europeans as "coolies," and Gandhi—the only Indian barrister in South Africa—soon became known as "the coolie barrister."

All this he learned quickly, in considerable consternation. Abdullah Sheth was his tutor and seems to have warmed to the stranger after a few days. Gandhi learned, for example, that the well-to-do Indian merchants and their staffs, mostly Moslems, had little to do with the much larger population of Indian workers who had been brought to South Africa under "indenture"—that is, as contract laborers for a period of five years. Illiterate, depressed, these workers were mostly from southern India. They were much in Gandhi's thoughts, but he had no contact with them for some time: his task was to work on a lawsuit for the firm of Abdullah Sheth.

The lawsuit was for a large sum and was highly complicated. Gandhi had to go through some severe study, involving a self-given course in bookkeeping, before he could understand it. Quite early he told his employer that he would try to settle it out of court. In all his professional career most of his cases were so settled. This was advisable because of the great saving in fees, he thought, but also because the suit was between relatives who had been and ought to be friends.

Three days after he had landed in Durban, his employer took him to a magistrate's court to see how it worked. Gandhi in those days wore his English clothes, but with an Indian turban. Decorum requires that the turban be kept on indoors or out.

The English custom of removing the hat on entering a house or courtroom is thus directly at variance with Indian proprieties. Gandhi entered the court with his turban on. Eventually the magistrate asked him to remove the turban; he refused and left the courtroom.

There was quite a little row about this incident; Gandhi wrote to the papers defending his right to wear an Indian turban at all times, and a controversy arose which made him known in Natal sooner than he might have been otherwise. But in this dilemma his self-respect as an Indian was, he felt, at stake.

When he felt that he understood the lawsuit, Gandhi notified Abdullah Sheth that he was ready to go to Pretoria, the capital of the Transvaal, where the case was to be tried. Abdullah was anxious; the journey was long; still the young barrister set forth in the train with a first-class ticket.

When the train reached Maritzburg, the capital of Natal, a white passenger saw him in the first-class compartment and summoned railroad officials. Gandhi was ordered to go into the van compartment, where Indians usually traveled. He refused and was forcibly removed from the first-class compartment. Because he refused on principle to travel in any other manner, he sat in the railway station at Maritzburg all night long in the bitter cold. In the morning he sent telegrams to the railway management and to Abdullah Sheth. When the next evening's train arrived, a sleeping berth had been reserved for him, and he accepted it.

Gandhi arrived the next morning at Charlestown, the end of the railway, where he had to take a stagecoach to Johannesburg, his next major stop on the way to Pretoria. At first the coach agent wanted to refuse him a passage, but on Gandhi's insistence allowed him to come along on the box outside with the coachman. The young barrister "pocketed the insult," as he said, but later on when the coach agent wanted to come out for air and told Gandhi to sit on the footboard so that he (the agent) could sit by the coachman and smoke, Gandhi refused. The man thereupon proceeded to beat him. The passengers protested in vain.

At Johannesburg there was a fresh incident: he could not be admitted to the Grand National Hotel. Indian merchant friends explained to him that no Indian could stay in any hotel in the Dutch Transvaal, which was much worse than English Natal, and that on his journey to Pretoria on the following day he would be obliged to travel third class.

Gandhi was as gently obstinate then as ever afterward. He wrote to the stationmaster of Johannesburg and stated his intention, then proceeded to buy a first-class ticket. The stationmaster, a Dutchman from Holland, sold the ticket, but asked Gandhi not to involve him in any trouble that might result. It was a lucky day, apparently; for when the guard on the train, taking tickets, ordered Gandhi to leave the first class, the only fellow passenger in the compartment, an Englishman, would not allow Gandhi to be evicted.

In Pretoria there was nobody to meet the traveler. He stood in the dimly lighted station and wondered what to do. Providentially a Black American befriended him and took him to Johnston's Family

Hotel, where Mr. Johnston, an American, agreed to give him a room if he was willing to eat his dinner there rather than in the dining room. Gandhi took the room; he was learning fast. Then Mr. Johnston found that his European customers were quite willing to eat in the same room with Gandhi, and he brought Gandhi downstairs with apologies.

The next day Abdullah Sheth's attorney, Mr. A. W. Baker, found board and lodging for Gandhi in the house of a poor woman willing to put up with the ignominy of an Indian guest for thirty-five shillings a week.

It seems to have been Baker's desire to convert Gandhi to Christianity. Baker was deeply religious; he had built a church in Pretoria at his own expense, and he had a daily prayer meeting to which he invited Gandhi at once. But Christianity was not really for Gandhi, then or afterward, and indeed, the result of some months of association with devout Christians, who gave him books to read and prayed for his conversion, was to turn him back to his own Hindu religion with renewed interest.

Gandhi, so earnest and hardworking, had never before found himself able to study religious literature or think what it was that he did believe. Now other lawyers were working on the Abdullah-Tyeb lawsuit, and his services were not, for the moment, required. Thus he found, originally through Christian influences but afterward through Mohammedanism and Hinduism, a whole world of thought congenial to him and opening up vistas toward what was to be, at last, his own religion, his own kind of universalist Hinduism.

He wished, during this period of waiting for work, to do what he could about the status of Indians in the Transvaal. Going to Tyeb Sheth, the person against whom his lawsuit was intended, he made friends, a characteristic move on his part. With his help Gandhi called a meeting of all the Indians in the Transvaal capital. It was held in the house of a leading Moslem merchant, and Gandhi made his first speech.

That, too, was characteristic: he wanted to help the Indians, but he began by telling them what they themselves should do. His most earnest plea was made for truthfulness in business, for many of the Indian merchants regarded truth as having little place in business. He went on to urge them to reform in respect to hygiene and sanitation. He asked them to obliterate all the distinctions of religion and race brought over from India (Hindu, Moslem, Parsee, Christian, Punjabi, and the like). And he suggested the formation of a permanent association to defend the rights of the Indians before the authorities.

Considerable interest was aroused; and the association was formed. Gandhi, after studying railway regulations, wrote in the association's name to the Transvaal railway authorities and reminded them that even under their own rules the Indians were entitled to travel in any class for which they bought a ticket. The authorities replied that first and second class would henceforth be open to Indians who were "properly dressed"—a matter of interpretation for the ticket seller.

Thus began, in 1893, and on the smallest scale, the mission of Mahatma Gandhi. The Indians were to discipline themselves, tell the truth, be clean, learn English, forget their internal differences—all this so as to achieve self-respect and set themselves free. This was pretty much what Gandhi was to ask of them for the next fifty-odd years. It was what he was soon to call "public work," a kind of service for which he would never accept any emolument. He did not think of this as political but as an effort for the general welfare of the Indians, beginning, as was Gandhi's way, with the Indians themselves.

There were, as he was learning every day, endless disabilities, humiliations, and hardships for the Indians of the Transvaal and the Orange Free State. Indians were actually excluded from the Free State, except in designated menial jobs. In the Transvaal they had no vote and could not own land except in special "locations." They had to pay a three-pound poll tax even to enter the Transvaal. They could not go out at night after nine without a special permit, and they could not walk on the public footpaths, but must take to the road with the beasts. On one occasion Gandhi was assaulted by a policeman somewhere near President Kruger's house for walking on the footpath.

Gandhi's growing concern over the predicament of the Indians was checked for a while: he now had to deal with the lawsuit between Abdullah Sheth and his cousin Tyeb Sheth. Patiently he worked on Tyeb Sheth, the friendly enemy, and upon the various counsel, until he got their consent to the appointment of an arbitrator; the case was argued, and Gandhi's client won. It was then his self-appointed task to persuade Abdullah, his employer, to allow payment of the claim in installments, and to persuade the proud Tyeb Sheth to agree. He said that if the whole sum had been exacted at once, Tyeb would have been bankrupt. He had his way, and the peaceful outcome was a solace to both sides.

Gandhi's year was up, and he prepared to go home after the case was settled. It had been a momentous year not only in his discoveries, but also in the arousing of his religious consciousness. He had read Tolstoy's *The Kingdom of God Is Within You*, which penetrated his being as none of the arguments of orthodox Christianity had done. Tolstoy's argument (that governments, police, armies, and so on would be unnecessary if men would live by the Sermon on the Mount) was in harmony with Gandhi's natural feeling. My belief is that Gandhi's early enthusiasm for the Tolstoy doctrine was later somewhat modified. He said to me, two days before he died: "Mind you, no ordinary government can get along without the use of force."

For the youth in South Africa, however, some of the blessings of experience (if blessings they be) were yet to come. He went back to Durban, where Abdullah Sheth arranged an all-day farewell for him, with a good many of the Indians of Durban present. In the course of the party, quite by chance, Gandhi saw a newspaper paragraph about the Natal legislature's Indian Franchise Bill. It was a bill withdrawing the right to vote from Indians. Gandhi, in amazement, asked if his Indian friends of Durban had done nothing about it. They had not. They were more or less reconciled to their status. He tried to tell them the seriousness of their situation if they lost the franchise. Their answer was a touching clamor for him to stay with them and tell them what to do.

Gandhi accepted for one month, on condition that they find the funds for a struggle against the Franchise Bill. He himself would accept no payment, but the costs of printing, law consultations, and travel must be paid; moreover, one man could not do all the work; there must be volunteers. He resolved to claim volunteers for the work from among young Indians born in South Africa who were for the most part Christians and educated and who did not associate much with the Moslem and Hindu Indians; and he actually succeeded in getting a good number of them to volunteer.

The first step was a telegraphed request to the speaker of the legislature to delay further debate on the Franchise Bill until the Indians could be heard. Then there was the drafting and copying out of the petition itself. The speaker gave them only two days and Gandhi with his volunteers worked night as well as day. When the two days were up, the Indian petition was presented in the legislature and discussed; it appeared in the press; it created a stir; but the Franchise Bill was passed.

This failure, however, only encouraged

those involved to further effort. The conflicting groups of Durban Indians had come together as one group for the first time. They now decided on a much bigger undertaking, a petition to London, to the secretary of state for the colonies (Lord Ripon), which would be signed by as many as possible of the Indians of Natal.

Natal was huge and the villages were widely scattered but ten thousand signatures were obtained in two weeks. One thousand copies were distributed in India, England, and elsewhere; the press was kept fully informed; both *The Times* in London and the *Times of India* (Bombay) supported the Indian claim to the vote. This was the first real acquaintance of England and India with the questions arising out of racial prejudice in South Africa.

Aside from Indian unity, organization, and communal effort, all new in South Africa, the brief campaign brought out a number of promises for the future. For example, the young men born in South Africa, once alienated from the other Indians, had come out for Gandhi. This may initially have been because of his London English, his London clothes, the fact that he was a barrister and a credit to the community; but his powers of gentle persistent persuasion must have come into play already.

After the excitement of the month past, it proved impossible for Gandhi to leave Natal. The Indians of Durban would not let him go. Too many people and things depended upon him. As he would not accept payment for public work, the merchants banded together and guaranteed him enough work as a lawyer to stay another year. It was his desire, for quite impersonal reasons, to live in a manner befitting a London barrister, to travel first class, and to compel respect; to do this he needed three hundred pounds a year, and the sum was provided.

The Law Society, made up entirely of Europeans, opposed his admission as an advocate of the Supreme Court of Natal. The chief justice declared that the law did not distinguish between "colored" and white people, and admitted Gandhi at once. As soon as he had done so, the chief justice said: "You must now take off your turban, Mr. Gandhi." And this time Gandhi yielded.

He proceeded at once to form a permanent organization among the Indians and decided to call it the Natal Indian Congress, a controversial name because the Indian National Congress, at home in India, had already begun to irk conservative and imperialist opinion, and such nationalism as existed in India was already firmly associated with the word "Congress."

There was no difficulty in obtaining the necessary subscriptions, but those who had signed for contributions were not always prompt in paying, and a good part of the work of Gandhi and his volunteers had to be wasted on collection of sums due. However, between two lifelong principles of his—no debts and no surplus—he so built the Natal Indian Congress that it was steadily solvent for at least twenty years. Accounts were kept with the greatest care. "Without properly kept accounts," Gandhi said, "it is impossible to maintain truth in its pristine purity."

Meetings of the Congress were held regularly, and Gandhi taught the members the rules of procedure. A library, a debating society, a special subsidiary body to bring together the educated young men born in South Africa—all were quickly brought into being. The effort to state the case for the Indians naturally fell principally upon Gandhi, and he produced at this time two pamphlets for the Congress: *An Appeal to Every Briton in South Africa* and *The Indian Franchise—An Appeal*. Both evoked many expressions of sympathy not only in South Africa, but in England and India. The question was ceasing to be local and becoming what it really was in fact, both general and fundamental.

At this stage of development Gandhi came into contact with the larger mass of Indians in South Africa, the indentured laborers. His work had thrown him entirely with the prosperous merchants and their staffs, but what he had already done was known throughout the Indian population.

One day a Tamil workman, trembling and weeping, appeared in his office. His mouth was bleeding and two front teeth had been knocked out. He held his turban in his hand deferentially—Mr. Gandhi was a barrister!—and poured forth his story. The man had been severely beaten by his master, a well-known European. Gandhi sent him to a doctor for a certificate of the injuries, and then took him to a magistrate, who issued a summons for the offending master.

The law governing indentured laborers was severe: a man could not leave his employment without risking criminal proceedings and imprisonment. It was akin to slavery in that the man had no freedom of action. Gandhi wanted the victim released from that particular indenture. He secured the agreement of the European master (who by that time was probably rather frightened) and then went to the protector of indentured laborers, a public official, who released the man to a new master Gandhi found.

The victim in the case was called Balasundaram, a name Gandhi never forgot. Balasundaram played a brief but decisive part in history because he acted, all unwittingly, as the key to Gandhi's greater mission.

The episode became legend overnight; there was a man, actually an Indian sahib, a barrister, a man of the great, who did not disdain to care about a poor coolie. The story went rapidly to southern India, and succeeding waves of Indian immigrants were told, even before they left India, that Gandhi was their friend. As for Natal itself, the indentured laborers adopted him and streamed through his office from then onward. Gandhi's immense popularity in southern India, which actually preceded his full recognition in the north, came originally from the story of Balasundaram.

He was himself very deeply moved. Not only the suffering of the laborer, but the humility of the man—the fact that he held his headgear in his hand—struck deep into Gandhi's heart. He felt, as before, that those who had no help elsewhere were the people he most desired to help. The pathos of the headgear struck him more particularly because he had gone through such a series of incidents concerned with his own. The humiliation to which he had objected was here accepted as natural by the stricken man, the defenseless. Gandhi had asked him at once to resume his scarf, and Balasundaram had done so hesitantly, but with a glow of pleasure. Such small things were Gandhi's secret power, more than his external skills in law or action. There was no indentured laborer in Natal who did not know all about this within a few days.

As HE conducted the campaign of the Natal Indian Congress and simultaneously earned his living at the bar, Gandhi continued to pursue his aroused religious interests. He began to study his own religion more carefully than ever before. His friend Raychandra in Bombay was of great use, corresponding with him during this period (1893–1896) and afterward. Under his counsel Gandhi read some of the Hindu scriptures, particularly the *Upanishads*. At the same time he read more books on India and on Islamic subjects, and he read those polemical works which Tolstoy had been pouring out. Oddly enough he never discovered, throughout his life, how much Tolstoy was a literary phenomenon; Gandhi never found out that the man who made the preachment could not himself obey it. If a man said that the Sermon on the Mount was the one single rule, Gandhi believed that to this man it was the one single rule. He seems always to have assumed the total sincerity of others as he extended the areas of literal sincerity in himself. Thus he came in the end to the essential error of all great souls: "I am a creature of nothing, devoid of special faculties for achievement, and yet I can do it, therefore why can all others not do it? What I, poor limited creature, can do must be much easier for others, or at least as easy." This was his greatest fallacy, and the measure of his failure in the world. He thought all others could do what he did. The error puts him with Socrates, the Lord Gautama Buddha, and the Lord Jesus of Nazareth. All of them believed that other men could do what they did. They were wrong, and so was Gandhi.

He had now completed three years in South Africa, and it was quite apparent that he would have to stay a long time if he hoped to bring to any good result the work that he had initiated. He made a compact with his friends in Durban: they would permit him to go home to India to collect his family and his possessions. Picking two devoted volunteers to run the Natal Indian Congress during his absence, he set sail for Bombay.

III
Satyagraha

ON THE way to India, Gandhi quite characteristically studied two Indian languages, Tamil and Urdu, with British officers of the ship. At all stages of his life British people instinctively liked him, made friends with him, helped him. He reciprocated the feeling, and it may truthfully be said that the British never had a more loyal and loving rebel than Gandhi in all their history.

In India he did his best to make known the questions that now interested him. He began by writing a pamphlet on the Indians in South Africa; it had a green cover and was known as the Green Pamphlet. It made a great stir and was commented upon editorially by newspapers in both India and England. In his own native place, Rajkot, he sent out these pamphlets (one thousand of them) by means of volunteers, and in this case he made use of small children. It was the first time he had thought of asking children to do this kind of work. Later on he was to rely upon them repeatedly for such enterprises; they were eager, happy to do it, and felt themselves made important by trying.

At this moment plague broke out in Bombay, and Gandhi volunteered his services, as usual, thus making his first acquaintance with sanitary arrangements in Indian houses. He found that the houses of the well-to-do were less sanitary than those of the very poor, and in particular of the untouchables, whom he saw now for the first time in their own homes.

He also met friends who would be useful thereafter, especially in Bombay—Sir Pherozeshah Mehta, the great Bombay lawyer, and Gopal Krishna Gokhale, the head of the Indian National Congress, who had the most influence upon him. Gokhale, who welcomed him as a son, was by all accounts a very remarkable man. The instinctive communication of the two men, wide apart in age, was immediate, and Gandhi ever afterward referred to Gokhale as his "political guru," his master in all those matters which had to do with public work.

There was a visit to Madras: wild enthusiasm. Gandhi was the protector of the slave laborers of South Africa, most of whom had come from the province of Madras. He could not speak to these people in their own language, and was obliged to use English, but, said he, "What barrier is there that love cannot break?"

In Bengal it was different: Gandhi had to wait for hours to see important editors or persons who could help the Indians of South Africa. Scarcely any Bengalis had gone to South Africa, so that the question seemed very remote. As usual, Gandhi found an Englishman (Mr. Saunders, editor of *The Englishman*) who espoused his cause and gave him office room and space in the newspaper for presenting his case. But his six months' leave came to an end; and collecting his wife, two sons, and a nephew, he set sail in December 1896 to return to South Africa.

Gandhi tells us how he dressed his wife and children on this journey. He wanted to compel the Europeans to respect Indians as Indians. Though he cared little or nothing about himself, he regarded himself as representative of the community. His wife and children could not really dress as Europeans, but they could dress as Parsees, which was the nearest thing in India to European. This meant coat, trousers, and shoes for the boys, a Parsee sari and shoes and stockings for poor Kasturba. None of them had ever worn shoes before, and it was a great pain: their toes got sore and the stockings smelled of perspiration, offensive to them. Gandhi also made them use a knife and fork, a custom which seemed an abomination to Indians who wished to eat with clean hands.

At Durban the boat was delayed for quarantine: there had been cholera in Bombay. This was comprehensible, of course, but during the five extra days ordered by the doctors quite different themes began to be heard. It was not merely cholera; it seemed that Mr. Gandhi was the point at issue.

The Natal white people had made up their minds that Gandhi was a troublemaker and should not be permitted to land. They wanted him and all the persons on his ship and on another ship that anchored at the same time, also full of Indians, to return to India at once. An ultimatum was served on the passengers at Christmas: they would return to India or run the risk of death. But all stuck to their right to land at Port Natal—a matter of principle in which Gandhi had instructed them.

When there was no further legal excuse for keeping the ships outside, they were authorized to enter the harbor and disembark their passengers. One of the Abdullah lawyers told Gandhi that it would be best for Mrs. Gandhi and the children to disembark, take a carriage, and go straight to the house of their Indian friend (Rustomji) with whom they were supposed to lodge. Gandhi himself should take his chances on foot. Gandhi agreed, and his wife and children were driven without incident to Rustomji's house. Then Gandhi got off the boat with the lawyer and walked a few feet, upon which some rowdy youths started shouting: "Gandhi! Gandhi!"

A crowd quickly assembled; Gandhi was showered with stones, brickbats, and eggs. His turban was torn off, and he was severely beaten and kicked by the mob. Then an English person saved him—Mrs. Alexander, the wife of the superintendent of police. She knew Gandhi, and seeing the little man beaten against an iron railing where he was clinging, half-conscious, she calmly stood beside him and opened up her umbrella between the mob and Gandhi and herself. The umbrella was strictly symbolic, but everybody in the mob knew Mrs. Alexander and nobody dared attack her. Gandhi was safe. Alexander, the police superintendent, arrived and was able to get him off to Rustomji's house under guard. There again a mob formed with the plain intention of lynching him. This time Alexander got him out of the house by the back way, disguised as a police constable.

For two or three days thereafter Gandhi was kept in the police station under guard. Then the white people found that none of the accusations against him were true. They had thought he had brought over all the Indians on both the ships; but he had had nothing to do with their migration. They had also blamed him for a very misleading article, sent out by Reuters from

India, which distorted what he had said of conditions in Natal. When all this was cleared up, a sense of justice prevailed, and Gandhi was more esteemed than ever among the Natal whites. He himself believed that his subsequent work was aided by the episode.

GANDHI was at a very curious transition just at the end of the nineteenth century. He was very active sexually (two of his sons were born in South Africa, and one he delivered himself because the doctor was late). Yet he had begun to feel that he could not fulfill his appointed tasks unless he abstained totally from sexual intercourse. This idea, very deep in Hinduism, is embodied in the word *brahmacharya,* "the learning of God," by which is meant self-control and an abnegation of sensual appetite. It took Gandhi many years to achieve; he did not feel strong enough to take the final vow until 1906.

Furthermore, at this time his ideas of his public duty were evolving slowly. His loyalty to the British raj was intense and was to remain so until the 1920s. When the Boer War came, Gandhi felt sympa-

54

thy for the Boers, but an overruling loyalty to England. Thus he organized and led an Indian medical corps (over one thousand men), which served with distinction, and received the thanks of the highest authorities.

Medical service was, as a matter of fact, congenial to Gandhi and remained one of his preoccupations. He gave two hours a day to a free hospital in which many poor Indians were treated, and in later years was quite capable of keeping a cabinet or a whole empire waiting while he took care of a leper. Applying bandages, giving enemas, caring for the sick in every way imaginable, were parts of what he felt to be his job.

After the Boer War was over, Gandhi again returned to India. Many expensive farewell presents were bestowed upon him and he resolved to put them into a bank as a trust fund to support public work for the Indians in case of need. Kasturba was very hard to persuade on this count, but as he had the children on his side he eventually won.

In India his first interest was to attend the 1901 meeting of the Indian National

Congress at Calcutta. Its purposes were social and political: it was to canalize the rising nationalism of the Indians, both Hindu and Moslem, into ways of moderation and legality. It was to do what it could for the general welfare and to express, as much as possible, the wishes of the country. As illiteracy was then very widespread (well above the ninety percent registered in later years), the inevitable result was that the Congress became an assembly of middle-class intellectuals, lawyers, merchants, and the like, who spoke for India in a notably timid and circumspect manner. Even so, it was the only national association that could speak for India at all, and Gandhi felt it to be the "life blood" of the country.

His main purpose was to present a resolution in support of the Indians of South Africa. But he had two or three days first to appreciate the difficulties of a vast meeting of his fellow countrymen. He did clerical work as a volunteer and kept his eyes and ears open. When it came time to read his own resolution, it was late; few persons listened; the resolution went through without a dissenting vote because Gokhale, the great man of the Congress, had approved it.

After the Congress meeting, Gandhi spent a month as Gokhale's guest in Calcutta, where he met many eminent persons to whom he could preach his gospel of help for the Indians of South Africa. He was horrified by the blood sacrifices at the Temple of Kali. The sheep or the lamb, he felt, was life even as the human being was life. He did his best to bring blood sacrifice to an end in India.

Finally he said his farewells to Gokhale and started for Bombay. For the first time, he traveled third class in order to study the conditions of the Indian poor. Now, too, for the first time, he adopted ordinary Indian clothing—the shirt and dhoti, or wrapped skirt. Indian third class is incredibly dirty, overcrowded, and unsanitary. Gandhi recorded his shock at the conditions he found. From then on, whenever he was in India, he tried to travel third class, partly to study the conditions there and partly as a protest against them. In later years the governmental authorities went to great lengths to ensure cleanliness and decorum on any third-class carriage that Gandhi used.

Back in Bombay he tried to return to the bar, but the Indians of South Africa sent an urgent cablegram: Joseph Chamberlain was coming to South Africa; Gandhi must "return immediately." This time he took with him four or five young men, including his second cousin Maganlal Gandhi, who was to prove one of the most useful lieutenants in the great struggle now about to begin.

Gandhi arrived in Durban just in time to draw up a paper seeking protection of Indian rights and present it. Chamberlain had come to Africa to get a big monetary gift and to reconcile, if possible, the lately embattled British and Boers. He had short shrift for the Indians, declared that the government in London could not control the self-governing colonies, and advised the Indians to "placate" the Europeans if they wished to live in Africa at all.

From Natal it was necessary for Gandhi to go immediately to the Transvaal, where Chamberlain was next due. The Transvaal, smarting under defeat, was a far rougher and tougher country for an Indian than Natal. What he saw in the Transvaal made him feel that the Indians there needed him far more than did the Indians of Natal. He resolved to stay and to set up as a barrister in Johannesburg. To his surprise the Law Society of the Transvaal made no objection (he was the only Indian).

His first task was to expose the shameless way in which Indians were being fleeced for reentry permits. Many had left the Transvaal during the war; to come back they were compelled to pay large sums, up to one hundred pounds each, for the permit. Gandhi patiently collected evidence of bribery. A trial ensued in which the guilty officers were acquitted by a jury, but were so thoroughly exposed that the abuses came to an end and the officers were dismissed from their employ. Gandhi's prestige as the Indians' protector rose to new levels.

Gradually Gandhi's system of living began to be patriarchal, even though he was in fact only in his early thirties. He took his office clerks to live with him, along with the young men he had brought from India and also, from time to time, various Englishmen and other Europeans. He was simplifying his existence in every way possible, materially speaking, and his guests had to conform to the rules of the house. He was up every morning at six, and he embarked on the diet of fruit and nuts which sustained him for a good many years thereafter. His religious interests were deepening, and he never ceased to read books on Hinduism at this time.

The next step was the foundation in 1904 of a weekly journal, *Indian Opinion*, in which for the next ten years Gandhi poured out his thought and feeling on subjects of interest to the Indian community. He was convinced that his success in South Africa—and *satyagraha*, itself, voluntary sacrifice—became possible only through the existence of this newspaper.

His immediate task in public work was the defense of the poor Indians, most of them indentured laborers who had served out their time, against dispossession of their land. The "coolie location," outside Johannesburg, was dirty and neglected, and perceiving its dangers to general health, the municipality proceeded to destroy the location. Gandhi was the lawyer for practically every Indian thus dispossessed. He tried some seventy cases and lost only one.

While he was in the midst of this litigation, there came an outbreak of black plague—pneumonic plague, worse than bubonic. Twenty-three Indians came down with the plague in one evening. Gandhi moved into the district at once, taking with him four Indian boys who worked in his office.

On the next day the municipality of Johannesburg gave him an empty warehouse as a hospital. The municipal nurse, a woman sent in on the second day, was not allowed by Gandhi to touch the patients for fear of giving her the contagion. Yet she got it a day or so later and died in a short time. Neither Gandhi nor his four assistants, who were in close contact with the patients, suffered any consequences. This strange immunity was to be repeated on numerous occasions throughout his life, when he nursed patients in cholera, leprosy, and other eminently contagious diseases.

Now the Johannesburg authorities decided that the coolie location, as a plague danger, would have to be burned to the ground. The Indian population was to be moved to tents in the great plain about thirteen miles away. Gandhi gave the municipality his full support in this project. The poor Indians were in a great fright, and as they had never had any dealings with a bank, they wanted to give all their savings, mostly pennies and silver coins which had been buried in the ground, to Gandhi. He gave a receipt for each sum, then had the coins disinfected and deposited them in his own bank. Later on he persuaded a good many of the Indians to use the bank. In their camp on the plains the Indians were merry after a day's uncertainty; Gandhi rode out to see them every day on his bicycle, and it was his impression that the open air did them good.

During the epidemic, Mr. Albert West, an English vegetarian whom Gandhi had met, had agreed to take charge of the *Indian Opinion* press at Durban. West remained an invaluable co-worker during Gandhi's stay in South Africa.

Mr. West on arrival in Durban found

that the bookkeeping had been so neglected that he could not be sure whether *Indian Opinion* faced a profit or a loss. Gandhi, startled at this, determined to go to Natal himself. On this journey to Durban he read one of the most decisive books of his life, John Ruskin's *Unto This Last*. In his autobiography, Gandhi says:

The teachings of *Unto This Last* I understood to be:

1. That the good of the individual is contained in the good of all.

2. That a lawyer's work has the same value as the barber's, inasmuch as all have the same right to earn their livelihood from their work.

3. That a life of labor, i.e., the life of the tiller of the soil and the handicraftsman, is the life worth living.

I arose with the dawn, ready to reduce these principles to practice.

Gandhi took from the book what he most needed—specifically, the idea of cooperative labor. As soon as he got off the train in Durban he told his loyal friend Mr. West that he wanted to move *Indian Opinion* to a farm—staff, presses, and all— where everybody would have a fixed work contribution and monetary allowance, equal for all. Within a week (backed by his friends among the Moslem merchants) he had bought a tract of land at Phoenix, fourteen miles from Durban. Within a month he had built a big shed for the printing press, using volunteer Indian masons and carpenters. From then on *Indian Opinion* was published at the Phoenix Settlement, which became the center of Gandhi's activity in Natal.

The land around the settlement was divided up into plots of three acres each, and each member of the cooperative was responsible for the cultivation of his own plot. Quick, cheap huts of corrugated iron were built. Every member of the community learned to set type and work the printing press, so that there was a plentiful supply of labor for the paper.

Gandhi was obliged to return to Johannesburg as soon as the Phoenix Settlement had been well started. Throughout these years, in fact, he had one foot in the Transvaal and one in Natal.

The moment the Zulu War broke out in Natal, Gandhi offered his services with an Indian ambulance corps. In actual fact

Gandhi's sympathies were with the Zulus, but he felt his loyalty to the British Empire to override everything else.

Somehow the conflict set up in his mind by the Zulu War worked itself out into a personal dilemma: brahmacharya, control of sexual appetites. Now he felt that the time had come to take the vow of chastity for the rest of his life. He was thirty-six (in the middle of 1906) when he took the vow irrevocably. His wife became his most devoted friend and helper. He was persuaded that this "self-purification" was necessary not only for his own release, but also for the birth of satyagraha, his distinctive creation, the idea that changed the world.

Satyagraha had existed, of course, before he found a name for it. His notions of sacrifice for the truth, voluntary abnegation and self-surrender in the service of the community, challenge to the unrighteous law or to the unjust application, all had been growing in him for years. It needed to be made quite plain and clear so that every ordinary Indian person (unlettered, but willing to learn) might absorb the idea and act upon it. Gandhi offered a small prize in *Indian Opinion* for a name that would crystallize his ideas of the nature and method of struggle. His cousin Maganlal won the prize by suggesting the word *sadagraha,* from *sat* (truth) and *agraha* (firmness or force), two Sanskrit words that had not been combined in this way before. Gandhi changed it to satyagraha, a more comprehensible form for masses of Indians with no knowledge of Sanskrit. From then on, the word and the idea grew; they were to liberate India and put an end to the greatest of empires.

THE actual beginning of the satyagraha campaign in South Africa may be dated from September 11, 1906. The government of the Transvaal had announced in the preceding month that it would introduce a bill calling for the registration of all Indians above the age of eight. They were to be fingerprinted and were to carry certificates with them at all times. If they disobeyed this ordinance, they were to be imprisoned or deported or both.

In Johannesburg the indignant Indian community called a mass meeting, at which the chairman called upon all present to take a vow, "with God as their witness," to disobey the law. This aroused Gandhi to a speech which—in spite of his lingering shyness—was one of the greatest in his career. He personally pledged himself "unto death," and warned the three thousand persons present that taking the vow might mean jail, hardship, cruelty, or death; but every person took the vow.

Gandhi himself had ample realization of the magnitude of the vow. Before offering satyagraha (the voluntary sacrifice), he decided to go to England to see if persuasion would do any good. But the law was passed in due course and went into effect on July 31, 1907.

Most of the Indians stood firm. Although Gandhi's concept of satyagraha was not yet fully understood by his followers, they understood that they could not register under the iniquitous law and keep their self-respect. Among the first summoned before the magistrate for not doing so was Gandhi, who (January 11, 1908) asked the judge to give him the heaviest sentence. The judge gave him the lightest—two months of simple imprisonment, specifying that it should be "without hard labor."

It was Gandhi's first term in jail. He seems almost to have enjoyed it as a holiday from his work. He read the *Gita* in the morning and the Koran in the afternoon; he read Ruskin, Tolstoy, Bacon, and Plato. But his term was all too short: General Smuts wanted to see him. The chief of police of Johannesburg came to the jail and fetched Gandhi—in prison uniform and without money or baggage—to Pretoria to see the prime minister of the Transvaal.

Smuts proposed a compromise by which the Indians would voluntarily register, and the objectionable act for compulsory registration would be repealed. The compromise was made. Then Smuts broke his word to Gandhi. After the latter had persuaded most Indians to register voluntarily, Smuts passed the Asiatic Act anyhow. This was a cruel blow. Gandhi now had to mobilize his resources for a more bitter and general struggle.

On August 16, 1908, at a mass meeting in Johannesburg, some two thousand Indian registrants burned their registration certificates in a cauldron of kerosene. Under the Asiatic Act this rendered them all liable to imprisonment. Selected volunteers were also sent across the border from Natal to the Transvaal without certificates. Among these was Harilal, Gandhi's eldest son. Gandhi himself defied the law and was arrested again on October 10, 1908.

During this second prison sentence Gandhi made another of his epochal literary discoveries: Thoreau. He read Thoreau's fiery essay, "Civil Disobedience," concerned with his refusal to support the American government (1849) because of slavery and the Mexican War. In jail, aside from reading, Gandhi was cook to some seventy-five other Indians and a volunteer for latrine duty.

The second prison sentence ended December 13, 1908, but upon his release he continued the satyagraha movement and was quickly sentenced for a third term (February 25, 1909) of three months at the new penitentiary at Pretoria. He had borrowed his Thoreau from the jail library in Johannesburg; now he seems to have found Emerson's essays in Pretoria. In his letters he recommends them to correspondents. It is striking that Thoreau and Emerson, who owed so much to the *Gita* and the *Upanishads,* thus returned to India. The *Bhagavad-Gita,* greatly treasured by Thoreau, was in fact the only book he possessed at his death. Gandhi by now had memorized a large part of the *Gita* in Sanskrit; he used to paste it up, couplet by couplet, on his shaving mirror and learn it during his morning ablutions. To find in the writings of far-off America—and by means of jail libraries in Africa—echoes of his beloved "song celestial" must have been a rare experience for Gandhi; he referred to it repeatedly afterward.

When he was released this time, Gandhi resolved to try his luck in London. He remained there from July to November 1909, ceaselessly talking, writing, and agitating for a hearing. The Union of South Africa was being formed, and the danger was that the new Union might extend the Transvaal legislation to the whole country and brand the Indians forever.

Under British pressure Smuts agreed, not too willingly, to repeal the objectionable Asiatic Act and to permit the limited

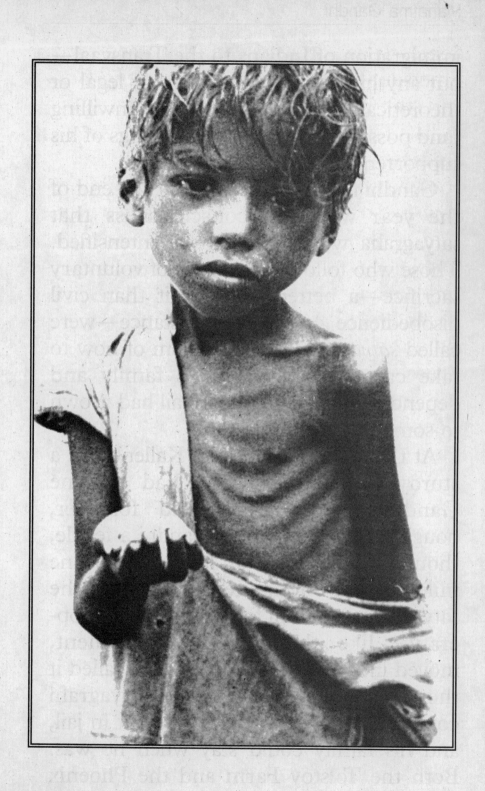

immigration of Indians to the Transvaal—
but anything like a concession of legal or
theoretical equality he was quite unwilling
(and possibly, in view of the feelings of his
supporters, unable) to grant.

Gandhi returned to Africa at the end of
the year with the consciousness that
satyagraha would have to be intensified.
Those who followed his ideas of voluntary
sacrifice—a better term for it than civil
disobedience or passive resistance—were
called *satyagrahis*. The problem of how to
take care of a *satyagrahi*'s family and
dependents while he was in jail had grown
to some dimensions.

At this juncture Herman Kallenbach, a
sturdy German Jew who had become
Gandhi's good friend and follower,
bought and presented to Gandhi a fertile,
thousand-acre tract of land twenty-one
miles from Johannesburg, for the
satyagrahis. Gandhi formed another cooperative like the Phoenix Settlement,
moved into it with his family, and called it
the Tolstoy Farm. Here the satyagrahi
could be at home when he was not in jail,
and his family could stay when he was.
Both the Tolstoy Farm and the Phoenix

Settlement became flourishing establishments, with many men, women, and children living in each, and the experiments in education, vocational training, diet, and discipline were ceaselessly interesting to Gandhi. Much of the "Basic Education" system, now gaining ground rapidly throughout India, was developed by actual work on the Tolstoy Farm and the Phoenix Settlement.

Gandhi's austerity, steadily on the increase, reached its permanent level on the Tolstoy Farm. There he vowed not to drink cow's or buffalo's milk, having read that cruelty was used to increase their production.

The visit of Gokhale, Gandhi's political guru, in the autumn of 1912 was a turning point in the long struggle for Indian rights. Gokhale was highly respected both in India and in England. In Pretoria, the two Boer generals, Botha and Smuts, now intent on the establishment of the Union without unnecessary difficulty, actually promised Gokhale that the worst of the Indian disabilities would be repealed. Gandhi was not prepared to believe this just yet, and he was right.

Smuts brought on the last battle by announcing that the European community in Natal refused to permit the lifting of the poll tax. Gandhi and his family and friends moved at once to Natal—to Phoenix Settlement—and prepared for the struggle. They were vastly aided by a Supreme Court decision in the Cape Colony declaring that only Christian marriages could be valid in South Africa. This made all Indian wives concubines, and their children bastards. It embittered the Indians more than anything that had gone before, and aroused the women, hitherto not active in the movement. Satyagraha was now to be enacted on a really large scale.

Gandhi decided that one group of women should offer sacrifice by crossing from the Transvaal to Natal without permission. If the "sisters" (as Gandhi called them) were not arrested by the border police, they would go to the coal mines at Newcastle and ask the indentured laborers to go on strike. This was what took place, and five thousand struck. However, a second group of sisters, crossing from Natal to the Transvaal, was arrested and sent to jail for three months.

Gandhi organized the miners' camp, obtained food and equipment for them, and then notified the South African government that his "army" was about to march across the border into the Transvaal and go to jail for doing so. His arrangements were precise and characteristic. Every precaution of hygiene and sanitation was taken. His followers were not to struggle, must engage in no violence, and must not resist arrest, flogging, or other indignities at the hands of the police.

After prayers on the morning of November 6, 1913, the march began. At the first stop across the border, Gandhi himself was arrested. He was released on bail, but the next day he was arrested again, and again released on bail. Two days later it happened again, and this time there was no bail. His arrest was followed by large numbers of other arrests. His army had its orders to continue, and it was arrested en masse for deportation to Natal. New volunteers arose in all parts of the country to court arrest. All of this, amply reported in both England and India, stirred up a storm.

The army, returned under guard to the

coal mines at Newcastle, refused, in spite of floggings and starvation, to go back to work. They were joined by others. The strike movement spread rapidly until fifty thousand indentured laborers were refusing to do any work. Thousands of free Indians, like Gandhi, were in jail.

The viceroy of India (Lord Hardinge) demanded a commission of inquiry, and the idea was taken up in London. Botha and Smuts released Gandhi. This was not what Gandhi wished, for he could actually do more good in jail than out. He attacked the commission of inquiry as being a "packed" body hostile to the Indians' rights, and announced that on the first of the year (1914) he and a group of Indians would march from Durban again to court arrest.

At this point the white employees of the South African railroad system went on strike. Perhaps these white workers felt that the Indians could help them; but Gandhi was against it. He called off his New Year's Day march, explaining that satyagraha must be pure and must not aim at humiliating the enemy. The government had declared martial law; he would forbear.

Perhaps he gained more for the Indians by this forbearance than if he had pursued his intended course. In any case, Smuts asked him to come to Pretoria and talk.

The early months of 1914 were devoted to a long, painstaking negotiation between Smuts and Gandhi. There is little doubt that these two men acquired a high regard for each other during their struggle. "You can't put twenty thousand Indians into jail," Smuts said, and indeed the jail system of South Africa had already proved inadequate to the problem. He clearly came to regard Gandhi with a respect bordering on awe and affection.

The Indian Relief Bill became law in July 1914. It declared Indian marriages legal; it abolished the three-pound poll tax on indentured laborers, canceling all arrears; it declared that the system of importing indentured laborers from India must cease in 1920; and it provided that, though Indians could not leave one province for another without permission, those born in South Africa might enter the Cape Colony.

Satyagraha had proved to be an irresistible weapon. It was surrounded by Gandhi with such severe disciplines of self-control and nonviolence that it represented something quite novel in the techniques of human struggle. It was years before its full meaning could be taken in by all the people.

Gandhi's work in South Africa was now completed. On July 18, 1914, he sailed for England with Mrs. Gandhi and his friend Mr. Kallenbach. Before he left, he gave Smuts a pair of sandals he had made in prison. These Smuts wore for twenty-five years, until Gandhi's seventieth birthday, when he sent them to Gandhi as a token of friendship. "I have worn these sandals for many a summer," Smuts said then, "even though I may feel that I am not worthy to stand in the shoes of so great a man."

IV
India—and War

WHEN Gandhi left South Africa forever at the age of forty-five, he was already a fully formed personality. He had adopted practically all those disciplines with respect to diet, hours of work, exercise, meditation, prayer, and silence which were to be his unvarying rule thereafter. The great achievements of *satya, ahimsa, brahma-charya* (truth, nonviolence and respect for all life, and self-control or chastity) had been made.

His external success in leading the Indians of South Africa to victory in their human rights was to a very considerable degree the result of his self-conquest in these matters. He felt, probably quite correctly, that he could not lead unless he was himself pure. It has been said that nobody can lead India without first "renouncing the world." Gandhi's renunciation was gradual, but by forty-five he not only had given up sex and the pleasures of food, but also had surrendered savings, possessions of all sorts, and all aspects of social consideration except those necessary for the self-respect of the Indian community.

He was small, gentle, sad, with mournful eyes, and with ears that stuck out at right angles, as always. His physical endurance was fantastic—sometimes he used to walk from Tolstoy Farm to Johannesburg and back on the same day, roughly fifty miles, to save money—and yet it was sustained on the slightest diet possible. He had already taken up the habit of fasting as a form of prayer, and giving fixed limits to his fasts. He would vow, for example, to fast for seven days in atonement for a sin committed by some of his followers. At other times he would fix no limit, but fast simply until he felt that the "inner voice" permitted him to cease. These great fasts were conceived and executed as prayers to God, either in atonement or in aspiration. But in later days, when so many governments were forced to yield on so many points because of them, they came to seem a form of political pressure.

The chief concomitant of satyagraha, as Gandhi developed it in South Africa and later in India, was loyalty to the opponent. You must never take unfair advantage of your opponent. He must always be aware of what you intend. He is, in fact, your friend, from whom you are temporarily separated by a disagreement. These precepts probably account for the circumstance, so often noted, that many of his opponents—

jailers, policemen, detectives, and the like—became his greatest friends.

THE First World War broke out two days before Gandhi landed in England from South Africa. He immediately set about the formation of all Indian ambulance corps for the British Army. He believed that because he accepted all the benefits of British rule, he had some obligation toward that rule. His loyalty to the British Empire was not to suffer any change for another five years. But he fell ill with pleurisy after a few weeks, and accepting the doctor's advice, he went home to India.

The return to India was in many respects a great surprise to Gandhi. He had been away most of twenty years, and he was surprised to be greeted by great crowds in Bombay (January 9, 1915). His previous visits home had produced no such excitement. But in the meantime he had been victorious in his South African struggle; and he himself had become Mahatma (Great Soul) to large numbers of people. He did not actually like the title. He refused to believe that there could be "greater" or "smaller" souls, and the reverence surrounding a mahatma was a nuisance to him in the prosecution of his work. Through many years he learned to endure it, and with it the pitiless attention of the entire country to every deed of his life—and the crowds, the unbelievable Indian crowds!—but the evidence is that he never really accepted the appellation.

Meanwhile his first year at home was spent, at the request of his revered political guru, Gokhale, in retirement from public life. Gokhale felt that this strangely powerful little man was an instrument of India's destiny, but wisely saw that he required time to grow familiar again with the country and its people.

The "family" from South Africa, Gandhi's twenty-five or more followers from Tolstoy Farm and Phoenix Settlement, were being cared for in India at Shantiniketan, in Bengal, the school and settlement of Rabindranath Tagore. The Mahatma now wanted to find a home of his own for this family. He found it, eventually, in the neighborhood of Ahmedabad in his native Gujarat province. The Society of the Friends of India supplied the money necessary for purchasing the land and building huts. Gandhi hoped that the rich merchants of Ahmedabad, his fellow Gujarati, would provide the funds to continue the work, and for some time they did.

Tagore's *ashram* (the Indian word for a settlement and school) consisted of about one hundred and twenty-five Bengali boys and a score of teachers. Gandhi's ashram, men, women, and children, belonged to several castes, sects, races, and religions. It included two Englishmen, William Pearson and "Charlie" Andrews. The difference between the two ashrams was like the difference between Tagore and Gandhi themselves—the Poet, as Tagore was called, remote, beautiful, sonorous, and rich; the Mahatma, small, busy, humble, and penniless.

Gandhi was called to the other side of India by the death of his "sure guide," Gokhale. This was a great grief to him, and it is likely it made him feel even more insecure during his first year back in India. His position was peculiar. All the political classes in India were highly aware of him; in many sections he was extremely well known for his work in Africa; yet he was personally unknown. And the probability is that he was not himself sure of what to do. He was content to build his ashram, remain silent on public questions, and study his surroundings.

The ashram, known as Sabarmati, was founded May 25, 1915. In the original ashram there were some twenty-five persons, all vowed to chastity, poverty, and a life of service, all committed to every form of communal work, including that usually performed by untouchables (scavenging, in particular, upon which Gandhi insisted). Not long after he had opened the ashram, he admitted a family of untouchables. As the kitchens and water supply and everything else in Gandhi's settlement operated by cooperative labor, the admission of a man, wife, and child from the untouchable outcastes was a revolutionary thing in India.

There were no servants in Gandhi's ashram. All were equal and all shared in the same work for the same pay. The Mahatma himself, with surprising energy, did manual labor, including the digging of latrines and the transport of excrement. This is the lowest labor known to India, and can be performed only by untouchables. His own performance of such tasks was forgiven by everybody, because holy men for thousands of years have been like that—humble, willing to do all work. For this reason holy men are supposed to be completely outside the caste system—they are too erratic to obey the rules of caste.

But the moment Gandhi admitted some real untouchables to his ashram he was in trouble, because this meant that others besides himself, caste Hindus, were cooking and eating with untouchables, drinking the same water and living an equal life with them. By bringing this about he offended his contemporaries to the depths. Consequently all his income was cut off. The neighboring rich Hindus who had given the ashram money were incensed at him. The storm spread, and Indian opinion everywhere was aroused against him.

He calmly decided to move with his family and followers into the untouchable quarter of the city, to become untouchables themselves. Such a thing, if it had happened, would have shaken India far more than anything yet. But it did not happen. A Moslem, unknown to Gandhi, appeared from nowhere and gave him a purse of rupees sufficient to sustain his ashram for a year. By the time the year was over, the storm had subsided, and even orthodox Hindus were willing to contribute to the support of Gandhi's work, as they continued to do throughout his life.

GANDHI'S year of public silence came to an end at the opening ceremonies of the Hindu University at Benares, on February 4, 1916. The university, to which fortunes had been given by maharajahs and other rich Hindus, had grown from slight beginnings twenty-odd years before, the original founder being Annie Besant, the brilliant Englishwoman and theosophist. After the grand opening ceremonies, Mrs. Besant herself presided over a meeting where Gandhi spoke.

What he offered, in his gentle, modest way, was a criticism of India. He began by saying that he regretted the necessity for speaking in a foreign tongue (English) at the opening of a Hindu university. He said self-government could come only through the masses of the people. He made severe references to the jewels seen on the Indian princes at the ceremonies, and to the general extravagance of the ceremonies, while most of India starved in dirt, and untouchability was rampant. He spoke of Indian lack of sanitation, of the intolerable conditions in third-class carriages on railway trains, of spitting, and of other things most unpleasant for his audience of upper-class Indians and British officials. Many notables left the meeting, and finally the disorder grew uncontrollable. When cries of "Sit down, Gandhi!" began to be heard, Mrs. Besant, who was no doubt the most scandalized of all, adjourned the meeting.

Gandhi had, in his way, thrown down the gauntlet. The attack upon Indian conditions was thoroughly in Gandhi's character. It was, however, quite new in India, where the fashion was to tell the Indians how remarkable was their culture, how ancient their tradition, how noble their aim. The speech was repeated throughout the country, from the Himalayas to Cape

Cormorin. It began to appear that a holy man, living like the poor, had spoken for the poor against the rich. He had not spoken against the British at all—merely as an Indian among Indians, talking about India. The echoes were heard.

The first results of Gandhi's emergence from silence were an increase of demands upon his time. He had much to do at his ashram, he was busy writing at the time, he was working to abolish indentured emigration, and he was already engaged in the search for the spinning wheel.* But he did as much as he could to satisfy these demands. The real opportunity— the Gandhian opportunity to accomplish a suitable task in a characteristic way— arose more or less by accident. An obstinate peasant sharecropper named Shukla had turned up at the 1916 convention of the Indian National Congress at Lucknow. He wanted the Mahatma to

---

*Presently Gandhi asked all Indians to cease buying British-made cloth and clothing, and he asked them to spin and weave their own material. He himself took to using a spinning wheel daily; and he called spinning "a sacrament" which turned the spinner's mind "Godward."

come to his district, Champaran, and see how abominably the indigo cultivators were being treated. The Mahatma had no time. Shukla waited—and followed the Mahatma wherever he went, even to the ashram, for weeks on end. And finally Gandhi went to Champaran.

In the Champaran district Gandhi found that the indigo workers were desperately poor, and he undertook a form of action peculiarly his own. He started in Patna, the capital of Bihar province, where a number of lawyers and Congress members had some sympathy for the sharecroppers and had (for fees) undertaken some of their court cases. The Mahatma asked these men to go with him to the Champaran district and give their services for nothing. They must be willing to go to jail, if necessary. It took a little time for Gandhi to win over a sufficient number. His next step was to warn the opponents (in this case the head of the indigo planters' association and the government district commissioner) that he intended to investigate the grievances.

From the tone of their response he knew that there would be trouble and in all probability jail for him. He proceeded just the same, in an orderly manner, with the taking of depositions from indigo sharecroppers as they came to him. His personality attracted such throngs of the downtrodden indigo workers that it was quite impossible to flog them for obeying his summons. In the dilemma the local magistrate decided to order Gandhi out of the district, and when the Mahatma politely refused to go, he was summoned to stand trial the next day. The magistrate was taken aback by Gandhi's attitude: the Mahatma simply declared that he was guilty as charged and asked for the legal punishment. Judgment was postponed, and in the meantime the government of India, somewhat disturbed over the wide attention given to these events, ordered the case withdrawn.

Gandhi then proceeded with his depositions. So many thousands of them were unnecessary, but he had realized from the start that these poor indigo workers, accustomed to starvation and floggings, needed above all things to be "free from fear." Therefore, to give them the sense of having a friend, to free them from the fears of the defenseless, he encouraged them all to tell their stories. It required from five to seven of the volunteers from Patna to be on duty all the time to take down the depositions.

In the meantime, as usual, Gandhi was busy with sanitary problems. The villages of the indigo workers were squalid with filth, vulnerable to every disease. Gandhi began his customary washing, sweeping, and cleaning, with six villages chosen to start the operation, and he started schools in these six spots.

And in all this work, of course, the usual detective from the Criminal Investigation Department was beside him, noting all down and making reports. These C.I.D. detectives accompanied Gandhi wherever he went for about thirty years, and he invariably treated them with great courtesy. Some became his devoted friends.

At length the government grew weary of the campaign in Champaran. It set up a commission of inquiry, with Gandhi as a member, and as a result the system by which three-twentieths of the land had to be worked in indigo for the benefit of the landlord was abolished by law.

The Champaran experience may be called the first triumph of satyagraha in India, even though the satyagraha involved was for the most part Gandhi's alone. He had gained an objective of importance to human welfare by his own distinctive means of truth, self-control, and nonviolence, but his methods had still been most imperfectly understood even by those who applied them. He had to spend hours a day explaining, even to his own volunteers. Still Champaran was, in practical action, the introduction of satyagraha to India. It was soon followed by the introduction of another characteristic peculiarity of the Mahatma's genius—a fast for a specific purpose.

There were times when Gandhi's opponents contended that his fasts were, in objective fact, little more than a kind of blackmail. As against this view the principal facts to be cited are: first and most of all, that fasting as a form of prayer was deep in Gandhi's psychological structure; second, that he took this punishment upon himself, but never wished to extend it to others; third, that he had already fasted a great many times, in prayer for various purposes, or in atonement for various actions by his own followers, before the world in general paid any great attention; and last, that he tried hard, when impelled to fast (and often by his inner voice), to avoid giving this form of prayer the aspect of coercion upon others.

The fast in 1917 took place as a result of responsibilities he had assumed toward the millworkers of Ahmedabad, who had come to him for advice. These were his own people, of course, to whom he talked in his native Gujarati. Their employers, the mill owners, were also his friends, and many of them had contributed to the upkeep of his ashram. Upon investigating, and talking to both sides, Gandhi decided that the mill hands' grievances were legitimate and that the mill owners were unwilling to give any satisfaction. Therefore he advised the mill hands to go on strike, but only on condition that they would pledge themselves to nonviolence (such as toward strikebreakers).

The mill hands took this vow daily for the next two weeks. With time the zeal for nonviolence declined, and the Mahatma, troubled, decided to fast until the mill hands returned to their vow. The fast lasted three days. After that time the employers and workers met and settled the strike.

The Ahmedabad fast has troubled even some of Gandhi's followers because it looked like a threat. This he never intended. "I fasted to reform those who loved me," Gandhi stated: that is, to keep the mill hands to their vow of nonviolence. Settlement of the strike was the result, not the intention.

THE end of Gandhi's life as a loyal subject of the British Empire was now not long in the future. As a final expression of this loyalty, he undertook to recruit soldiers for the (British) Indian Army during the summer of 1918. He did so, however, in the full expectation that his effort—and India's—would be rewarded by a "share in the partnership" of empire, which is to say, in the language of 1918, by home rule. He further asked the London government to make some provision for the restoration of the Moslem Caliphate, destroyed by the defeat of Turkey.

He then embarked on a long, arduous

tramp from village to village in the Kheda district of Gujarat, trying to enlist men for the Army. He had engaged in a satyagraha campaign shortly before in this district in aid of peasants who were being sold out for tax arrears. It had ended with a partial victory, the government agreeing to remit taxes for the very poor. During the campaign Gandhi had felt the full support of the people.

Now it was a grievous disappointment to him to find that when he went among them as a recruiting agent for the Army he was greeted with incomprehension and even hostility. "What about nonviolence? How can you ask us to take up arms? What good has this government ever done to India?" Questions like these were fired at him in village after village. They would perhaps not have impressed themselves so deeply on his consciousness if they had not found echoes in its depths. He himself had asked the same questions. Now he redoubled his efforts, worried and fretted over his inability to make the people understand his point of view. As a result he succumbed to a severe attack of dysentery.

He was not a good patient: he refused medicines and almost any treatment. He fasted; he refused to change his nuts-and-fruit diet even when he was willing to eat; his body diminished at a startling rate. He would not eat eggs, and the doctors ran into the vow when they recommended milk. At this point Kasturba had the final say. "Your vow was against cow's or buffalo's milk," she said. "It did not include goat's milk."

He accepted goat's milk and lived. Thereafter he continued to drink goat's milk, though it worried him that he might be breaking the spirit of his vow in honoring the letter.

During this illness a message arrived from the viceroy saying it was no longer necessary to recruit soldiers: Germany had surrendered. This relief from a task he must have disliked intensely may have contributed to Gandhi's recovery.

During this winter after the war, the report of the Rowlatt Committee was published. The committee had been appointed to study Indian sedition. Its report recommended an extension into peacetime of all the wartime rigors in suppression of free speech, freedom of the press, and the right of assembly.

Gandhi, too feeble to act at once, studied the document with mounting indignation. If this was India's reward in time of peace, what hope could there be for home rule? But against the protests of all Indian leaders, the principles of the Rowlatt report were embodied in an act early in 1919.

This was the turning point in Gandhi's life as a political force in India and the world. He had never taken any direct part in politics. Now he faced a political action of great importance from which he did not flinch. It seemed to him that the time had come for an application, in India itself and on a large scale, of the principles of satyagraha. To prepare the ground he traveled through India. Handicapped by his physical feebleness, he found the travel fatiguing, yet he covered a great deal of territory and put a large part of India into the frame of mind for a movement of nonviolent protest. He, the humble and loyal subject of the King-Emperor, was becoming a rebel. He was not ready to renounce his allegiance to the British raj, but he was approaching that culmination with a speed he could not have believed possible only a short time before.

V
Into Rebellion

WHEN the Rowlatt Act became law, Gandhi was in Madras staying with C. Rajagopalachari (known later as Rajaji), one of the stoutest of his lieutenants in the decades about to begin. On the morning after the signature of the act Gandhi said to his friend: "Last night in a dream the idea came to me that we should ask the whole country to observe a general *hartal*."

Hartal is a day of abstention from economic activity, a day of mourning, of prayer and contemplation, sometimes also of fasting. Under Gandhi's interpretation it was to be a day of fasting and prayer. (Curiously enough, the American Revolution began in much the same way: the "day of fasting and prayer" which Thomas Jefferson and his friends proclaimed for Virginia on June 1, 1774.) He did not expect the response to his appeal to be general. He thought Madras and Bombay, Bihar and Sind might answer his call. He decided upon April 6 as the day of hartal.

The results astonished everybody, including Gandhi. The whole of India observed the day. Nobody in the great cities went to work, banks could not operate, ships were neither loaded nor unloaded, public transportation and the post office were paralyzed. The complete cessation of activity proved to everybody, including the bewildered British, that a new force was abroad in the land. Gandhi himself, with Mrs. Sarojini Naidu, one of his oldest friends and followers, spoke in a mosque in Bombay on April 6. Together they sold copies of two books forbidden by the government: Gandhi's *Hind Swaraj* and his translation of Ruskin's *Unto This Last*.

The excitement went far beyond what Gandhi had intended, and it did not stop on April 6 as he had asked. India was in turmoil. Gandhi himself tried to continue his journey on to Delhi, but was arrested on the train and turned back to Bombay. The news of his arrest, running through India like wildfire, caused huge crowds to collect in various cities. In Bombay itself an immense mob gathered and was charged by the mounted police with many casualties. In Ahmedabad, where the mill hands were Gandhi's special children, the news of his arrest aroused a mob to violence, and one policeman was killed. This disturbed Gandhi more than the similar news from elsewhere, because he thought the Ahmedabad workers had really understood satyagraha. "A rapier run through my body could scarcely have pained me more," he said.

Then, on April 13, came the Amritsar massacre. As a result Gandhi decided that the time for satyagraha had not come, and he called off the movement. In atonement for what had happened he would fast and pray for three days, and he would not go on until his principles were sufficiently understood to make the satyagraha pure— a sacrifice, not a violence.

No act of his life was more bewildering to the masses in India than Gandhi's abandonment of the satyagraha movement at this moment. It took a long time for Indians in general, Hindus as well as Moslems, to understand that the frail little man meant simply what he said, and that no power on earth could induce him to pursue an action if he felt that it violated his principles.

AMRITSAR was the holy city to the Sikhs. It was the scene of events on April 13, 1919, which have never been forgotten in India. In that crowded city an unprecedented show of friendship between Hindu and Moslem had taken place during the hartal. However, in fear of the great crowds that had assembled, the Punjab government ordered the deportation of the two local Congress leaders, one Hindu and one Moslem.

Furious crowds ran amok; three English bankers were killed; others were assaulted. Brigadier-General Reginald E. H. Dyer was ordered to Amritsar and as his first act (April 12) prohibited public meetings. The proclamation was read to the people at various points of the city, but it has never been established that its provisions were known everywhere. In any case, a public meeting took place on the 13th in the Jallianwalla Bagh, an open space in the middle of the city. The crowd, estimated

by the British official report at somewhere between ten and twenty thousand,
filled all the space at one end and the
middle.

General Dyer entered on the raised
ground at the opposite end with twenty-
five Gurkhas and twenty-five Baluchis, all
armed with rifles, and then, without giving
any warning or ordering the crowd to dis-
perse, simply opened fire and kept on fir-
ing for ten minutes. As the exits from the
Jallianwalla Bagh are few and very narrow,
it was impossible for the crowd to get
away. By the official British estimate, 379
were killed and 1,137 wounded. As the
troops fired 1,650 rounds, this means that
almost every bullet hit a man.

Dyer further ordered that all Indians
passing through a certain street, where
the English headmistress of a school
had been beaten by a mob on April 10,
must crawl on all fours; any Indian in a
vehicle had to get out and crawl; any
Indian was ordered to salute or salaam
any English officer in these districts.
A whipping post was installed at the
spot where the schoolmistress had been
beaten, and this was used for flogging

102

such Indians as disobeyed any of these orders.

Dyer after this was asked for his resignation and retired to England. Indignation in England reached a high pitch, almost as high as in India, and the government in London declared that the order for Indians to crawl "offended against every canon of civilized government." Still, the massacre at Amritsar convinced many Indians of goodwill that there was no hope in British government. It pushed Mahatma Gandhi, in his great grief, much farther into politics (and much sooner) than he might otherwise have gone. And truthfully, too, it inflicted many Englishmen of goodwill with a sense of guilt and a desire to do better by India in the future. Edwin Montagu, the secretary of state for India, and Lord Chelmsford, the viceroy, were such men, and the Montagu-Chelmsford Reforms, giving India a constitution and a share in government, were proposed in that same year, 1919. But the bitterness of Amritsar was responsible for many of India's vicissitudes in the next twenty years—for the widespread belief that the British were never to be trusted; for the difficulties of any negotiation.

Gandhi wanted, above all, to go to Amritsar, but the government had restricted his movements. It was October of that year before Lord Chelmsford telegraphed him that he was free to go "any time after October 17th." In Amritsar he settled down to make his own inquiry into the massacre. Wherever he went, he was received by those delirious crowds who then and thereafter were never to leave him. Thousands of Punjabis filed before him to tell their stories, and he listened patiently, though he rejected anything he thought unproved. The principal result of the inquiry, in Gandhi's life, was that it entwined him more closely into political life than before; having made this inquiry, he could not refuse to take part in the annual meeting of the Congress that year in Amritsar, or in the Hindu-Moslem conversations on the caliphate. The process that had begun with his dream in Madras was quite relentlessly leading him into the central position in Indian politics.

The progression was accelerated by the question of the caliphate of Islam, considered vital by the Mohammedans of India. Gandhi had been by instinct and deliberate intention a friend of the Moslems all his life. He once said in South Africa, long before he returned to India, that the final test of his satyagraha would come on Hindu-Moslem unity. Now an opportunity was offered to make that unity real. He left Amritsar for Delhi in November 1919 for the Moslem Conference, to which he had been officially invited.

Gandhi was on the platform at this fateful Moslem Conference. The Moslems of India had already passed resolutions condemning the British for being too severe with Turkey; the time had now come to think of some method of making their desires felt. All expected that the final peace terms dictated to Turkey would emasculate that old Moslem state and destroy the caliphate of Islam, the center of the Moslem world.

Gandhi's contribution, when it came his time to speak, was the single momentous word "noncooperation." (He could not very well propose to Mohammedans the idea of satyagraha; the word itself was

Sanskrit and not suited to the English-speaking Moslems of this conference.) The Moslems had proposed a boycott of English textiles. This was not in itself a sufficient action; what was needed, Gandhi told them, was a firm noncooperation in all other fields: a refusal of British employment, British honors, British schools or courts. So grave a step should not be taken, however, unless the British terms of peace with Turkey were as severe as expected.

The word and the idea of noncooperation dominated Indian public life for years afterward. And yet in a new test that came within a month, Gandhi favored cooperation with the British.

The Montagu-Chelmsford Reforms were announced on the day before the Indian National Congress met at Amritsar. The constitutional system devised was unsatisfactory to all other Indians, Gandhi said, "and was not wholly satisfactory even to me," but he thought it wise to accept the proposals in good faith and try them out as a beginning.

When Gandhi discovered that the Congress did not wish to accept the Montagu-Chelmsford Reforms, he tried to retire to his ashram rather than argue it out. They would not let him go away—any decision taken in his absence would have been almost meaningless to the people of India, because the mere fact of his absence would have indicated disapproval. He stayed, and his views prevailed; the Congress passed a resolution commending the reforms; and Gandhi from this time forward was the unquestioned spirit of the Indian National Congress, even when his wishes ran counter to the wishes of the impatient youth of the country.

Gandhi himself, however, rapidly lost faith in the good intentions of the British. Aside from Edwin Montagu, nobody in the government in London seemed to realize what the abolition of the caliphate meant to the Moslems of India. A ruthless peace treaty was dictated to Turkey. The Hindus of India at the same time were flouted by the fact that General Dyer's pension (paid by India) was continued after his retirement to England, and by the fact that a large purse was collected there as a gift to him in sympathy after the Amritsar massacre.

These episodes and the continued enforcement of the Rowlatt Act finally drove Gandhi into the acceptance (April 1920) of the presidency of the Home Rule League. This was a symbolic deed, placing him on record as an opponent of the existing government. It was much farther than he had ever gone before.

The time for active noncooperation had now come. Gandhi wrote to Lord Chelmsford, giving courteous notice that he had advised the Moslems and Hindus "to withdraw their support from Your Excellency's government." The viceroy said that noncooperation was "the most foolish of all foolish schemes."

It was far from being a "foolish scheme" as it worked out. Beginning August 1, Hindu and Moslem committees, working together, scoured the country and induced millions to give up their British clothing and even jobs. Gandhi himself was incessantly moving about India, immune to fatigue, preaching his home-rule gospel in the Hindi word *sivaraj* (self-rule). Noncooperation was confirmed by the annual Congress meeting at Nagpur in December. At Nagpur, Gandhi produced a constitution for the Congress (which had had none before): it created the system of village, district, and city units, the executive All-India Congress Committee of three hundred and fifty, and a Working Committee of fifteen. Thus the body of upper-middle-class lawyers, bankers, and pundits, brought into being originally by the British, became a mass organization with its roots deep in Indian life.

Gandhi's tours during late 1920 and the greater part of 1921 took him everywhere in the country that could be reached by railroad, and into many districts where the railroad did not go. It was his habit to ask for the sacrifice of foreign clothing, and great bonfires of clothes soon burned all over India. Many fires were actually started by him; he himself applied the match. Men and women were taking to the spinning wheel, which now began to be produced in quantity, and the Mahatma also pleaded that they all get into homespun as soon as possible.

At that time he wore homespun, but the

garments themselves were conventional enough: a white cap (known thereafter as the Gandhi cap), a dhoti or loosely draped trousers, and a vest. It was not until September 1921 that he took the final step and adopted the dress of the poorest of the poor—a loincloth and, in cold weather, a homespun shawl.

During this period money was collected on a very great scale. A spirit of sacrifice swept over India. This was perhaps the highest, as it was the first, of these general passionate assertions of belief in the Mahatma's way to freedom. It is remarkable indeed that, in the midst of the great crowds and with all the excitement, violence did not occur anywhere for many months.

Gandhi traveled for a large part of the time with Mohammed Ali Jinnah, younger of the two brothers who were acknowledged leaders of the Moslems. It was a high point, too, of Hindu-Moslem unity. Yet in September 1921 Mohammed Ali was arrested and Gandhi was not, though they were walking together to a meeting at the time. The arrest was made because Mohammed Ali had asked Moslems not

A GANDHI PORTFOLIO

Gandhi with associates in South Africa, about 1900

With his wife, Kasturba, in 1896

Gandhi and Mrs. Naidu on the Salt March

A rousing reception by English millworkers

Nehru and Gandhi in Bombay, 1946

Gandhi's funeral pyre, January 31, 1948

to join the British Army. Gandhi, in great distress at the loss of his Moslem friend and fellow worker, asked the Congress Working Committee (October 5) to pass a resolution declaring it the duty of every Indian soldier or civilian to quit government service—thus sharing whatever guilt Mohammed Ali had incurred.

The Prince of Wales visited India at the end of the year. Perhaps it was thought that he would calm the tempest, but instead he added to it. His visit aroused even more emotional tensions among the Indians themselves, and violence broke out. In Bombay nationalists attacked those Indians who had gone out to welcome the prince, and the ensuing riots were a terrible additional grief to the Mahatma. He undertook to fast as a prayer for peace until the violence should cease, and took no food for five days.

It is often asked why the British authorities refrained from arresting Gandhi in 1921, at a time when others were being arrested on a very large scale for doing what he asked them to do. By the turn of the year some thirty thousand Indians were in jail for obeying Gandhi's wishes (sedition, it was called).

It often has been said that the government was fearful of the results if the Mahatma was sent to prison. But it is known now that the new viceroy, Lord Reading, was almost alone responsible for the Mahatma's immunity. Lord Reading was a very exceptional man who had started life as a messenger boy and who had risen to his eminence by his own efforts. On his arrival in India in April of 1921, he proceeded to talk to Gandhi at great length, though they were both criticized by their own friends for consenting to the interviews. The details were all published by Reading's son in a biography that appeared long afterward (1945), complete with the viceroy's own letters on the subject.

In these six curious conversations, Gandhi attempted to inculcate his ideas of truth, nonviolence, and love on the worldlywise viceroy. Reading, though obviously startled at first, was quick to recognize the sincerity, courtesy, and, as he says, "distinction" of his visitor. He remained for many months unwilling to order Gandhi's arrest, sometimes standing out alone against it while the government in London demanded it.

The British were not alone in being puzzled by the Mahatma's course during 1921 and early 1922. Many Indians wanted to begin an armed rebellion. They were restrained by the knowledge that without Gandhi's approval the masses would not move.

The arrests continued until practically all Indian leaders except Gandhi were in prison. In the annual Congress meeting at the end of 1921 there was little to do except what the Congress did do: elect Gandhi as the "sole executive authority."

His slightest word now was law for millions. India, and a large part of the world besides, waited anxiously for what he would do next. The more impatient nationalists were urging him to go beyond noncooperation into outright civil disobedience. Civil disobedience on a vast scale, involving over three hundred million people, might very well lead to violence, and no doubt the advocates of violence counted upon that.

However, out of his endless self-com-

116

muning and meditation, the Mahatma brought forth a new idea. He would try a campaign of straight, nonviolent civil disobedience, under his own direction, in one circumscribed district. He chose the small district of Bardoli, in the Bombay presidency, for this experiment. It had a population of eighty-seven thousand, mostly in small villages, where the danger of violence was less than in cities. Even in a small district, the total paralysis of all British authority would be a solemn warning to the government. Gandhi hoped that the warning might be heeded and that no more extreme measures would be needed.

He therefore courteously wrote Lord Reading on February 1, 1922, of his decision. He then went to Bardoli to speak to the people. While he was thus busied, the news reached him (February 8) of a dreadful atrocity.

It occurred at Chauri Chaura in the United Provinces. By Gandhi's own account, written in his weekly magazine *Young India*, a legal procession had taken place there without police interference, but after it was over some stragglers were molested by constables. The stragglers called for help. In Gandhi's words: "The mob returned. The constables opened fire. The little ammunition they had was exhausted and they retired to the thana for safety. The mob, my informant tells me, therefore set fire to the thana. The self-imprisoned constables had to come out and as they did so they were hacked to pieces and the mangled remains were thrown into the raging flames."

This horror so depressed the Mahatma that again, as in 1919, he felt compelled to cancel the entire campaign of civil disobedience. In penitence he fasted for five days while both India and Great Britain looked on in amazement. To the Indians who protested, the Mahatma said patiently: "The drastic reversal of the program may be politically unsound and unwise, but there is no doubt that it is religiously sound."

Lord Reading, who had held off for so long against those who wanted Gandhi arrested, now decided, rather mysteriously, to give the order for arrest, and it was executed on March 10, 1922, at half past ten at night.

The Mahatma had anticipated his own arrest for a long time and had published an appeal, one day before the arrest took place, asking the people to be calm if the event occurred. The British—misunderstanding as usual—thought that his imprisonment "like an ordinary mortal" would be a "blow to his prestige." They remained unaware, even at this late date, that such imprisonment was a calculated part of the satyagraha. They also seem not to have realized (at least the viceroy did not) that India's quiet and good order were in obedience to the Mahatma's wishes rather than to the power of the British raj.

The trial took place in Ahmedabad on March 18, 1922. Gandhi and the printer of his magazine, Mr. S. G. Banker, were charged with writing and publishing three seditious articles in *Young India*. They were, indeed, seditious: one of them declares it in so many words ("sedition has become the creed of the Congress"), and it also declares it a sin for any soldier or civilian to serve the government. The attention of the whole country (and, for the first time, of the entire world) centered upon Gandhi on the day of the trial. He did not defend himself against the charges—indeed, he stated that he was more seditious, and had been more seditious for a longer time, than the government's case charged. He asked the judge to impose the highest penalty.

The Mahatma's statement had a tremendous effect at the time. His behavior still had, in 1922, the element of surprise—people in general seem to have thought he would defend himself somehow, or at least ask for mercy. The judge, Mr. C. N. Broomfield, was obviously embarrassed and regretful. "It will be impossible to ignore the fact that you are in a different category from any person I have ever tried," he said. The sentence imposed was six years of simple imprisonment. "If the course of events in India should make it possible for the government to reduce the period," the judge added, "no one will be better pleased than I."

Gandhi was led away between kneeling, weeping spectators.

It is worth pointing out once again that imprisonment was not only welcome to

Gandhi, but absolutely essential. His system depended on it. Moreover, he never asked others to do anything he was not willing to do himself. Possibly the cleverest thing the British could have done would have been never to arrest him at all; he might have abandoned public life if he had been immune to punishment while others suffered. In any case, the British were not clever, so (as the Mahatma would say) "the contingency did not arise."

GANDHI was lodged in solitary confinement in Yeravda Jail from March 20, 1922, to January 12, 1924. He said himself, in one of his letters from jail, that he was "happy as a bird." His life outside of prison was now so totally public that incarceration genuinely appealed to his solitary and contemplative nature.

The British were extremely courteous to him, and when they realized that he had taken a vow to spin every day, they broke their own rules and allowed a spinning wheel to be brought into the cell. He spent four hours each day at it. The wheel no doubt had a fundamental mystic significance, as it does throughout the Indic and

Buddist world, but for Gandhi it had also an almost immeasurable practical importance for "the economic salvation of impoverished India." The rest of his day (four in the morning to eight at night) was given to books, correspondence, and meditation.

This happy existence was brought to an end by a sudden appendicitis. The dilemma of the British was painful. They could not permit him to die in jail, but neither could they risk an unsuccessful operation. They transferred him in haste to the Sassoon Hospital in Poona, where the Mahatma signed a declaration that he had consented to an operation, and that, whatever happened, the people of India should not make it a pretext for agitation. This precaution was highly necessary, for at the mere rumor of his illness excitement began to rise all over the country.

The operation, by a colonel of the British Medical Corps, was successful, though performed under difficulties, for the electricity went off and the job had to be done by the light of a hurricane lantern. The government then decided that Gandhi had been in prison long enough, and on February 5 he was released. In the midst of great national rejoicing, he went to Juhu Beach, near Bombay, to convalesce in the house of a well-to-do friend.

Gandhi's term in prison (almost two years) had undone much of his most cherished work. The Congress Party had passed into the hands of the activists, C. R. Das and Motilal Nehru, father of Jawaharlal; all the boycotts were dead or dying: lawyers were returning to their practices and students to their colleges; noncooperation had ceased and there had been no civil disobedience since Gandhi had himself canceled it. But worst of all in Gandhi's eyes, Hindu-Moslem unity had been shattered, and there had been communal riots and murder in a number of places.

Under these circumstances Gandhi, who did not want to split the nationalists into factions, decided to leave politics and devote himself to what he called "constructive work." He adhered to this line for several years, but in point of fact everything he said or did had some influence on politics because the masses would have no other guru. His constructive work itself had vast political effects—the spinning wheel, for instance, and his work for the untouchables. He held that the key to *swaraj* (self-rule) for India was not in British, but in Indian hands. India would be free when it was purified, and not before.

In this task of "purifying India" it was obvious that the first thing must be a restoration of friendliness between Hindus and Moslems. As soon as his strength was partially restored, Gandhi resumed the editorship of his weekly magazine, *Young India*, and in it he returned again and again to the subject of deteriorating Hindu-Moslem relations.

In the summer of 1924 things went from bad to worse between the two communities. Mobs got out of hand in cities. When Gandhi went to a meeting of the Congress Working Committee that June and was made to understand that a considerable number of his own associates did not believe in his nonviolence, he wept publicly. They had followed his nonviolent campaign two years before because it had seemed to be getting results, not because they had believed in it as a principle.

On September 18, 1924, therefore, Gandhi had recourse to his supreme remedy and declared a fast of twenty-one days to pray for peace between Hindu and Moslem.

His physical condition made this an extremely reckless undertaking, and yet it seems clear that nothing else could have brought peace to India. The Mahatma had been writing and speaking on the subject ever since his release from prison, and the situation had grown steadily worse. He felt that people no longer listened to him. The "craze for darshan," as he called it— the desire of the masses to receive the mystical blessing that is supposed to come from the sight of a saint or even of a great leader of men—got in the way of his work. And it was indeed true that many gazed upon the Mahatma with reverence and with love, but listened to not a word he was saying.

The sources of Gandhi's power over the masses of Indians were numerous and complex, but high among them must be named the instinct for symbolic action. Certain of his most characteristic acts (such as this fast, and later the Salt

March) carried the stamp of a peculiar genius, one that knew how to dramatize the truth. This twenty-one-day fast was grim torture part of the time and profoundly serious all of the time, yet it conveyed to the most ignorant villager the truth of a great sacrifice for peace. Long before the fast was over, Hindus and Moslems, with prayer and weeping, had pledged themselves by the millions to keep the peace.

Mohammed Ali, Gandhi's friend of the 1921 campaign, had a house in Delhi, and it was there, sheltered by Moslems and cared for by Moslem doctors, that the Mahatma chose to undergo his fast. His great friend, the Christian missionary Charles Freer Andrews ("Charlie"), acted as his nurse. The prayers and hymns at the beginning and the end of the epic endeavor were Moslem, Christian, and Hindu. In every respect the dramatization of the Mahatma's truth was carried out so that the whole world could see what religious unity might achieve. The thing in itself, however, held the imagination of the world for those three weeks. The fast had tremendous immediate results. They were all, unfortunately, based upon fear for Gandhi's life; and in stony fact the enmity between Hindu and Moslem did not really diminish. No symbol of such incontrovertible purity had been offered the world for a very long time. The fragile little man seems to have had some inner assurance that he could fast three weeks without a danger of suicide, and he ended the fast exactly as planned, on Wednesday, October 6, at midday.

IN THE years preceding the great struggle that reached its climax in the Salt March (1930), Gandhi devoted himself almost entirely to his constructive work, and most of all to the spinning wheel. More Indians were learning to spin, and more homespun was being worn. In 1925 the All-Indian Spinners' Association was formed. Gandhi himself made incessant long tours throughout the country, always pursuing his aim of the "purification of India." His teaching was not always received by the minds of his audiences, but his moral authority was as supreme when he ignored politics as when he took an active part. Nothing of which he really disapproved could get far in Indian political life.

The years 1924–1928 are remarkable, as Louis Fischer has pointed out in his *Life of Mahatma Gandhi,* for the fact that in all of Gandhi's voluminous speaking and writing there is little reference to British rule. He was at this period intent on "swaraj from within"—that is, on preparing India, by "purification" and endless teaching, for the pure satyagraha that would someday be possible and would bring freedom. In this preparation the British had no part: it was Indians who had to be made ready from within, Indians who must learn to be clean and truthful and to spin and weave their cloth and walk uprightly with their God. The time for the British would come later, when Indians had been made ready.

Gandhi was much plagued during the 1920's by various outbursts of excessive reverence touching on worship. He did not like it. One tribe, the Gonds, had deified him outright, to his horror. He was represented in temples from about 1924 or 1925 on. His dislike for these excesses of the Indian religious instinct was strong.

Most of all, he seems to have been

embarrassed by legend and miracle. He tried to laugh them out of existence. A man traveling on a train with him fell out, landed on his head, and came up smiling. His miraculous escape, he said, had been due to the fact that he was traveling with the Mahatma. The Mahatma said: "But in that case you wouldn't have fallen out at all." A poor man in Bengal came to him wearing a photograph of the Mahatma on a chain around his neck; the man had been paralyzed, he said, and by endlessly repeating the name of Gandhi, he had been cured. "It was God who cured you, not Gandhi," the Mahatma said sharply, "and kindly oblige me by taking that photograph off your neck."

When he first came out of jail, Gandhi intended to retire from political life. The spontaneous protest that arose from the whole country delayed him a bit; he accepted the presidency of the Congress for 1925 on one condition: that the Congress should take to wearing homespun, and every member of Congress was to spin an hour each day. The Congress—then badly split in political views—could not do without Gandhi; to preserve their unity they all accepted *khadi*, and from 1925 onward it became the official wear for all Indian nationalists.

In 1926, after his year's presidency of the Congress, Mahatma declared a year of "political silence," during which he vowed to say nothing on political subjects and to remain in his own ashram. There is no doubt that he needed a rest, body and soul. He was certainly not idle during the year; his voluminous correspondence and *Young India* alone were enough to keep him busy.

On the sexual questions that filled *Young India* Gandhi made a long series of pertinent answers during the year. He recognized the need for birth control in India, but wanted to see it brought about by self-control and not by artificial contraceptives, which were repugnant to him on religious grounds. He ceaselessly advocated late marriages, vegetarianism, exercise, prayer, and work as means to controlling sexual desire. He attacked child marriage as vehemently as he did untouchability and other evils; the existence of child widows (who could not remarry under Hindu law) was a great horror to him. He gave the

130

British figures for 1921: 329,076 widows under sixteen in India, 85,037 of them between the ages of five and ten. He permitted girls in his ashram to marry only after they had reached twenty-one, and in print he advocated twenty-five as the marriage age for boys.

Lord Irwin (later Lord Halifax), the new viceroy, arrived in India on April 1, 1926. Gandhi did not mention this in *Young India,* and it was October 1927 before the viceroy sent for Gandhi. By this time the Mahatma had finished his "year of political silence" and was again touring India. Now he journeyed to Delhi to see the viceroy and was confronted with a strange bit of paper announcing that Sir John Simon would soon arrive in India at the head of a parliamentary commission of inquiry on Indian conditions, with the power to recommend reforms. Gandhi accepted the paper and departed without comment.

The Simon Commission was doomed from the start because it contained no Indian members and was responsible only to the British Parliament. It was the creation of Lord Birkenhead, then secretary of state for India, whose oratory had made him famous, but who was singularly unsuited to the realities he now faced. "What man in this House," Birkenhead asked in the Commons in 1929, "can say that he can see in a generation, in two generations, in a hundred years, any prospect that the people of India will be in a position to assume control of the Army, the Navy, the Civil Service, and to have a Governor-General who will be responsible to the Indian government and not to any authority in this country?"

Boycotted by all responsible groups, the Simon Commission produced a political dead letter.

On February 28, 1928, Mahatma Gandhi returned to the very plan he had adopted and discarded six years before: a campaign of civil disobedience in the single district of Bardoli, in the Bombay presidency. It was to be a campaign to the end, for the government had decreed a twenty-two-percent increase in taxation for the peasants of Bardoli, and they could not pay it.

Gandhi directed operations from his ashram. Sardar Vallabhbhai Patel, a brilliant Bombay lawyer who had now been his follower for some twelve years, was the field general for the struggle. It went on from February 28 to August 6. The eighty-seven thousand peasants of Bardoli refused to pay their taxes.

The government fumed and raged. Cattle, carts, possessions were seized, and many peasants went to jail. Land was taken, too. The peasants held firm, and there was no violence at all. Money poured in from all over India and abroad to help the peasants keep alive. On June 12, when the struggle had continued for three and a half months, Gandhi proclaimed a hartal for all India in sympathy for Bardoli. Again, as once before, nobody went to work, and India was completely paralyzed. These immense warnings to the British were brought about with no violence whatsoever.

On August 6 the government gave in, repealed the increase in taxes, released the Bardoli prisoners, returned the confiscated land, and promised to make good on animals or property that had been seized.

The significance of the victory, promising greater victories on a larger scale whenever the Mahatma wished to bring them about, was not lost on India. Talk of complete independence was becoming common. Swaraj (self-rule) was too vague a term for the young men. Subhas Chandra Bose, then in the early stages of his career as a nationalist, was a frank believer in violence as a political weapon. Jawaharlal Nehru, though not bloodthirsty like Bose, also wanted independence as the declared aim of the nationalist movement.

Gandhi distrusted all this hotheadedness because he feared that it might lead to violence, in which he knew that the dangers to India would be very great. He went to the annual Congress meeting (Calcutta, December 1928) in a mood of caution. He was unable to put down the revolt of the young men, and compromised by asking for a delay of one year: that is, if India had not attained swaraj by the end of 1929, the Mahatma promised to support a declaration of complete independence. With this the young men had to be content.

Gandhi spent the year touring India, trying to prepare the people for a gigantic

134

effort of satyagraha in the months to come. He did not talk politics much; he tried instead to explain his principles more clearly so that he might be able to count on truth and nonviolence when the hour should strike. Meanwhile, after a journey to London, the viceroy, Lord Irwin, made a statement favoring a Round Table Conference of British and Indian representatives to study Indian constitutional progress, with dominion status as the aim. This produced a storm in London, and the position of the Labour Party was much too weak to hold against the Tory thunder. When Gandhi and the other leaders went to see the viceroy on December 23 he was forced to tell them that he could give no pledges—he could not "prejudge" the decisions of the Round Table Conference.

This was, in effect, the real decision. Gandhi now had no recourse. At the annual meeting of the Indian National Congress at Lahore he accepted the principle of a declaration of complete independence from the British. That Congress meeting was for the first time presided over by Jawaharlal Nehru, then just forty years of age. Gandhi retired to his ashram afterward to write the Declaration of Independence of India, proclaimed on January 26, 1930.

VI
The Salt March to Victory

FROM the moment of the Declaration of Independence it was known throughout the world that Gandhi would soon engage in a new campaign against the government, but nobody knew what form it would take. Gandhi himself was at a loss, it seems, for a time. Whatever he did had to be nonviolent, injuring no Englishman; it must be loyally notified in advance to the opponent and carried out with rigid discipline in every part of the country. When Tagore visited him early in the year and asked him what was coming, the Mahatma told the poet that he could not see any light in the darkness: the means eluded him.

They did not elude him for long. From February onward those who read *Young India* realized that the Mahatma's thoughts were dwelling on the salt laws. Salt was a British government monopoly in India; nobody could make it or buy it except from the government. Two articles in *Young India* analyzed the salt laws and their iniquity as an example of foreign rule, foreign exploitation. Then, on March 2, 1930, Gandhi wrote his famous letter to the viceroy. It begins:

> Dear Friend, Before embarking on Civil Disobedience and taking the risk I have dreaded to take all these years, I would fain approach you and find a way out.

The letter proclaims his central principle ("I cannot intentionally hurt anything that lives, much less human beings"), but then proceeds to indict the British administration for its exploitation of India. He asks the viceroy "on bended knee" to consider these things and discuss them. If no discussion is possible, "on the eleventh day of this month I shall proceed with such co-workers of the ashram as I can take, to disregard the provisions of the Salt Laws. . . . It is, I know, open to you to frustrate my design by arresting me. I hope that there will be tens of thousands ready, in a disciplined manner, to take up the work after me."

Lord Irwin was faced with a tremendous problem, and we can have no doubt that he relied heavily upon cablegrams to and from London. A great part of the Labour Party was openly in favor of independence, or at least dominion status, for India. The world at large waited with intense interest. The main question for Lord Irwin, a man of rare quality, was whether or not to arrest Gandhi. If he went to jail, there was no telling how violent the coming movement might become. And yet not to arrest him was to court disaster.

Years later Lord Irwin (by then Lord Halifax) told me that his personal regard for "the little man" had never faltered, and that "the little man" had never once broken his word. Lord Halifax was a very religious man, and the conflict in his own breast must have been painful. In the immediate situation created by Gandhi's letter, the viceroy decided to sidestep. He had a secretary write the simple answer that His Excellency regretted to learn that Mr. Gandhi intended to act in a way "clearly bound to involve violation of the law and danger to the public peace."

Gandhi waited, prayed, meditated, while the whole world grew more attentive to his slightest word. Nobody knew what exactly was coming. His natural sense of drama prompted him to keep his own counsel until the great day arrived. Then, on March 12, 1930, he and seventy-eight members of his ashram started to walk from Ahmedabad to Dandi, on the seacoast two hundred miles away. Followed by great crowds, he went some of the time barefoot and some of the time in sandals.

The excitement throughout India has perhaps never been equaled. The Salt March lasted twenty-four days. The little old man in the loincloth was the center of the world's attention when he started out; by the time the Salt March ended, no other topic anywhere aroused such universal interest.

Gandhi was happy and healthy, as always when he was doing something he regarded as God's work. Some of his disciples grew sore and weary, but he never flagged. He thought twelve miles a day, the most they could manage in such a procession, no strain at all. At each village he would talk to the people, telling them that a great ordeal was at hand, and that they must live purely, tell the truth, wear only homespun, wash themselves regularly, forswear alcohol and drugs, give up the abuses of Hinduism (such as child marriage), and prepare to break the salt laws when the signal would be given them.

The villagers sprinkled the roads to keep the dust from his feet; they strewed leaves and branches in his path; they followed him to the next village before turning back home. The procession went on and on, while the government sat back, aghast at the power of this strange new movement.

On April 5, 1930, Gandhi and his immediate followers prayed all night long. In the early morning they went down to the sea. The Mahatma dipped into the water and picked up some salt from the shore. It was only a pinch of salt, but it was enough. He had symbolically broken the law and defied the empire.

Salt was the commonest of necessities. Salt was something every peasant could understand. Salt was God's gift, and the wicked foreign government had stolen it from the people.

The disciplined execution of the salt campaign was the high point of satyagraha as a whole. Demonstrably it hurt nobody; it was perfectly nonviolent; it was merely illegal. The government was compelled to act precisely as Gandhi had foreseen, and with the results he had foreseen.

The Mahatma was not arrested at once. The whole country burst into a flame of action as soon as the signal had been given on the seashore at Dandi. Everybody made salt, sold or bought salt, did everything possible to contravene the salt laws. The government began arresting people from one end of India to the other, but others constantly took their places. Neither the police nor the Army could adequately deal with a situation in which virtually the whole population was breaking the law. Nor were the jails of India able to hold all the lawbreakers.

Gandhi remained in camp with his seventy-eight followers for the weeks that followed. He did not again pick up any salt; millions were doing it for him all along the immense seacoast of India. The Congress

Party organized the illegal sale of salt, quite publicly, throughout the nation. The government went on with the campaign of repression, until by the end of a single month over sixty thousand persons were in jail for breaking the salt laws. Censorship was imposed on the Indian press. One by one the leaders of India went to jail, Nehru, Rajaji, Devadas Gandhi. On May 5 Gandhi also was arrested. There was no charge and no trial. He was taken to Yeravda Jail. There he was happy with his spinning and his books.

The salt campaign continued. Gandhi had intended to raid the Dharasana Salt Works, and had so informed the viceroy. This act was carried out by Sarojini Naidu, whose radiant personality shines through the whole Gandhian epic. The well-known American correspondent Webb Miller was present at the Dharasana raid, and he wrote a description of it:

> Suddenly, at a word of command, scores of native police rushed upon the advancing marchers and rained blows on their heads with their steel-shod lathis. Not one of the marchers even raised an arm to fend off the blows. They went down like tenpins.

From where I stood I heard the sickening whacks of the clubs on unprotected skulls. The waiting crowd of watchers groaned and sucked in their breath in sympathetic pain at every blow. Those struck down fell sprawling, unconscious or writhing in pain with fractured skulls or broken shoulders. . . . The survivors, without breaking ranks, silently and doggedly marched on until struck down.

This astounding scene was repeated for several days thereafter, and on all these occasions the violence was entirely on the side of the police. Sarojini Naidu was arrested the first day.

The government was in grave difficulty now; all work was handicapped by the resignations of numerous Indians in the offices; revenue was declining rapidly; the jails were packed (one hundred thousand political prisoners) and the police were weary; there seemed no issue from this dilemma except by giving in to Gandhi. Gandhi, when approached in Yeravda Jail, said he could not discuss terms without consulting members of the Congress Working Committee. The government then transported its most notable prisoners by special train to Yeravda Jail to talk with the Mahatma. As a result a communiqué was issued that an "unbridgeable gulf" separated the Indian leaders from the British on terms for peace.

There was a Round Table Conference on India in London in November 1930, but it was quite useless because no leader of consequence except Mohammed Ali Jinnah was willing to attend it. The time had come for the government to give in, and it did. The Indian leaders, beginning with Gandhi, were set free unconditionally on Indian Independence Day, January 26, 1931. The Mahatma wrote at once to the viceroy, thanking him for this act and asking if they could not talk things over.

The Gandhi-Halifax (or Gandhi-Irwin) conversations had the historic importance of being the first in which Indian and Englishman spoke as equals, representing countries which henceforth would deal with each other as equals.

Winston Churchill saw this most clearly when he made his celebrated invective in the House of Commons, speaking of "the nauseating and humiliating spectacle of this . . . seditious fakir, striding half-naked

144

up the steps of the viceroy's palace, there to negotiate and to parley on equal terms with the representative of the King-Emperor."

Irwin, so tall, so infinitely *grand seigneur*, must indeed have made a striking contrast to the dark little man in the loincloth whose greatness was of another kind, and whose unique demeanor treated everybody he met as an equal.

The Mahatma made good progress with Irwin. They ended their series of conversations with a high mutual regard in spite of a great deal of hard bargaining and weary disagreements. Irwin was obliged to consult London at every stage, and Gandhi had to keep the Congress Working Committee fully informed and in agreement. The Gandhi-Irwin Pact, signed March 7, 1930, made no stipulation on the future status of India, but restored peace to India; civil disobedience would be called off, political prisoners released, salt made free along the seacoasts, and the Indian National Congress agreed to be represented at the second Round Table Conference in London.

The pact itself, however, as others have

quite accurately pointed out, was more important than any of its contents. Its essential character is that of an agreement between equals, and in this respect it constitutes a tacit acknowledgment of independence. The seventeen transitional years that followed may have made many Indians impatient and caused others to doubt British good faith, but the main point was gained in 1930 and all the rest was detail.

Gandhi stood now at the apex of his career, politically speaking. The annual meeting of the Congress elected him as its sole representative at the Round Table Conference in London, and he sailed on August 29.

The conference brought Gandhi squarely into the center of the world's attention. The press of the period, in all nations, reflects the intense curiosity he had aroused, though his clothing and diet commanded more space in the American press than his ideas. He could not alter his habits just because he was on a mission to the West. He traveled to England as a deck passenger, with his own goat, which he milked. He would not go to a West

146

End hotel in London, but stayed at a settlement house in the slums, because he liked to live among the poor.

And they liked him to be there. He was followed in the streets by friendly crowds, and often by children. It is much to the credit of the English character that during all this visit nobody showed any open hostility to Gandhi—in fact, few native-born English heroes have been so warmly greeted by the multitude. Detectives must have been scattered about in these crowds, but they had no work to do. It seems Gandhi's transparent honesty, his simplicity, and his evident friendliness toward all human creatures won the people's hearts and caused them to ignore the political differences that had brought him to London. Even in Manchester, which was in the midst of a terrible crisis of unemployment and depression brought about partly by his boycott of foreign cloth, he was welcomed by cheering thousands.

The Gandhi legend, now in its full maturity, multiplied incessantly during these weeks and filled the press of the world with stories, some true and some false, but all more or less in character.

Everybody of note and many of no note wanted a Gandhi interview: scholars, theologians, and scientists, as well as politicians or journalists. Bernard Shaw, the Archbishop of Canterbury, the King, the Queen, the youngest American newspaper reporter, the children in the streets—all were the same to Gandhi, and he treated them exactly alike. The loincloth, the goat, the almost toothless grin, the unfailing good humor, and the love of innocent laughter—all became familiar to the whole Western world. His own remark on the subject of his clothes, "You wear plus-fours and I wear minus-fours," went around the world.

Gandhi's time in England (almost three months) was spent more in an effort to get the English people into sympathy with India than it was on the Round Table Conference itself. This, of course, he did attend, as the sole Congress representative, but there was little likelihood of a firm agreement because he was obliged at the outset to make it clear that the Congress wanted complete independence for India. This was contrary to Article 2 of the Gandhi-Irwin Pact, which had reserved

148

defense, foreign affairs, and certain national debts for British control. The Congress had repudiated Gandhi on this, and he was now under instructions to say so. To the English it seemed that the repudiation was Gandhi's; he had signed the pact and now was going back on his signature. To Gandhi it was probably apparent that he could not get complete independence for India then, and that the best course would be to prepare the English people to grant it in the future.

He talked incessantly to every kind of audience, visited Oxford and Cambridge, Lancashire and Eton, and a large number of organized groups in London. His main effort was to explain the meaning of independence for India, and his definitions were remarkably like what eventually took place. He would cut India off "from the Empire entirely, from the British nation not at all, if I want India to gain and not to grieve. The Emperorship must go and I should love to be an equal partner with Britain, sharing her joys and sorrows, and an equal partner with the Dominions. But it must be a partnership on equal terms."

Gandhi's work was deeply felt in England, and when independence did come, England freely granted it, and India one year later chose to remain in "association" with the Commonwealth. This was a precise fulfillment of Gandhi's plea in 1930.

The Round Table Conference itself, as a body to plan India's future, started with hardly any chance of success, as it was composed of inherently divisive elements. Lord Reading, at the outset, defined its purpose as being "to give effect to the views of India while preserving at the same time our own position, which we must not and cannot abandon." The viceroy (now Lord Willingdon) had sent to London a handpicked collection of reactionaries and factional representatives whose ideas and interests were all against any form of real union in India. Each faction wanted to vote separately, as a faction—Moslems voting for Moslems, Parsees for Parsees, and so on—in the legislative elections to be set up under the new constitution.

This was contrary to every principle or wish Gandhi had. He wanted no separate electorates—Indians were all Indians and should vote as Indians. The perpetuation of India's divisions would, he foresaw, lead to more and greater trouble. British prestige was, in spite of everything, high in India, and because the British had appeared to condone factionalism at this conference, nothing could be easier for an agitator from then on than to claim British support or approval.

The conference ended on December 1, 1931, in complete failure. By dividing the Indians more sharply than ever before, it probably made things a good deal worse.

THE news Gandhi learned on his return to Bombay was anything but good. The government had started a new campaign of repression and arrests in the north and northwest because of a Congress campaign against paying rent. Jawaharlal Nehru had been put in jail two days before Gandhi's homecoming. Gandhi tried at once to see the viceroy (Lord Willingdon), but the viceroy obviously did not want to see him. The homecoming was December 28, 1931; and on January 4, 1932, the Mahatma was arrested again. This time, as the time before, no charges were made and no trial was held; he was in Yeravda Jail at the government's pleasure.

His usual jail happiness was impaired and finally extinguished by the decision of the British government to create, in the new constitution for India, separate electorates not only for Hindus and Moslems, but also for the "depressed classes," the untouchables. For these people, the stepchildren of Hinduism, Gandhi had labored all his life, but he did not want them used as a means of dividing Indians from one another. Nevertheless, in spite of Gandhi's numerous protests, the British government went on with the scheme, which Ramsay MacDonald, the prime minister, announced in London on August 17.

Gandhi's response was terrible. He declared (August 18) in his letter to MacDonald that he would be compelled to fast "unto death," beginning September 20.

The fast began on September 20 at noon. Many millions of Indians fasted on that day; the country was in mourning. The Indian leaders hastily began to negotiate some kind of settlement which would induce Gandhi to cease fasting. He was not strong at this time, and even the first twenty-four hours visibly sapped his reserves. On the fourth day he was thought to be sinking, and serious fear for his life fell upon the whole country. Ambedkar, the untouchables' leader, who was not a Gandhi follower, was the most difficult for the Hindus to deal with, and yet no compromise settlement would be worth making unless it bore his signature. He visited Gandhi in jail, and the general lines of an agreement were hammered out in long, labored discussions of all the leaders and signed by them on September 24. The Mahatma approved of the compromise, but he could not cease fasting until the British government had also approved. On September 26, it was simultaneously announced in London and Delhi that the British government would accept the Yeravda Pact. The Mahatma's fast ended that day, when he accepted a glass of orange juice from his wife, Kasturba.

The fast had an electrical effect on Indian society. In demonstrations throughout the country, caste Hindus mingled with untouchables and ate meals with them; temples were thrown open to the untouchables; pledges to work against discrimination were made and sent to Gandhi's prison. The six days of the fast were treated as a period of mourning throughout India, and the end of the fast was the occasion for national celebration.

Gandhi had asked the Hindu mind to "banish untouchability root and branch." For this larger objective the agreement on a combined electorate was not in itself very important, but the great movement throughout Hindu society to meet Gandhi's wishes was a vital force. The Mahatma's most permanent objective, the purification of India, which always seemed to him more important than anything in politics, was advanced by the fast of 1932 more than by decades of preaching or teaching.

And, too, it seems to have turned the Mahatma's own mind more firmly toward those nonpolitical purposes which commanded his adherence. He referred to these purposes as his constructive work. From the fast on until the outbreak of the Second World War, Gandhi left politics to others and spent most of his energy on his

work for the untouchables, for women and children in villages, for "Basic Education," and for the spinning wheel. These activities, like nursing, appealed to his innermost nature. He could walk from village to village barefoot, month after month, with apparently indefatigable energy, preaching against untouchability, telling the people to be clean and to love one another. And at the outset of this period, for self-purification he undertook a fast of twenty-one days. On the day it began, the government released him from prison, as his death there would have been a calamity for the British raj. It did not seem possible that he could survive a fast of three whole weeks, when only six days of abstinence from food had brought him to death's door six months earlier. And yet the long fast, unaccompanied by the anxiety of the six days in September, left him as well as ever—he would have said, better.

He founded the Harijan Sevak Sangh, a society to improve the lot of the untouchables by model villages and schools and in other ways, in February 1933, while he was still in prison, and at the same time

156

started a weekly paper called *Harijan* to take the place of *Young India. Harijan* was his own word for the untouchables; it means "children of God." From that time until his death he never ceased to do everything he could, in the most practical way, for these oppressed victims of the caste system. One of his endearing habits in later years was to give his autograph—which was constantly in demand—in exchange for five or ten rupees for the Harijan work. Anybody who wrote to him, from any part of the world, could get the signature, but he firmly collected the fee.

Gandhi's ideas of "Basic Education" have been carried out on a very large scale in several provinces since his death. He had been much impressed by Mme. Montessori and her methods in London in 1930, and his own system may owe a good deal to her. He started, as always, with the mass level, the level of the poor Indian villager whose maintenance standards (food and clothing) he emulated. Such a villager cannot afford to lose the work of his children. Therefore the school must combine learning with useful work, which should be remunerated. That is, if a boy

157

can make a good bench or a pair of sandals he ought to be paid for them, and his schooltime must be apportioned between useful arts of this sort and ordinary learning.

Gandhi in his unceasing movement about India brought all his ideas to the people as nobody had done, in all probability, since Gautama Buddha. It is quite possible to find places in India which Gandhi never visited. The country is enormous and the villages are innumerable. But almost any Indian one meets anywhere, including the poorest, has a memory of at least one sight of the Mahatma.

GANDHI was out of politics now, but politicians were forever consulting him; he would not scruple to make them wait outside while he doctored a beggar or administered to a leper. His approval was necessary for any decision of importance, and his disapproval was fatal to any idea or activity. Jawaharlal Nehru, recurrently president of the Congress, said that Gandhi was "the permanent Super-President." When Gandhi consented to Indian participation in the legislatures set up under the new constitution, Congress candidates were triumphant in many provinces and took part in the government. This was, in Gandhi's eyes, a prelude to independence, perhaps a training for it.

The Second World War was the occasion of his return to public affairs. When war was declared, the British government brought India into it at once without consulting any Indian. This offended all opinion in India.

The viceroy (by this time Lord Linlithgow) asked Gandhi to come to Simla the day after war was declared. Gandhi had watched the progress of fascism in Europe with much foreboding, and he was clear in his condemnation of Hitler's system: it was "naked ruthless force reduced to an exact science." In the Simla interview he pledged his moral support to England and the Allies, and declared that "my whole heart is with the Poles in the unequal struggle in which they are engaged for the sake of their freedom."

These declarations were as far as he would go in supporting the war; he did not intend to take any active part and would not even have defended India against aggression. Thus he was out of step with both British and Indian political leaders. The Congress felt that India could support the war effort on certain political conditions. Gandhi was never willing to bargain on a principle. "Whatever support was to be given to the British should be given unconditionally," he said.

Nevertheless the Congress leaders went ahead with their manifesto of September 14, 1939, which condemned Hitler's aggression but also blamed the Western democracies for their imperialism and concluded that "a free India" would gladly associate itself with other free nations. This manifesto (the work of Jawaharlal Nehru) did not represent Gandhi's views, but once it had been issued Gandhi asked the country to support it, hoping that this "departure from the nonviolent method will be confined to the narrowest field and will be temporary."

The viceroy replied to the Congress manifesto, obviously on orders from London, that England could not yet define war aims; he cautioned India against too rapid advances in self-government. The

Congress thereupon voted to abstain from any help to England, and asked the Congress members of provincial governments to resign.

Gandhi's delicate conscience did not like even the appearance of taking advantage of England's difficulties, and above all, he wished to cling to nonviolence. Meanwhile the rush of events in the spring of 1940 threw India, too, like most of the world, into apprehension; Hitler seemed to have conquered Europe. There was some panic, some runs on British banks. Gandhi asked the country to be calm and said that if Britain had to die, it would be "heroically." He seems to have had a very accurate notion of the last-ditch courage and toughness of the British.

Nehru, however, in his desire both to aid the war effort and to get some advantage for India out of doing so, was in control of the Congress Working Committee, ably assisted by Rajaji. The Mahatma knew his nonviolence did not suit the mood of the moment, and all he could do was let the resolution pass, in which the Congress promised to "throw its full weight" into the defense effort if India was given independence and an Indian government.

Winston Churchill was prime minister in London, and the independence of India was never an acceptable idea to him. Also, it may be historically doubted whether the crisis of a desperate war was the correct moment for such a difficult operation as the transfer of power.

In any case, the answer to Congress was a firm negative, accompanied by the statement that Britain could not yield power to an Indian government to which large sections of the Indian population objected. This was a reference to the non-Congress and anti-Congress Moslems, who had been organized into a new and vital opposition by Mohammed Ali Jinnah.

Congress now swayed in the direction of nonviolent noncooperation again. It must have been all too evident to Gandhi that the political leaders adopted his principles only when they thought it advantageous to do so. Nevertheless, the Mahatma welcomed them back on his side, but cautioned them against doing anything to embarrass the British. He went in behalf of the Congress to see the

162

viceroy, proposing that the Congress should be free to work among the people even though it would not support the war effort. This, too, was refused.

Gandhi's conscience could not permit him to do any real harm to the British at such a moment, but neither could he accept this total denial of any rights to India. He decided upon a small-scale campaign of disobedience. In something like a year, 23,223 persons were jailed for speaking against the war effort.

Japan's entry into the war at the end of 1941 brought this phase of India's war experience to an end. The British government released the prisoners; Gandhi's views were no longer in control of Congress; the Japanese Army was sweeping across Southeast Asia and might soon be in India.

However, the United States and Russia were both now aligned against Hitler, and the United States against Japan as well. There was no longer any real doubt in high quarters that eventual victory was assured. But American opinion, always rather pro-Indian, was not happy over England's treatment of India; it seemed too much at variance with the declared purposes of the war. Much evidence has appeared in recent years to show that President Roosevelt never let the subject of India drop for long in his correspondence with Mr. Churchill. Strong elements in England itself agreed with Roosevelt rather than with Churchill: the Indian contradiction, it seemed plain, would have to be solved sooner or later, and the sooner the better for Allied purposes.

It was at this point that Churchill sent Sir Stafford Cripps to India to discuss possible constitutional changes with Indian leaders. Cripps arrived in New Delhi with definite proposals for dominion status, which includes the right to leave the Commonwealth at any time. This was to come when the war was over, and was to be accompanied by a provision allowing any province or area to secede from the Indian Union and form a separate dominion.

The only thing in the Cripps proposals that Gandhi could have accepted was dominion status. The rest—special status for the Indian princes and the threat of "vivisection," or partitioning of India—he

164

could not accept. The final article on the war effort was antipathetic to nonviolence. Consequently Gandhi rejected the whole Cripps proposal at first sight and went home.

Nehru and Rajaji continued the talks, as did the leaders of many Indian factions and minorities, but in the end the proposals were not accepted. Cripps went back to England on April 12. Churchill, obviously, had already gone so far beyond his own true convictions in this matter that he must, one feels, have been glad that the Cripps mission failed, the "dissolution of his Majesty's empire," as he called it, was for others to bring into history.

Perhaps Gandhi wished to face the threatened Japanese invasion with a passive resistance on a mammoth scale, and thought he could only do so if India was free to make the attempt. Without freedom, without a national government, India would of course be defended by British and Allied forces in the conventional manner, and though Gandhi did not wish to impede them, neither would he aid them.

Gandhi's thinking at this point was far

different from that of his closest political friends and followers, all of whom wanted independence precisely so that they could fight the war. Nehru, in particular, had been an anti-Fascist for years, and wanted to fight "in every way possible." The prerequisite was immediate independence for India, and the Working Committee so resolved at Wardha on July 14. If this was refused, the resolution declared, the Congress would be "reluctantly compelled" into a campaign of civil disobedience.

The final decision was taken by the All-India Congress Committee meeting in Bombay, August 7–8, 1942. In Gandhi's mind it did not mean that civil disobedience should begin at once; he wanted, as usual, to try negotiation first, and was actually working on a letter to President Roosevelt when he was arrested the morning of August 9, and taken to his last prison, the palace of the Aga Khan at Poona. With him were also arrested most of the other Congress leaders.

These arrests ended any hope of a peaceful, nonviolent campaign of civil disobedience. The Indian people were now leaderless and did not have the calming

166

power of Gandhi's voice and example to deter them from excesses. Gandhi was kept without newspapers during the first part of his imprisonment, and actually did not know, except from his jailers, what was going on in the country. Bands of Indians were tearing up railroad tracks, engaging in acts of violence, cutting telegraph wires, and attacking policemen. In some districts the movement, now completely out of hand, wore the aspect of armed rebellion.

When Gandhi began receiving newspapers, he could see that the governments both in Delhi and in London were engaged in what he called "distortions and misrepresentations," the purport of which was to make the Mahatma and the Congress responsible for the disorder in India. It was a typical effort of war propaganda, and he resented it very much. Therefore his first letter to the viceroy (August 14) was not much like Gandhi; five pages long, it was filled with accusations. Linlithgow replied very briefly that he could not accept this criticism.

On New Year's Eve, Gandhi again wrote to the viceroy and said that he was hurt that such an old friend should have jailed him without a hearing. He said that he was not responsible for the violence in the country, but that the government itself was. He had decided to fast, and he announced that it would begin February 9 and last twenty-one days.

The viceroy wrote back with unusual bluntness: "I regard the use of a fast for political purposes as a form of political blackmail." This was very strong language, considering how careful the Mahatma had always been to define his fasts. In his reply he said: "Despite your description of it as 'a form of political blackmail,' it is on my part an appeal to the Highest Tribunal for justice which I have failed to secure from you. Posterity will judge between you as a representative of an all-powerful government and me a humble man who has tried to serve his country and humanity through it."

The government tried to get out of this dilemma by releasing Gandhi; if released, he said, he would not fast—thus implying that he might engage in some other activity. He was just as troublesome to the viceroy in jail as out of it, but it was thought safer to let him fast while still confined at the Aga Khan's palace.

This fast (February 10 to March 2, 1943) was a terrible one for everybody in India, and the government was in fairly continuous hot water from all directions. It became necessary to allow the crowds to pass through the palace and see the Mahatma with their own eyes, the fear of his death having gripped the country. He sank steadily after the first week, and it seems to have been universally expected that he would die before the twenty-one days were over. Kasturba herself seems to have thought so.

Gandhi's own unhappiness during the period in the Aga Khan's palace—August 1942 to May 1944—was extreme. Violence was rampant over India, officially ascribed to his own doings. If he had not been arrested, he felt, he might have prevented the outbreak.

To this daily misery two great personal griefs were now added—first, the death of his devoted secretary, Mahadev Desai; second, the death of Kasturba herself, his lifelong companion, the wife of his youth. The Mahatma's sorrow in both cases was extreme, but he tried to express it in the *Gita* terms of detachment—not, perhaps, with much success. He had been living with Kasturba at this time for sixty-two years, and although she, as a devout and simple Hindu woman, had not been able to follow him in all his experiments with truth, she had absorbed much of his teaching without question. Both Mahadev and Kasturba were cremated in the prison courtyard and their ashes were buried side by side in the grounds.

After this personal tragedy the Mahatma suffered two severe illnesses, first malaria and afterward an intestinal trouble. The great Bengal famine of 1943 had come and gone while he was in prison; the disaffection of the Indian masses toward British rule was stronger than ever; it became obvious that if he died in prison very serious results would probably ensue. The new viceroy, Lord Wavell, released Gandhi, Patel, Mrs. Naidu, and their associates on May 6, 1944.

THE story of the next three years is essentially the tale of Gandhi's last struggle to save India from what he called vivisection. He had always worked toward national unity in the vast subcontinent. Now there appeared on the horizon, just when the liberation of India was at hand, the most serious of all threats to India's unity, a militantly nationalistic Moslem movement aiming at the creation of a separate nation.

That movement was recent: the very name of the new nation, Pakistan, had not yet become generally known. Moslems and Hindus had lived in all parts of India for centuries, mixed together in the villages and towns. They were substantially the same people, and most Moslems were descendants of Hindus who had been converted to Islam at various periods (and usually by the sword) in previous centuries. The languages of the south were the same for Hindu and Moslem alike. In the north a language distinction existed between Urdu, the Moslem language, and Hindi; and yet even these two languages used to be mutually intelligible.

Gandhi could see no reason why a separate Moslem state had to be. His famous expression on the subject, used to Mohammed Ali Jinnah, was: "You can cut me in two if you wish but don't cut India in two." Jinnah, on the contrary, declared that the Moslem nation already existed and must have its rights. One hundred million Moslems in a nation ruled by three hundred million Hindus would be submerged, he said.

Gandhi tried very hard. He knew, as he slowly recovered from his illness, that independence must be near, and could perhaps come now if he could unite the Moslems and the Hindus. Long years before, in South Africa, he had foreseen that the "crucial test" would be this. As soon as he was able, he wrote to Mohammed Ali Jinnah and proposed to talk over a compromise.

Those conversations took place in Jinnah's fine house in Bombay during the summer of 1944. Jinnah wanted the areas of big population to vote on secession from the Indian Union, but only Moslems should take part in such a vote: this meant that in a number of key provinces, where Moslems and Hindus were almost equal in population, the Hindus should be disenfranchised altogether. Gandhi was prepared, for the sake of peace, to let units of predominantly Moslem population vote for secession if they wished to do so after independence, but he hoped for a common administration in foreign affairs, customs, and the like.

Jinnah, an extremely able and successful lawyer, had once been a vigorous Congress Party worker, but he was personally jealous of Gandhi's unique position and disliked Jawaharlal Nehru. He was vain, as anybody knew who ever talked to him, and one element in his character must have been an unwillingness to play second fiddle to anybody. He made a militant anti-Congress force out of the Moslem League and adopted the Pakistan idea (which dates from 1936) as his war cry. In this new state he wished to put the provinces of Sind, Baluchistan, the Punjab, the North-West Frontier Province, Bengal, and Assam, and consequently, of course, a huge Hindu minority that thus would have nothing to say about its own fate. In less than ten years Jinnah had transformed the whole situation in India, so that to most politically active Indians it now appeared that the antagonist was not the

British at all, but the Indians of another religion.

Lord Wavell called all the leaders to Simla at the end of June 1945, when Churchill was still prime minister, and put before them a scheme that would have made the Viceroy's Council entirely Indian, made up of Indians chosen by the viceroy from lists drawn up by all parties. Moslems and Hindus were to be represented in "equal proportions," though Hindus outnumbered Moslems three to one. In effect, this was self-government, preserving only a vestige of the old empire, and the Congress leaders were prepared to accept it. Jinnah refused, seemingly because Wavell had named Moslem members of the council, whereas he alone should have had that right.

Events moved fast thereafter. Churchill was defeated in the British elections; a Labour government came to power and called Wavell home. On his return to India he announced a new plan: elections would be held for the provincial and central legislatures as a prelude to a new constitution. The election results might have been foreseen: the Congress won in districts with Hindu majorities and the Moslem League in Moslem areas.

To solve the problem of this tug-of-war, Clement Attlee decided to send three members of his cabinet to India—the Cabinet Mission—with authority to draw up a scheme for the transfer of power from British to Indian hands. The mission published its decisions on May 16, 1946. It had studied the ground carefully, and it took full account of Jinnah's demand for a separate Moslem nation. Its report points out that any line drawn for the partition of India would leave large minorities on each side, whereas lines drawn through the middle of provinces would violate local geography, economics, and traditions. In consequence, instead of partition, the ministers recommended a federal government with majorities of both Moslems and Hindus required for anything that concerned the religious communities. An interim government was to prepare the way for a constituent assembly.

There was a period of uncertainty, in Gandhi's mind as in others, about these proposals. Gandhi felt he had failed in his main mission in India—that Indians had not understood nonviolence and therefore he could not take up any kind of civil-disobedience campaign again. He thought the best thing for the Congress leaders to do would be to go into the constituent assembly and make the best of it.

The uncertainty lasted well into 1946. Jinnah might have entered the provisional government, but refused because he would allow no Moslem except one of his own to be in it; the Congress, too, had Moslem candidates. Finally the viceroy asked Nehru to form the provisional government, which came into being on September 2, 1946. This great event, which caused Gandhi to refer to Nehru "as your uncrowned king and Prime Minister," was treated by Jinnah and the Moslem League as the signal for mourning and the display of black flags. There had been terrible Hindu-Moslem riots in Calcutta the month before, with at least five thousand killed and over fifteen thousand wounded; these were followed by outbreaks in a dozen different places in the new nation.

One of Gandhi's last great marches took place as a result of the intercommunal violence, which now, perhaps more than ever before, grieved him to the depths. He chose East Bengal for a long walk through the villages. He had been living in a hut in the untouchables' quarter in New Delhi, where members of the new government could consult him more or less at will. The outbreak of violence in East Bengal had particularly aroused him because it had occurred in small villages, where, as a rule, Hindus and Moslems had always lived together without trouble. He decided to walk through the Noakhali and Tippera districts, where the murders had occurred.

The journey across India was done in a special train, as had become usual when the Mahatma traveled, for enormous crowds gathered at every station, and an ordinary train was so delayed that it upset the entire schedule. His special trains were made up of scrupulously clean third-class carriages.

Gandhi reached Noakhali on November 7, and stayed in the district until March 2, 1947, walking from village to village. These were very poor villages of the delta country where the Ganges and the Brahmaputra rivers run together, and there were neither roads nor transport. Gandhi himself stayed a few days in each village, or sometimes two days, and then walked on to the next, through country that had been cruelly hostile to Hindus, and with only three companions. For a large part of the time he walked barefoot. Sometimes the villages were half in ruins; there had been much looting; a good many frightened Hindus had gone away. The Mahatma kept on just the same, and the Mohammedans gathered by the thousand to listen to him. He preached his old message of brotherhood, purity of heart, forgiveness for injuries. Before his pilgrimage was over, a very great improvement had taken place in the relations of Moslems and Hindus in the Noakhali and Tippera districts. He now departed for Bihar, where there had been terrible bloodlettings, and the dead, mostly Moslems, were said to be over ten thousand. He carried the same message to Bihar, where the Hindus were the wrongdoers; and it was generally his way to be a little more severe with Hindus, his own people, than he ever was with Moslems. "I would forfeit my claim to being a Hindu," he said, "if I bolstered the wrongdoing of fellow Hindus or of any other human being."

But while he was on this long journey of compassion, watched by all of India, political affairs had reached a decisive phase. The Labour government was bent upon an immediate transfer of power in India, and for the first time named a date: "not later than June 1948." For the final negotiation and the actual transfer of power Mr. Attlee made an extremely auspicious choice as the last viceroy: Admiral Lord Mountbatten, a man with the skill, charm, and intelligence required for the unparalleled task.

Mountbatten arrived in Delhi on March 22, 1947, and immediately invited Gandhi and Jinnah to come to the palace. Independence had, in fact, come; all that remained to be done was to fix its terms. As Gandhi left Bihar for Delhi on what was to be the last of all his journeys, he must have thought that this was the end of a very long road, and in spite of all his sorrow, he must have had some pang of joy in the birth of freedom.

VII
Sacrifice and Fulfillment

THE Mahatma's ordeal reached its most acute stage during the six or eight months before his assassination, mainly because of the partition of India and the wave of human misery that followed.

Gandhi got on well with Mountbatten, as did all Indian leaders. It was not Mountbatten's fault that the fundamental condition of Indian independence now seemed to be partition. Jinnah, leading one hundred million Moslems, would accept nothing else. Mountbatten told him that he could have partition, but not at the price of taking vast numbers of Hindus and Sikhs into Pakistan against their will: a line of partition would have to be drawn that would cut through the Punjab and Bengal, two provinces he had claimed in their entirety. Nehru, Rajaji, and the rest of the Congress leaders would accept this as the price of independence. Gandhi conceded their right to do so, but partition never received more than his passive acceptance. This (the acceptance) occurred at the prayer meeting in Delhi on June 4, 1947, and settled the fate of the British Empire.

But all through that awful summer and winter the Mahatma was in storm and travail. There were riots and murders more or less everywhere. He felt his life had been wasted, had resulted in no achievement. Moslems were killing Hindus and Hindus were killing Moslems wherever the balance of numbers made massacres possible. It has been estimated that several millions (as many as seven or eight) lost their lives in this unprecedented mass murder, and something like fifteen million people were uprooted from their homes and hurled from Pakistan to India or from India to Pakistan.

No greater suffering for Mahatma Gandhi could have been devised. This is what he had given his life to prevent. He took his weary way again to Calcutta, where mass violence had been prevalent, and there drove or walked through the streets, talking to the people. He got there six days before the transfer of power from British to Indian hands.

On the actual day of India's liberation,

August 15, 1947, he passed his whole time in silence, fasting, and prayer. The effect of his own presence restored peace to Calcutta, but it was still not complete; the Mahatma declared a "fast unto death" or until Calcutta had returned to sanity. Within seventy-three hours Calcutta had returned to sanity. And it remained sane: during all the horrors of the next month or two in other parts of India, peace remained in Calcutta.

Gandhi left Calcutta on September 7 for Delhi, intending to go to the Punjab, but he was implored to stay in Delhi at the government's wish. He remained in Delhi, the capital of the new nation. The city was torn by evildoing of the most barbarous character. Murder was rife. No street was safe. I arrived there on the heels of the worst bloodshed and heard endless tales of it. The Moslems had almost completely been driven out or murdered by the time I got there. The Mahatma was ceaselessly active, and wherever he went there was peace, but he could not be everywhere at once. Hindus and Sikhs were being murdered in Pakistan at the same time and on the same scale. The Punjab was perhaps the worst of all, and there the Mahatma wished to end his Indian pilgrimage, as he had in one sense (at Amritsar) begun it.

It was not to be. He began his last fast on January 13, 1948, for peace in Delhi itself. "If Delhi goes, India goes, and with that the last hope of world peace," he said. He would fast until death or until Delhi was at peace.

Those days were strange and solemn. The streets that had run with blood were filled with penitents of all religions, praying for the life of the Mahatma. Never shall I forget them. I spent much of my time reading Sophocles and talking to some of the Indian leaders. The fear of Gandhi's death was prevalent everywhere, among foreigners as much as among Indians.

The last fast ended with a pledge from all the principal leaders of Hinduism in India to keep the peace with their Moslem brethren. The Mahatma accepted a glass of orange juice from an old Moslem friend, Maulana Abul Kalam Azad (January 18, 1948).

For twelve days Gandhi recuperated from his fast. He was carried to his evening prayer meeting in a small, improvised wooden chair for the first few days, but thereafter walked in his sandals down the garden, leaning on "the girls" (his granddaughters or a granddaughter-in-law). Thus he walked on Friday, January 30, shortly after five in the afternoon. I was standing there waiting for him to come and noted by my watch that it was five twelve when he appeared. This was unusually late, for he was due at five; and the official version says that he appeared at five past five. He mounted the few steps that led to the small terrace at the end of the garden, which he had appropriated as prayer ground. Nathuram Vinayak Godse, a young ultranationalist Hindu, bowed before him, receiving his blessing, and then shot him dead.

THE assassination of Gandhi was designed by its perpetrator to remove an obstacle to war. It was thought by Godse and his fellow conspirators that only Gandhi was preventing war between India and Pakistan, a war which, they considered, India would inevitably win, thus reuniting the country by force.

What the assassin achieved was peace, not war. The revulsion against war which swept over the entire subcontinent was tremendous, and it was certainly sincere. It was just as true in Pakistan as in India. In after weeks I was on the North-West Frontier itself, where the semibarbarous Pathans have no regard for peace. In certain villages I was asked to describe how Gandhi died, and I saw tears in some very tough eyes. The whole of India and Pakistan mourned the apostle of peace, and thereby brought about a psychological condition in which war became totally impossible.

This may have preserved the peace of the world for the duration of the present situation. Atomic energy already had rendered war a horror to all informed men of any imagination, but it had not yet been sufficiently understood throughout the world. It needed another two years, and perhaps three, to deliver its dreadful message. If Pakistan and India had gone to war in 1948, they might have dragged the whole world into it before it had gone very far.

The Mahatma's sacrifice was therefore

a fulfillment. He restored peace to "Delhi, India and the world," as he had prayed. His death fulfilled his life, in a manner that has been characteristic of religious drama since the beginning of history. No less than Jesus of Nazareth, he died for all mankind. There could have been no better end for a life that was all devotion, all sacrifice and love. The man had no equal in our time, this one who treated all men as equals. Of all that we have known, he was the wisest and the best.

ABOUT THE AUTHOR

Vincent Sheean began his illustrious journalism career early. In 1920, straight out of the University of Chicago, he became a reporter for the Chicago *Daily News*, then the New York *Daily News*. By 1922 he was a foreign correspondent for the Chicago *Tribune*, and by 1925 he had gone freelance, writing as a political journalist as well. All in all, from the end of World War I to the Korean War, he covered most of the world's significant events.

Sheean excelled also as the author of biographies, other nonfiction works, novels, and short stories. He published *Mahatma Gandhi* in 1954, just a few years after the great leader's death. Later he wrote about the Mahatma's successor in *Nehru: The Years of Power*.

THE PRESIDENT'S LADY

by
Irving Stone

What price does a woman pay when her husband steps into the frightening glare of high public office? How does she feel when their private life becomes public property, to be gossiped about cruelly and smeared in opposition newspapers?

No woman ever learned the penalties of fame more dramatically than Andrew Jackson's devoted wife, Rachel. In *The President's Lady* best-selling author Irving Stone tells her true and touching story: the story of a love affair that survived every kind of reverse, and of an innocent woman who became an issue in one of the most bitter presidential campaigns in American history.

CHAPTER 1

THEY emerged from the dark woods and were suddenly in the hot September sunshine. At the bottom of the hill their horses stopped to drink from the shallow stream.

"Would you like to rest for a spell, Rachel, and freshen up? We'll be home by sundown."

"I'd rather push on, Samuel, if it's the same to you."

He seemed relieved. Why was her own brother so constrained with her? No matter how serious the charges, she had expected support from her family.

They crossed the bottomlands and made their way up the trail to a timbered knoll. She paused for a moment to let the cool wind of the uplands blow through her abundant black hair, refreshing her. For the first time in the four days since they had left Harrodsburg she began to feel clearheaded.

It's strange, she thought, during the long week that it took for my husband's message to reach the Cumberland and for my brother to come for me, I was too wretched to worry about anybody but myself. Yet the moment we were on the trail for home I began to think about Samuel and how hard he has taken my misfortune. If I greet my mother and brothers and sisters with the same stricken face I showed to Samuel, I'll make them all as wretched as I was.

I must think this thing through, come to some sort of understanding with myself before we reach home. Was I really guilty of misconduct? If so, how? If I wasn't guilty, then why has this happened to me?

She looked across at her brother, the change in her mood communicating itself to him. She saw Samuel's warm brown eyes, so quick to pain and hurt, proffering her a tiny tentative smile. He had not been judging her; his confused and troubled expression had been but a true reflection of her own.

Though she had not seen her family for three years, there had never been any question in her mind as to which one of her seven brothers would make the dangerous trip to fetch her. She and Samuel were the youngest and gayest of the Donelson family; when her father was home he had taught her to read and write, but when he was away on surveying trips or treaty-making with the Indians, she and Samuel had studied together from the leather-bound handwritten arithmetic book. Samuel had been clever with books, and their father, who was an intensely religious man, had imagined that at long last he had a son who would follow in the footsteps of his great-grandfather, the clergyman who had helped to found the first Presbyterian church in America.

"Why has Lewis done this, Rachel?" Samuel cried out, released at last to discuss their difficulty. "What was his provocation?"

"Provocation? Well, a letter. Sent from Virginia to Crab Orchard, to be delivered to me secretly. Lewis intercepted it."

"But what could be in such a letter?"

"I never read it. According to Lewis, a proposal that I elope with Peyton Short to Spanish Territory. Also a credit for me to buy anything I might need for a trip down to New Orleans."

Samuel gazed at her in bewilderment. "When did all this nonsense start?"

Tears came into her eyes. She said to herself, Samuel is right; perhaps if I could find my way back to the beginning of our troubles . . . When *did* they start?

Probably at that house-raising, when Lewis had suddenly become enraged because she was laughing heartily at a story told by one of his friends, an amusing fellow who insisted upon keeping his lips close to his listener's ear. Lewis had yanked her unceremoniously by the arm and taken her away from the party.

Before their marriage her husband had told her that he loved her for her bubbling good spirits, for the way her warm liking for folks somehow made them come alive. Then why had he turned against her? It had not been very long after the abrupt withdrawal from the house-raising party that Lewis Robards began accusing her of being too friendly with the young men of the neighborhood. Had she smiled too warmly upon greeting this one? Her husband had said so in unmistakable terms later that night. Had she danced with too much vivacity at her first anniversary party? Lewis's face had gone purple with rage when he locked the door of their bedroom and turned to accuse her.

After each quarrel she had lain awake saying to herself, If Lewis no longer likes me to be friendly, then I must be more reserved. If he doesn't want me to dance or sing, I will be quiet.

She would mind her resolution for a number of days, then forget herself and be gay with old friends . . . and Lewis would join in the fun making, his arm fondly about her, until a day or a week later, when he would again seize upon some harmless incident to stage a humiliating scene in public.

But her real difficulties had not begun, she remembered, until there was a series of Indian attacks around Harrodsburg, with a half dozen killings. Lewis's mother, who had managed the plantation since her husband's death, decided they had better take in a few young men to help defend the stockade.

The first boarder was a plump lawyer from Virginia with a rather loud voice. Peyton Short was a man who liked to talk, and he had chosen Rachel as the object of his monologues. On warm summer evenings the Robards family sat out on the front porch; Peyton Short usually managed to pull his chair up close to Rachel's to tell of the day's doings. Lewis became uneasy.

"Rachel, couldn't you avoid him? He's so confoundedly . . . present."

"Yes, I'll try."

But she found that Mr. Short was not the kind of man one could easily avoid. One evening Lewis found them alone on the dark porch; her mother-in-law had just gone inside, and Rachel was looking for an opening in the encircling ring of words. Accusing her of having a tête-à-tête, Lewis went straightway to his mother and demanded that Peyton Short be put out of the house. Mrs. Robards refused to listen to his "patent foolishness."

They had little peace until John Overton came to live with them. He was a distant cousin of the Robards', a little fellow with straw-colored hair and a pale skin, possessor of a dry sense of humor, which for a fair time soothed the distressed household.

But then, for Rachel, a new element entered into Lewis's jealousy: his outbursts seemed to bear no relationship to

196

the immediate goings-on: his most violent attacks came when she had not exchanged ten words with Peyton Short in as many days. Once, Short stopped her, and said:

"You'll never find happiness with Lewis Robards. He has neither the sense to love you nor the pride to protect you. But not all men are such fools, Mrs. Robards."

She had not understood him, but a few weeks later, after Peyton Short had gone home to Virginia, Lewis had burst in upon her, thrusting the crumpled Peyton Short letter into her face.

She reined in her horse, feeling ill, as though she were back in her room at the Robards house, waiting—waiting for any one of the paralyzing eventualities: news from Virginia that her husband had been killed in the duel to which he had challenged Short; word that her family had received her husband's letter requesting that someone be sent to fetch her but had decided not to interfere, that she would have to remain unwanted in a house where her husband had renounced her, or that one of her brothers would arrive and take her away, to . . . what?

SAMUEL HELPED HER off the horse. She sat down at the base of a big tree. Her brother kneeled in front of her.

"Are you taken bad, Rachel?"

"Just give me a few moments to rest, Samuel."

"Is there something I can do for you? A drink of water?"

"I'll be all right."

She understood why Samuel had been unable to ask questions or offer sympathy: separation of husband and wife had never happened in their part of the country. Everyone on the Cumberland would know that she had been repudiated. What would be her position among her neighbors? Would she be an outcast?

She could see these uncertainties reflected in Samuel's eyes as he leaned over and smoothed her hair back from her forehead. She simply could not reach home in this state; yet there were just a few more miles before they reached the Donelson stockade.

Often in the past four days she had imagined that she was thinking her way through to the core of the problem, but it always eluded her. Now fragments began to fit together, broken bits of action and explanation. One of her husband's characteristics was to go away for a night, giving an offhand reason or excuse. But all along she had had an inkling of the handsome young mulatto who was a Robards house servant; at intervals she had surprised a fleeting smile on the girl's face, had caught something intangible between her and Lewis. She realized now she had sensed the bitter truth . . . even though she had rejected the evidence. By the same token, couldn't that be the reason for Lewis's conduct? She relived the scene in her upstairs bedroom, with Lewis shouting, "I've written your mother to send someone to get you out of my house. And I'm leaving tonight for Virginia to kill Peyton Short!"

Mrs. Robards had taken Rachel in her arms and turned to her son with blazing eyes to tell him that he had gone stark mad. Lewis's sister insisted that Rachel had never given Peyton Short anything but hospitable courtesy. John Overton had said in his shy manner: "Lewis, I could write you a letter tonight inviting you to join me in horse stealing and murder, but that would hardly make you a horse thief or a murderer." But it was his mother who had said coldly to Lewis, "All this arises from your own improper conduct."

Rachel rose, walked to where the horses were drinking, and stood with one hand grasping her saddle, the other clenched tight as there rushed into her mind the formerly unrelated evidence: her husband had left her side, sometimes even their bed, to go out to the slave quarters; inevitably when he had returned he had accused her of a crime against their love and marriage . . . transferring to his wife his own capacity for betrayal.

Her hand fell from the saddle and she stood with her head lowered. After a time a feeling of relief came over her: if she could not live with her husband, she could at least live with herself. She had not injured her own dignity or self-respect.

She loosened a strap on the saddlebag, took out her traveling kit. Glancing down at her dress, she saw that it was soiled. From the saddlebag she took a fresh blue linen dress, then slipped out of the rumpled one, kneeling at the side of the creek in her white petticoat. She was small-boned, barely five feet two in height, with rounded shoulders; her hips were delicately modeled and her waist both slender and short, allowing for unusually fine long legs.

She scrubbed her face, neck and arms, then removed the small combs that held her long black tresses in place, and brushed the cool water through her hair. She gathered the bulk of it low on her neck, tied it with a white ribbon and sat on the bank in the warm afternoon sunshine, gazing into the mirror. Her enormous brown eyes, set wide apart and framed by thin curved black brows, had recovered from their days of weeping: they were soft and clear. Her face, usually on the round side, was now slender-cheeked.

I'm only 21, she thought. Surely life can't be over for me?

She put on the blue linen dress and then called out to her brother who was washing his own hands and face in the creek.

"We can go now, Samuel. I'm feeling much better. I'm really anxious to see Mother and the family again. You haven't told me very much about French Lick. Are there a lot of new settlers?"

He helped her into the saddle and mounted his own horse. They went swiftly down the trail. She turned to look at her brother and saw that he was smiling at her.

"You'll never recognize the old place, Rachel. They've even changed the name to Nashville. There must be about forty new cabins there, with two taverns, a store and a courthouse. It's really quite a big town you're coming home to."

RACHEL'S mother was already known throughout the Cumberland as the Widow Donelson. Her joy in this reunion was restrained, for Colonel Donelson had been killed since they last met; and now her youngest daughter was in trouble.

The Widow Donelson's family, the Stocklys, had settled in Virginia sometime before 1609 as original members of the Virginia Company; they had been large land- and slaveowners. When she married John Donelson and went with him to the western frontier of Virginia she took with her a substantial dowry, education and family tradition. They had come in handy, all three, in clearing the wilderness, raising

11 children, building a prosperous plantation and managing it while her husband served three terms in the Virginia House of Burgesses.

She sat now with her daughter in the big room beneath the oblong porthole windows, sunlight flooding over their faces, so amazingly alike in coloring and bone structure. Across the room the tall wooden cogwheeled clock sounded the buzzing whir of inside works before clanging out its metallic strokes.

"It seems so strange to me," said Mrs. Donelson. "I remember Lewis as a gay and carefree young man."

"Yes, we all thought so." Rachel's voice was soft and unhurried. Both she and her mother had carried over the musical intonations of Virginia.

A familiar step sounded outside the room. Rachel had always been told that she was the prettiest of the Donelson girls, but looking up, she realized all over again that her sister Jane was the truly beautiful one of the family, a willowy figure with fluffy blond hair and light green eyes. Jane had waited until she was 26 before marrying—an age called middleyeared on the frontier—waiting until she found Colonel Robert Hays in Nashville, then knowing instantly that this was her love.

Mrs. Donelson watched Rachel and Jane greet each other warmly, for these two younger of her four daughters had grown up as close friends. When their mother was called from the room, Rachel's calm left her and she sought refuge in Jane's arms.

"It isn't only the disgrace of being put out of my husband's home, Jane; that's bad enough when you consider it has never happened to anyone we ever knew. But what am I to think about the future? Do I remain Mrs. Lewis Robards all my life, and yet never lay eyes on my husband again?"

Jane chose her words carefully as she asked the all-important question. "Rachel, do you still love Lewis?"

Did she still love Lewis? She certainly had suffered at his hands, had lost her romantic illusions. Now, after three years, she understood her husband: his unfocused quality, his unwillingness to relieve his mother as manager of the prosperous

Robards plantation or to involve himself for long in any task; his inability to have confidence in himself . . . or her.

"If only we had children . . ." she replied resolutely. "Perhaps children are what he needs to settle him down, to give him a sense of permanence."

THE Widow Donelson's station was some ten miles north of Nashville. The following morning, thinking to divert Rachel, Samuel suggested that they ride into the town.

Their first stop was Lardner Clark's store, a double-sized log cabin, the only light coming from the open front door. There were long counters on either side; on the left, piles of clothing, pans, dishware, candles; on the opposite side, sugar, salt, spices, whisky, smoked meats; and at the back, the shelves containing axes, cowbells, rifles, powder and shot.

Several acquaintances greeted Rachel warmly, expressed their delight at seeing her again and wished her a happy visit with her family. One young wife said:

"You'll come visit us soon as you settle?

Sam, you be sure to bring her now; there's so few young people around."

Rachel squeezed the young woman's hand. Then she felt a pair of eyes staring at her from the back of the store.

"Why, it's Martha Dinsmore, from Harrodsburg."

She started toward Mrs. Dinsmore, but she saw that the woman's expression was forbidding. Rachel stopped short. Mrs. Dinsmore turned away with no sign of recognition.

The blood rushed to Rachel's head. She thought she heard Mrs. Dinsmore say: "Where there's smoke there's bound to be fire."

Did I really hear those words, she asked herself, or is it just my imagination? How could the news have come down the trail so quickly? If Martha Dinsmore knew and could feel this way, there would be others.

She felt Samuel gripping her arm.

"Rachel, you mustn't pay attention to people like that. There are always a few who get pleasure from believing the worst."

"I'll never expose myself again. I'm going to stay home until it's all over."

CHAPTER 2

RACHEL stepped out into the yard, which was enclosed by a high stockade fence sheltering the spacious two-story main house and its outbuildings. It was the first of March, five months since she had come back to the Donelsons'. She walked to the kitchen to inspect the sides of venison, bear and buffalo that were broiling on their spits, the wild turkeys and geese roasting on their suspended hempen cords. It was a double birthday, for her oldest brother, Alexander, who was 40, and her youngest, Samuel, exactly half that age.

Rachel was the only one of the four daughters now living at home; the Widow Donelson had turned over the household management to her, pretending to want a winter of rest. Rachel had been thankful for the busiest months of her life, supervising the making of the soap and candles, carding and spinning the wool into yarn, stuffing the new pillows and mattresses.

She stood in the open door of the cabin watching Moll, the deep-bosomed, gray-haired Negress who had helped to raise her, and who had been

207

bequeathed to Rachel in her father's will.

She stepped into the kitchen where Moll was basting the turkeys. "Have we plenty of meat roasting, Moll? It's beginning to look as though I asked the whole Cumberland Valley."

"And about time, Miz Rachel," said Moll. "I don't take to you lockin' yourself up like you done . . . not even one dance or quiltin' bee or house-raisin'."

"I really haven't wanted to see . . . outsiders," she murmured. She went to the open doorway of the kitchen and stood gazing at the young apple and peach orchards which her seven brothers had planted. Beyond was the pasture with a herd of 30 milk cows and the family's 20-odd horses. Their new home was coming to look more and more like the Virginia plantation they had been obliged to sell back in 1779, when her father had suffered reverses. That was when the entire family had set forth on the flatboat *Adventure* for the voyage down the Holston and Tennessee, then up the Ohio and Cumberland rivers, a 2000-mile journey through wild country and uncharted waters. Now they had built the most prosperous

plantation in the Cumberland Valley.

She started back toward the main house. Suddenly she stopped, seeing a figure framed in the open doorway of the guest cabin. The man had his back to her; he turned and she exclaimed in astonishment: "Why, it's John Overton!"

Through her mind flashed the thought, He comes from the Robards'. He will have news for me . . . perhaps a letter. . . .

Eagerly, she crossed the yard to greet him.

John Overton was a small man. His chin was bony and turned up, his nose was bony and turned down, his eyes were a light vapor gray. Yet after an hour of talking with him, Rachel always believed him to be a beautiful human being. Behind Overton's seemingly transparent eyes there was at work a first-rate brain: fast, logical, humorous, yet with the flinty incorruptibility of his Scottish ancestors. Inside himself, where he lived and breathed and fought, he was a big man; only newcomers were deceived by his unlikely shell.

"How good it is to see you again, Rachel."

"And to see you, John." She hesitated a moment. "Are you passing through our country on business?"

"No, I've decided to settle in Nashville and open my law office here. So of course I came straight to the Donelsons' and asked your mother if she would take me in."

A slow flush crept up Rachel's cheeks: Overton's coming directly to the Donelsons' was an act of faith on his part. A man of his rigorously ethical nature would never have come here if he had considered his relative Lewis Robards injured. She felt deeply grateful. "I'm happy you are going to be part of our family, John."

They faced each other in silence. Rachel knew Overton brought news from Harrodsburg for her. Was his news good or bad? She knew that she did not want to, could not, in fact, hear what he had to say

210

now. Perhaps when the party was over.

"I must finish my tour of inspection," she said abruptly. "Once again, John, the heartiest of welcomes."

THE guests had departed; her family had retired, exhausted from the daylong festivities. Now everything was quiet in the big room, the last of the candles extinguished, the fire banked and cooling. She stood at a porthole, slipped a wooden bolt and opened the heavy wooden shutter, gazing out at the March night. She felt lonely and sad; her family had done everything they could to make her feel welcome, yet as she stood trembling at the window she felt not only unwanted but rejected. With John Overton and his news at hand she must try at last to determine her feelings about Lewis.

She had loved Lewis Robards; he had seemed to her the handsomest, most romantic figure she had ever met, one of the most admired of the war heroes in Kentucky. He had wooed her with ardor and impetuousness. She had loved him during the first peaceful year of their marriage.

And now? Did she think of him harshly?

Or did she pity him, think of him as ill? That was the way his mother explained his rages. Mrs. Robards had said: "It's something the war did to Lewis. He was so happy during the years we were fighting: life was a great adventure for him then. But when the war ended, when he came home to . . . inaction, he felt as though the best part of his life had already been lived. He became bored, morose, irritable. That was why I thanked God for you, Rachel; I was sure that with you he would find happiness."

Yes, she felt sorry for Lewis. She murmured half aloud to the dark room and the sky: All my hopes are tied up in my marriage; without it I am nothing, I have no place, no future. I want my husband back and a home of my own. . . .

SHE watched the sunrise. When she heard the first stirrings throughout the house, she walked across the yard to speak to Overton.

"John, I feel sure that Lewis has asked you to bring a message to me. I appreciate your not saying anything until I was ready."

212

Overton bowed slightly.

"Rachel, Lewis has cleared you completely. I've heard him tell his friends in Harrodsburg that he has been the blindest fool."

A deep breath escaped her, one that seemed to have been long held in pent-up suspense.

"Your husband told me how much he loves you and wishes to live with you again. He requested that I use my exertions to restore harmony."

"You can imagine how happy I am to hear this, John. And the duel with Peyton Short? Neither of them was hurt?"

She saw John's jaw set a little.

"There were no serious results."

Silence fell. Rachel perceived that there was something unpleasant here, something in which Overton had been offended.

"Please go on, John," she said softly.

"I told Lewis that I would undertake to restore harmony, providing he would put down his jealousy and treat you kindly as other men treat their wives. He says that if you will come back to him he will never again cause you unhappiness."

213

She tried to separate her tumultuous feelings. Now that her husband had declared his confidence in her, she would go back to him, of course. But could she feel secure in Harrodsburg where Lewis had humiliated her so often by his torrential scenes? Could she return to the Robards' home where that young slave girl would be in daily evidence? Her face was averted while she was thinking; now she turned back to Overton.

"John, there is nothing I want more than to be with my husband again, but I'm convinced that our problems at the Robards' home make it impossible for us to live there happily. My father registered a fine piece of land for us just a few miles from this station. Would you write to Lewis and tell him that I reciprocate his feelings, but that I feel we have a far greater chance of success if he will come here to Nashville where we can build on our land and start an entirely new life for ourselves?"

RACHEL heard a hammering on the front-door knocker, gentle at first, then insistent. When no one answered, she left her bedroom and came down the rough plank stairs. She opened the door and saw a tall young man with a thick mop of sandy-red hair. Apparently he had grown a little discouraged, for he was half turned. He was an odd-looking creature in an ill-fitting black homespun suit, and seemed the tallest man she had ever laid eyes on, surely some six and a half feet, she thought, and with a thinness to match his height.

The back of his head seemed disproportionately massive to the slender features which she could see in profile, with the high forehead and flat-ridged nose; but then everything about him seemed a little disproportionate: the incredibly long face, the long thin neck which appeared too delicate to support such a heavy head; the oblong torso and the gangling arms and legs. He looked like a youth whose figure had stretched to its outermost limits and would now require a full decade to fill out; yet he held himself rigidly erect, and there was a suggestion of power, too, as though this scraggly body were having difficulty containing its own force.

The man wheeled sharply. She found

herself gazing up into the largest and most brilliant pair of blue eyes she had ever encountered. He seemed to be towering at least three heads above her, yet there was nothing formidable about him; rather she felt a warm glow and discovered to her astonishment that both she and the young stranger were smiling at each other.

"Please forgive my intrusion, ma'am, but I am Andrew Jackson of Nashville," he said. "A good friend of John Overton's."

"But of course, Mr. Jackson. We've been hearing tales of your exploits ever since you came here. I am Mrs. Lewis Robards."

He bowed slowly from the waist, acknowledging the introduction. She noted a scar on the left side of his forehead, saber-thin, arching from his hairline down to the thick undisciplined eyebrow. "I've come to ask a favor, Mrs. Robards. Since I reached Nashville, beginning of last November, I've been living at the inns. John Overton tells me there's room in the cabin he's occupying. Do you think your mother would take me in? I am a crack shot with a rifle and have had considerable experience in fighting the Indians."

"Well, Mr. Jackson, we certainly are glad to have all the protection we can get. Our neighbor Captain Hunter was killed last week by some Creeks." She hesitated. "But I am not the mistress of this station. My mother is in Nashville for the day."

She saw him turn and gaze wistfully at the full saddlebags on his horse; he had brought his possessions with him. He was a bold man, sure enough, but she also felt that he was lonely.

"You said John Overton will share his cabin with you?"

"Oh yes, we have just formed a partnership. He said we could hold our office right here."

"But aren't you attached to the court? An officer . . . ?"

"Indeed I am, ma'am; Judge McNairy and I brought that court with us from North Carolina. I carry the hifalutin title of attorney general; that only means I prosecute criminals where and as I find them. Rest of the time I'm just like all other lawyers, looking mighty hard for cases."

"In any event, you must stay to supper with us, Mr. Jackson. The family will want to meet you. Why not take your things out of the saddlebags and bring them over to the cabin meanwhile? Then you can turn your horse out in the canebrake."

He did as he had been bidden. Rachel walked across the yard with him while he supported the bulging bags on his bony shoulders, a rifle under each arm. She pushed open the door to the cabin.

Andrew Jackson stood in the middle of the room, the top of his massive red head barely an inch beneath the crossbeams which held up the roof, gazing at the field-stone fireplace, then at Overton's books, at the racks of pistols and powder horns and the colorful striped cotton curtains at the windows.

"This is about the prettiest cabin I've been in," he said softly. "Are you superstitious, Mrs. Robards? I am. For instance, I like to start new ventures on a Tuesday, like today, but I'll never begin anything on a Friday."

"That wouldn't be the Irish in you, by chance?"

He grinned, rubbing the freckles that ran like a speckled band straight across his nose and high cheekbones.

"My mother always said I carried two

218

things that gave my Irish away: my face and my temper."

He went down on his haunches beside his bags, took out a half dozen books, packets of ammunition, tea, tobacco and salt, two blankets and some spare clothing, which he hung in the cupboard.

"I'll just unpack a few possessions. Then if your mother should say no, I'll come over quietly and slip them into my saddlebags."

Rachel watched his quick, awkward movements which somehow had considerable grace in them; and she was aware of a tiny smile, not on her lips, but somewhere inside her head.

At that instant the young man turned, rose, stood towering above her. They gazed at each other in silence, even as they had in that first surprised moment at the front door.

She had refused all invitations to parties in the neighborhood; she had not wanted anyone to think that she did not grasp the true implication of her situation. But now, with her husband on his way to her, she felt free again and happy.

Sunday was gathering day for the Donelson clan. At the head of the polished split-log table sat Mrs. Donelson surrounded by her large family. Rachel's regular seat was next to Samuel's. Across from her were Robert and Jane Hays, and next to Jane sat Stockly, the lawyer and politician of the family. John Overton sat next to Rachel, with Andrew Jackson across from him. At the very foot of the table was Severn—the ailing member of the Donelson family—hollow-cheeked, and with a severe cough.

The spring term of the Davidson County court was to open the following morning, and Samuel, who was fascinated by the two young lawyers, was asking endless questions about the law.

Samuel had been drifting aimlessly this year not knowing whether he wanted to be a teacher or preacher or perhaps surveyor. He had taken on a new vitality since the lawyers had entered the family circle. To encourage this interest, Rachel, too, began asking questions about court procedure. John Overton said:

"Samuel, I heard your mother say that you were riding up to Nashville in the

220

morning to do some shopping at Lardner Clark's. Mr. Jackson and I have a number of interesting cases to try, so why don't you bring your mother and sister to court?"

"Won't Judge McNairy be upset at having lady visitors?" asked Rachel.

"Surprised, perhaps," replied Overton, "but on the pleasurable side. Besides, my partner is an officer of the court and I'm sure he'd be glad to intercede for you."

The next morning Rachel and her mother donned their severe black-wool riding dresses for the ten-mile ride into town. In Mr. Clark's general store they bought a loaf of sugar and some whole spices to be ground at home. Several of the women greeted Rachel, hugging her and saying how well she was looking. Then they walked up the rutted street to the courthouse.

Samuel took each of the women by an arm. As they went toward the open door Rachel drew back with an instinctive shudder of distaste: the interior was filthy, the doors askew, the window shutters sagging. At the end of the small room was a long table behind which sat John McNairy, the judge. There were also a number of split-log benches for the spectators and litigants, who now turned to gape at the two ladies standing in the doorway.

"I think we had better go," said Rachel, feeling self-conscious.

At that moment Jackson and Overton came from the end of the courtroom. "Here, let me make you comfortable," Jackson said.

He pulled a bench into line, wiping it vigorously with an enormous colored handkerchief, and they sat down. At that moment a man named Hugh McGary burst into the courtroom, his face hard-set with anger.

"Andrew, I'm not going to need you for that case against Casper Mansker. I'm going to kill him right here in the courthouse and take possession of that slave. We had a written agreement, then he goes and loses the bill of sale on purpose."

Jackson rose, put a long-fingered hand on McGary's shoulder and said in a placating voice:

"Now, Hugh, I think this can be settled peaceably. Casper Mansker is one of the oldest settlers around here and everybody says his word is better than a bushel of salt."

222

A voice behind Rachel called, "Did I hear someone ask for me?"

"Yes, Hugh McGary and I were looking for you, Mr. Mansker," Jackson replied quickly. "My client and I have just been thinking we ought to find a friendly compromise. Let's go sun ourselves on the south porch, gentlemen, then we'll really be settling this matter out of court."

Rachel saw Jackson link his arms through old Mr. Mansker's and McGary's, and take them not so much by physical force as by force of will out of the court's jurisdiction.

"He isn't at all like the stories they tell about him," commented Mrs. Donelson. "He's really quite gentle."

"What stories have you been hearing, Mother?" asked Rachel.

"Well, there's the story of that bully in Sumner County who purposely stepped on his foot in the public square, and then came back to step on it a second time just to make sure Mr. Jackson knew it was on purpose."

"And what did our peaceable Mr. Jackson do?"

"Why, he picked up a rail from the top

of a fence and knocked the man down."

Just then they heard a tremendous clatter of hoofs and the noise of a shouting band. By turning her head, Rachel could see a group of men in filthy buckskin shirts carrying rifles, their faces grimy, hair uncombed. She watched while they sprang off their horses, several of them picking quarrels with men standing on the porch. She had not noticed that Andrew Jackson had returned to the courtroom. Now he extracted a court citation from a sheaf of papers he was holding in his left hand, walked to the door and cried in a strong voice:

"First case on the docket is the *State* versus *Spill Cimberlin*, charged with theft, disturbing the peace, assault and contempt of the court."

Rachel rose so that she could see through the doorway to the crowd beyond. Spill Cimberlin, one of the men who had just ridden up, shifted his rifle to a more comfortable position under his arm, came within a few inches of Jackson and stuck his face forward. "There ain't no damned court on this whole frontier that's man enough to try me."

"That's no way to speak about your own courts, Spill," replied Jackson. "The law is here to protect you as well as to punish you. But if you've done wrong, you're going to be punished."

"And who's going to punish me? A skinny green saplin' like you?"

There was a silence during which Rachel watched the muscles in Jackson's jaw work up and down. He turned, went a short distance to his saddlebags, pulled out his two pistols and cocked them as he whirled about. He walked straight at Spill Cimberlin, the guns aimed at the man's head. Rachel went cold; Cimberlin's rifle needed only the slightest bit of raising. When Andrew got within three feet of Cimberlin he said in a voice that carried the length of the main street of Nashville:

"Step up to the bar of justice and be tried by His Honor, or I'll blow your meager brains out."

There was a breathless hush. If Cimberlin was going to do anything, this was the second when he must fire. But the man slowly sagged at the shoulders. Excited talk broke out; Rachel turned to her mother.

"Would Mr. Jackson really have shot him?"

"Mr. Cimberlin seemed to think so," replied Mrs. Donelson with a smile.

As they were leaving court after adjournment, Jackson fell in step beside Rachel.

"Weren't you frightened?" she asked. "Mr. Cimberlin could have killed you."

"Oh, I was just showing off," he replied. Andrew Jackson seemed obviously pleased with himself. "Besides," he went on, "I like to graze danger."

THAT evening at supper, they lingered at the table with the light of the pine logs on their faces. Mrs. Donelson asked: "Don't you have any family of your own here in the West, Mr. Jackson?"

"No, Mrs. Donelson, I'm an orphan. Have been since I was 14. My father died a few days before I was born. Hugh, my older brother, died after the battle of Stono Ferry. My mother rescued my younger brother Robert and me from the British military prison at Camden, but Robert died two days after we got home, of infected wounds and smallpox."

He stopped abruptly; his long expressive face became suddenly very red while the livid scar on his forehead stood out like a silver scimitar. "When I pulled through the smallpox, my mother heard that two of my cousins were lying sick in a British prison ship off Charleston, so she gathered up all the medicine she could find and made the journey there. I don't know how many days she spent in that prison hold trying to cure the boys, but she contracted ship fever, too, and didn't get very far on the way home, just a couple of miles out of Charleston. I don't even know where she is buried. It's an unmarked grave in an open plain. I've searched several times, but nobody seems to know."

His voice trailed off, the enormous head was lowered. For the first time Rachel sensed the tenderness in the man and his overpowering need for love. When he looked up again there were tears in his eyes.

"That's why, Mrs. Donelson, I think the greatest thing in the world any man can have is a family, the bigger the better."

"I wish I had another daughter for you."

228

"Seeing as how there are no more Donelson girls," said Rachel, "as soon as my husband and I are settled in our new house, we'll scour the countryside and give a lot of parties. Unless there is some girl waiting for you back in Jonesboro or Salisbury?"

He gazed at her, smiling, from across the hearth.

"Oh, sure, ma'am, dozens of them, whole jury panels full."

"What are their names?"

"Names? Oh yes." He ran his thin tapering fingers through the mass of red hair, pulling some of it down over his forehead. "Let's see, there was . . . Why, of course, Susan Smart, in the Waxhaws, used to tell me I had agreeable eyes and that I was a leaning-forward fellow. Then there was Nancy Jarret in Salisbury. Pretty girl, Nancy. Could ride a horse as fast as a March wind. But her mother didn't approve, said I drank and gambled too much."

"And did you?"

"Oh, I suppose so. I was a wild lad in those days. But there wasn't much else to do when taverns were the only place a man could find to live. When I was 16 and my grandfather left me a legacy of 300 pounds, I went to Charleston and lost that money on the racing ponies so fast my head is still spinning. But I don't even gamble anymore, and won't . . . until I can build me the finest stable of racing horses on the frontier."

IT WAS from John Overton later that the Donelson family got its real grasp of Andrew Jackson's character.

"He towers over all the other men I've ever known. You've noticed that scar on his forehead, of course."

There was a general nodding of heads.

"Back in 1781, it was, Andrew and his two brothers were fighting under their uncle, Major Crawford, against the British Dragoons. One day, Andrew's young cousin Thomas Crawford was made a prisoner. As Andrew entered the Crawford home to tell them what had happened, a company of Dragoons surprised the family. The British officer commanded Andrew to clean his high jack boots, which were crusted with mud. Andrew was only 14 but he cried out: 'Sir,

I am a prisoner of war and claim to be treated as such!' The commanding officer lifted his sword and swung it down on Andrew's head. Andrew threw up his arm, which was gashed to the bone; that's how he saved his life, but the tip of the sword cut his forehead."

"What did Mr. Jackson do about that?" Rachel asked.

"Just what you would expect: the British officer ordered him to lead them to the home of a man named Thompson. Andrew avoided the regular road and led the British across an open field; Thompson could see them from half a mile away and escaped. Somehow the English officer didn't like that, either. He made Andrew march 40 miles to a military prison without allowing him even a drink of water."

CHAPTER 3

IT WAS a magnificent May afternoon, some weeks later, the air filled with the fragrance of honeysuckle, when Rachel saw Lewis Robards come down the trail leading three heavily laden packhorses. He appeared heavier, and from the lines in his face

231

rather older than the passage of months should have warranted. She ran quickly to the door to welcome him.

Lewis was greeted warmly by everyone except Samuel, who could not wipe from his mind the picture of his sister's tear-streaked face when he had taken her out of the Robards' home eight months before. But as the day progressed Rachel saw with anxiety that her husband was very uncertain of himself. After supper the men fell to talking about the difficulties of clearing titles farther out in the wilderness.

"Speaking of titles, Lewis," said John Overton, "I've checked that six-forty in Clover Bottom where you and Rachel plan to live. The records are clean and legal."

"Thank you, John, but I'm not as much concerned over the title to the land as I am about Indian raids. It's still pretty wild country, isn't it?"

John replied gravely, "Yes. There have been several attacks out that way in the past month. Two children were killed."

"Then it would hardly be safe to expose Rachel to such danger, would it?"

There was an uncomfortable silence.

Yet she knew that none of her brothers considered Lewis a coward.

"If you will permit me an opinion, Captain Robards," she heard Andrew Jackson say, "I've always felt that the Indians never attack where they know a man is fast with his rifle. Your presence would be all the protection Mrs. Robards would need."

Lewis flushed with pleasure at the compliment. Rachel felt her own anxiety ease. She sat back quietly as Lewis told the first news of George Washington's inauguration as President a couple of weeks before on April 30, 1789, in New York.

"After Mr. Washington took the oath, the chancellor of New York cried, 'Long live George Washington, President of the United States,' and the crowd thundered back, 'Long live George Washington, President of the United States.' "

"Sounds too much like 'Long live the King' to me," growled Jackson. "We're a new country, with a new kind of elected executive. Why don't we make up our own saying?"

As Andrew spoke, Rachel was thinking hard. Her husband was already much attached to John Overton; they had remained friends at the Robards' home even after Overton had defended her. Now Andrew Jackson and her husband had gotten off to an excellent start, thanks to Mr. Jackson's compliment. However, they were all going to live together here in fairly close quarters, until the new Robards home was built. She resolved to give up the warm, informal relationship she had enjoyed with the young lawyers during the past months. Every life had to be lived inside its own boundaries and if her husband's nature formed the palings which closed them in, then she would try to live happily and securely inside that fence.

During the next weeks Rachel and Lewis rode out daily to their land, studying it with a view to clearing and planting. They saw the family only at dinner. She greeted John Overton and Andrew Jackson formally when they met, then moved on to whatever chore she was doing.

At dinner she no longer listened with interest to the legal discussions, even though the law firm of Overton and Jackson had converted the Donelson cabin into the most active law office west of the

Blue Ridge. Samuel's career problems had been solved: he was now reading law in the guest cabin. When it came time for Colonel Donelson's will to be probated it seemed only natural that John Overton should handle it; when Overton and Jackson were paid in barter for their services, paid such things as woolen cloth, country-made sugar or tobacco, they brought the stuff home to the Donelsons to be thrown into the family larder.

Late one afternoon Rachel was crossing the yard from the dairy cabin when Andrew Jackson rode in. She didn't know how he accomplished it so quickly, but before she had gone three steps, he stood directly in her path, his eyes searching hers.

"Mrs. Robards, have I said or done something to offend you? You know I have only the deepest—"

She hastened to reassure him.

"No, no, it's nothing you've done, Mr. Jackson. It's just . . . that since my husband's return I've been so busy. . . ."

As she raised her head she saw in his eyes an expression that was rather like Moll's the day she had told Rachel she was living like a prisoner. Jackson quickly veiled his feelings, said, "Please forgive me for embarrassing you, Mrs. Robards," and was gone.

It was two months after his coming to the Donelsons' that Lewis Robards suddenly told Rachel he had decided against developing the land at Clover Bottom.

"But Lewis, you promised—"

"What do I need another plantation for?" he demanded. "I've already got one back in Harrodsburg."

"Then what do you want to do?"

"Why must I do something? Would you think it more important if I went around blabbering like those two walking lawbooks you're so attached to?"

Rachel pulled back.

"I'm sorry, Lewis, I didn't mean to hurt your feelings."

"Why don't they move into Nashville and build themselves an office there? It surely can't be convenient for them to ride ten miles into town and back every day."

"But they're both alone, and they're happy here with us."

His skin grew dark; for a moment it

seemed as though he would hold back, but the temptation was too strong.

"And you're happy with them."

Rachel took a deep breath. It was so painfully familiar.

"Oh, Lewis, let's start the cabin at Clover Bottom."

"So now you want to run away?" His voice had grown louder with every passing sentence. "Well, I'm not going to let Andrew Jackson drive me out of here."

Rachel was shocked. There was a knock at the door. It was Mrs. Donelson.

"Lewis, for shame!" she exclaimed as she entered the room. "You've been shouting so loud that everybody downstairs has heard you."

Lewis stormed out of the house, jumped on one of his horses and rode off at a killing pace. A few hours later he was back, contrite. He asked, "Am I forgiven?" and Rachel replied, "Yes, of course." To avoid further trouble she stopped eating in the dining room with the rest of the family.

The peace lasted for two, almost three weeks. Then one noon, when she was in the kitchen with her mother and Moll, making a meat and vegetable hotchpotch, Lewis burst in, shouting:

"I won't stand him around here any more. You get that fellow off this place or I'll run him off myself!"

Rachel could only stammer: "What man are you talking about?"

"You know who I mean. Andrew Jackson. He insulted me. If it had been in my home, I would have shot him dead!"

"Mr. Jackson? But he admires you, he wouldn't insult—"

"He admires my wife, not me. He's trying to make me look ridiculous so he can get you away from me."

She sank onto the log bench by the fireplace. She caught only fragments of her mother's questions and of Lewis's loud replies. Apparently Andrew had made a generalization about some absentee land cases and Lewis had taken the remark personally. She did not know when Lewis left, but when she turned around from the fireplace she saw John Overton standing in the doorway.

"Forgive me for intruding," he said, "but I heard the—the commotion. Is Lewis at it again?"

Mrs. Donelson nodded with grim hopelessness, then left the kitchen.

Rachel spoke. "John, I must ask you to do something dreadful."

"You want us to go?"

"No . . . not you . . . just Mr. Jackson."

"We'll both go, Rachel." He put his hand out and covered hers. "But I'm reluctant to do this; Lewis Robards is probably the only man on the frontier who doesn't understand the implications of insulting Andrew Jackson."

He began pacing up and down the kitchen.

"In another month Andrew and I start on circuit. No one in Nashville will think it strange if we don't come back to the Donelsons'. But if we are obliged suddenly to move out, people are bound to ask why. I shall ask Lewis to let things go along until we leave for the next court session at Jonesboro."

It took only a few moments for them to reach the Robards' bedroom.

"Lewis," Overton began, "when I left your home to come to Nashville I agreed to serve as your emissary because I thought you had learned your lesson. And now you are behaving in the same unmanly fashion."

"John, I've always trusted you," cried Lewis, "and now you are turning against me."

"As your cousin," interrupted Overton, "I feel it my duty to hit you over the head with a tree trunk. But as your attorney I'm going to give you some advice. There has not been an untoward word or gesture between your wife and Andrew Jackson. If you drive him out of here you will have to go around again as you did at Harrodsburg, apologizing and explaining that it was nothing more than your imagination."

"You may interpret it that way," replied Lewis, his voice dry and harsh. "But I'm beginning to think that maybe I was right about Peyton Short, after all."

Rachel sat stunned and sickened.

"I beg your forgiveness, Rachel," said John, "for everything that has happened. Andrew and I will be gone in the morning."

Rachel slept fitfully. When she awakened she drew the curtains and saw her husband and Andrew Jackson in the courtyard. Lewis had his fist raised as though to strike Jackson; Jackson drew back several steps. Her husband lowered his arm. Jackson turned and walked to the horses, where Overton was waiting. They mounted and disappeared out the gate.

She dressed hurriedly, and ran quickly into the yard.

"Your chivalrous Mr. Jackson!" snorted Lewis. "He said he apologized if he had done anything to offend me, but that he couldn't leave without first telling me that you had done nothing to warrant my anger. The man is a coward, Rachel; I offered to thrash him and he refused to fight."

Rachel turned toward the house. Andrew Jackson knew that if he and Lewis Robards rolled on the ground like a couple of drunken brawlers the whole of Nashville would hear about it by nightfall. He had afforded her a protection her husband had not cared to provide.

QUIET descended on the Donelson station, but it was the wrong kind of quiet. Rachel's brothers were avoiding Lewis.

She knew what they would have to do

to ease the strain: start building the cabin at Clover Bottom. After several days of argument on the subject with Lewis, Rachel was forced to say firmly:

"Lewis, I cannot feel comfortable here any longer. I am a married woman and am entitled to live under my own roof. Everybody will help us make a clearing and erect our cabin."

"I don't need charity," he replied; "I'll hire my own workmen. I'll pay for what I get and be beholden to no one."

He bought two husky slaves in Nashville and hired the town's carpenter to see that the cabin was built to Rachel's specifications. Once they had moved in, Lewis hunted, molded bullets, cleared the thickets. But when winter came on and darkness fell early, he spent the long afternoons simply sitting by the fire, staring at the flames.

Finally they were shot at by Indians. Lewis stacked large piles of bullets beneath each porthole, stayed awake nights with his guns loaded and cocked, grew thin and jumpy. During the first heavy snowstorm he caught cold and came down with fever. Rachel sent for

Samuel, who rode out to the clearing, wrapped Lewis in bearskins and carried him to the Donelsons'. There Lewis made a good recovery, but remained in bed. Rachel sensed that the day he was completely well would be a difficult one for them both. She had imagined that his lethargy was part of his convalescence. Now she began to perceive that the spirit had gone out of the man.

In early April he informed her that he had to go back to Harrodsburg. She was puzzled both by the offhand way in which he spoke and by his choice of words.

"You *have to,* Lewis? Is something wrong?"

"Well, Mother hasn't been feeling well . . . and there are a number of business matters that have to be settled."

On the morning of his departure Rachel and Mrs. Donelson walked him down to the front gate. Lewis kissed them both on the cheek, thanked them for their hospitality and rode off.

Rachel leaned heavily against the gate. Was she not again caught in the halfway point between being married and unmarried?

TWO WEEKS HAD passed when John Overton and Andrew Jackson came to call and were promptly invited for Sunday dinner. Overton managed to get a few minutes alone with Rachel first.

"Rachel, do you know what Lewis's plans are?"

"No."

"Then I'd better tell you what I heard. Lewis is telling his friends that he'll be damned if he'll be seen in the Cumberland again, that he hates the valley, the people and the life here."

She thanked him. There was no shock to her in this news, only the confirmation of what she had suspected.

Later, at dinner, she heard her mother ask from her position at the head of the table: "John, how are you and Mr. Jackson getting along over at Casper Mansker's?"

"Well, the Manskers are showing us every courtesy, but we have no room for our office; we are practicing law across the bedcover."

"I don't mind that so much," said Jackson. "I can practice law in a hayloft. But the cooking is bad. John and I lie awake nights thinking of Sunday dinners like this."

"We haven't had any tenants in your cabin since you left," said Stockly Donelson blandly. "Wouldn't you like to move back into your old office?"

"There's nothing Andrew or I would like better," said Overton. "But is it . . . wise?"

"For my part," replied Mrs. Donelson quietly, "I can tell you that I was heartily against your moving out in the first place. However, the question of what is wise or unwise in this particular case must rest with Rachel."

All eyes turned on her. She found that there was no hesitation in her mind. Why should so many Donelsons be controlled by one absent and hostile Robards? She turned to the two lawyers. "I know of no reason why you shouldn't come back. Move into your cabin again, gentlemen. We enjoy having you here."

AFTER dinner a number of them walked into the orchard to see the first blossoms on the peach trees. They had gone only a few steps beyond the fence when

Andrew Jackson fell into step beside her.

"I want to thank you for your kind invitation, Mrs. Robards, but I just can't move back here. There's never been any young woman whose friendship has meant so much to me. That's why, for the time being, I think I had better continue living at Mansker's. I feel that I must do this to protect you, Mrs. Robards."

Rachel turned an unsmiling face up to him. "I don't think you need concern yourself about Lewis Robards."

He studied her, perplexed, his lips a little parted. She thought how peculiar it was that one could look at a man's face every day for months and not really know its detail until a moment of crisis. It was not a symmetrical structure: the high arched forehead was too narrow, the nose long and jutting. These things she saw vividly, certain that they were not the ingredients of handsomeness. Why did it seem to her the most attractive face she had ever known?

He managed to speak: "I don't understand."

"I don't believe he's ever coming back to Nashville. . . ."

246

IT WAS THE MOST beautiful spring anyone could remember in the ten years of the Cumberland settlement. The redbud and dogwood trees already showed pink and white on the green hillsides, and the yellow jasmine was rich with summer-like fragrance.

Rachel found her naturally buoyant spirits coming back in full force—that tremendous need to be gay, to sing and make jokes, to be happy over the simple fact that she was 22 and alive in a beautiful springtime.

Once she joined John and Andrew Jackson and the pretty blond daughter of a settler who had just arrived in Nashville, walking along the river road with the warm sun streaming onto their faces. She liked to walk; her long slim legs kept pace with Andrew's tempered stride.

John and the girl were up ahead. Rachel and Andrew Jackson talked about what they wanted out of life. For Rachel this was not difficult to tell, though it had been so difficult to achieve. She wanted a husband with whom she could live in love and peace; children; a home up here on the bluff overlooking the lazy green Cumberland.

It seemed that Mr. Jackson had no desire to become a great lawyer.

"I haven't the talent for the law that John has," he said. "Oh, I do well enough, but the law isn't something I've wanted all of my life. What I really want to be is a planter. And I'd like to raise blooded horses."

"But the law is an open door to politics," protested Rachel. "We're going to become a state within a few years. Wouldn't you like to be a Congressman, or governor, perhaps?"

"No," he said quickly. "I have no political ambitions. I even surveyed a beautiful site down near Natchez in the Spanish territory when I was there on business last year. I might settle there." He turned to gaze at her. "But now I just want to live here in the Cumberland."

One day that spring a party of traders came in from Harrodsburg; they carried a packet of letters for Mrs. Lewis Robards. Rachel read them through swiftly.

First, Lewis assured her that being home again had brought a complete

248

return of his energies; that his mother's illness had left her feeble and he had taken over the management of the plantation; and that he had now sold a number of slaves, both male and female. He apologized for having caused her anxiety, assured her that he loved her, and wouldn't she come to Harrodsburg as quickly as possible?

How carefully the letters had been designed to dispel her fears! The subject of the young slave had never been discussed between them, yet apparently he had sensed her knowledge of the relationship and was assuring her that the girl had been sold. And he was making it clear that, since he had assumed the management of the plantation, he would now be responsible and occupied. In all of her days of determination not to return to Harrodsburg she had never once imagined that her husband would use this approach. She was glad that Lewis still loved her; she was grateful to him for being willing to reconstruct his life. This was her only chance for a home of her own, for children. She must try again.

CHAPTER 4

SHE reached the Robards home late in the afternoon with the bright sun lighting up the rambling stone house. She had anticipated being met by Lewis where she branched off the Kentucky Road, but no one had been there to greet her. The leader of the trading party she traveled with insisted upon escorting her directly to the house, but there was no sign of welcome here, either. She tied her horse to the hitching post and walked up the four broad log steps and into the house.

She was escorted into the library. She found Lewis sprawled across a chair in a perspiration-soaked linen shirt and wrinkled woolen trousers, his booted legs stretched in front of him. His eyes were bleary and his face red from drinking. She stood with her back against the door, gazing at her husband in bewilderment. He made no effort to rise.

"It didn't take you very long, did it?"

"Take me long? Five days, instead of four; there was a sick woman traveling with the party."

"I was no sooner out of sight than you invited him back to the blockhouse."

All of Rachel's hopes and dreams crashed at that moment. "Lewis, what are you saying?"

"Friend of mine came in from Nashville, told me that Andrew Jackson was living at your house again."

"Mr. Jackson is not living at our station, Lewis. He thought it would be better if he did not live there since you had once demanded that he leave."

Lewis pulled himself heavily out of the chair and stood with his face close to hers. "Then you admit that you invited him back?"

"Mother wanted him, and so did the boys. After all, it is their house; he is like a member of our family."

"Yes," replied Lewis with a leer, "an intimate member."

Sick at heart, she realized that for the first time he was accusing her directly of infidelity. She turned, went out into the hall and up the stairs to her mother-in-law's bedroom.

She needed only one look at the thin face framed in the nightcap on the pillow to know that Mrs. Robards was seriously ill. She went to her side and kissed her. Mrs. Robards cupped Rachel's face in her hands.

"Rachel, my dear, there's nothing in the world I've wanted more than to have you become mistress of this house."

"Yes, darling, I know that."

"Lewis was a good boy; we loved him devotedly, my husband and I . . . but there can be no life for you here."

"You mustn't exhaust yourself. I'm going to stay here and help nurse you. . . ."

"No, Rachel," the older woman interrupted. "We must get you back home . . . at once." She closed her eyes for a moment, then whispered, "He promised me he would sell the slave girl, but he brought her back yesterday. He has been doing nothing but drinking and shouting. You must write your family at once to send for you. In the meantime, you can stay in that little room yonder."

During the long warm days that followed, Rachel nursed Mrs. Robards, feeding her, at the doctor's orders, chicken broth and a medicinal tea. She saw nothing of Lewis. Her hope for her marriage was gone.

One day, standing at the square window of her little room, she blinked her eyes hard. She saw a figure on horseback come up the road, riding fast, but sitting his horse with ungainly ease—and looking for all the world like Andrew Jackson! Her letter to her family saying that she was leaving Lewis forever had gone from Harrodsburg ten days ago, and she had expected that someone would arrive for her. But surely it would have been one of her brothers? Surely they would not have sent Andrew Jackson?

But it was indeed Andrew. He pounded on the door with his fists; it was as if that pounding were coming from her heart.

EXCEPT for necessities, her possessions had never been unpacked. She went quickly into her mother-in-law's room to bid her farewell, telling her that it was Mr. Jackson who had come for her and that she wanted to get away before Lewis could return; that she dreaded the thought of another duel.

"You need have no fear of that, my

dear," replied the old woman. There was a quality in her voice that brought Rachel up short.

"But Lewis fought a duel with Peyton Short."

Mrs. Robards turned her head slightly on the pillow. She had been a proud woman all her life. She could not look at Rachel in this painful moment.

"This is a sad thing for a mother to have to reveal about her son. But you are entitled to know. When Lewis found Peyton Short in Richmond, Mr. Short asked Lewis if he insisted on fighting a duel or if he would accept a money settlement."

"A money set— But for what?"

"For damages done to Lewis's feelings because of that letter. Lewis said he would consider a settlement. Mr. Short paid him a thousand dollars in sterling."

Rachel felt her face flame.

Tears welled in Mrs. Robards' eyes. Rachel kissed her mother-in-law's cheek hard and fled from the room.

Alongside this news all concern about Andrew Jackson's having come for her was forgotten. By the time she reached the front door her chestnut mare had been saddled and brought to the front of the blockhouse. She and Jackson exchanged a quick glance of greeting; it was not until they were several miles on their way to the Kentucky Road that he first addressed her.

"Shall we light straight out for Nashville or wait for the next party? There has been some Indian activity along the road during the past few weeks."

"How did you come?"

"Alone."

"Then that's the way we'll go back. I'd like to get distance between us and Harrodsburg as quickly as we can."

It was a little before sundown when they reached an inn. Rachel had a room to herself, while Andrew had to share the last available bed with two other men.

By the time the sun was over the horizon, they were on the road again. For the first time she realized how seriously Jackson was on guard, his whole being cocked at every tree and bush as they went through a copse of cedars. Suddenly he pulled in his horse.

"Can you shoot straight?"

"Sometimes."

"Take this pistol. Indians, perhaps only

three or four, have been paralleling our course through the woods. They've just pulled out ahead of us to get to that spot up above. Do you see that fallen tree about 20 yards this side of the open space?"

"Yes."

"I'm going to pull off the road just beyond that log."

He started his horse at a medium pace. She followed behind him. When he passed the big cedar log he gave his horse the spur and dashed into the woods. She came behind him as quickly as she could. He fired his rifle, then called to her, "Use your spur!" and in an instant they were out of the clearing and back onto the trail.

"I missed," he said, "but it served the purpose. They'll leave us alone from now on." He turned to her. "Were you scared?"

"No, I didn't see anything. Besides, I was too interested in watching you. If I'd been an Indian, I'd have been sure there was a whole militia regiment behind you."

"That's the best tactic," he replied, pleased. "It will bring you out unscathed nearly every time."

She joined his laughter at the use of the

word "nearly"; and the laughter dissipated the tension between them.

That night they stayed in the one-room log cabin of a family which had come over the Wilderness Trail with Daniel Boone. It had a divided loft for sleeping rooms, chickens and dogs in the hard-packed-earth yard, and children running in and out of the open door. There was cold broiled ham, milk and hoecake for supper served on a tree stump in the yard. Rachel shared a bed with several daughters of the family on the ground floor, while Andrew climbed up the rough-hewn ladder to the loft.

On the third day the Indian danger was past and so was the threat of Lewis Robards' catching up with them. They let the horses set their own pace, riding side by side. The day was soft and warm; they listened to the sounds of the wildlife about them, feeling a sense of peacefulness and of companionship.

JACKSON had brought her an invitation to stay at the blockhouse of her sister Jane and Colonel Robert Hays in Haysboro, and Rachel was glad to be going there

258

instead of to the Donelsons'. Jane's off-hand manner would have a remedial effect upon her. Jackson turned her over to Jane, waved aside their efforts to thank him and rode off for Nashville.

Rachel's sanctuary lasted two days, long enough for Lewis Robards to reach the Hays plantation. He came along the dog-trot, chatting in an amiable voice with Jane.

"You have company, Rachel," called Jane, as though an acquaintance had just ridden out from Nashville.

"Aren't you going to welcome your hus-band after he's ridden more than 200 miles to see you?" Lewis's voice was charming. He wore a smartly fashioned suit and white silk shirt.

"The kind of welcome I had when I reached Harrodsburg?"

"I behaved badly, Rachel. I had been inflamed by the stories I'd heard."

"What kind of man believes every chance story that gossips may care to repeat about his wife?"

"My kind of man, I guess: a little stu-pid, a little hysterical."

"And you don't take it amiss that it was

Andrew Jackson who brought me here?" asked Rachel bluntly.

"Certainly not," he replied. "If it was more convenient for your mother to send Jackson, then there is no reason why he shouldn't have come."

Lewis went to her impulsively, with one of his tenderest smiles. "I trust you, I love you," he said, "and I want you to come back with me. This won't ever happen again, my dear. I give you my word of honor."

"No, Lewis. You've broken your word many times before. It would do no good."

He peered at her intently. "No good?"

"I bear you no ill will, Lewis, but I have no affection left for you, none at all. I could never live with you again."

His placating manner vanished.

"I don't believe you! Besides, you *are* my wife and you must do as I say. We will return to Harrodsburg in the morning."

His voice had risen. She replied with a firmness he had never before heard.

"Lewis, I never intend to see you again."

There could be no mistaking the finality in her voice. He stood close to her, a tight-clenched fist in front of her face.

"Then it was true."

"What was true, Lewis?"

"My suspicions of you and Andrew Jackson! The fact that he came to Harrodsburg for you clinches the case!"

"But it's only a few moments since you told me that there was nothing wrong in Mr. Jackson's coming for me."

"That was before I knew."

"Knew what?"

"That you were in love with him."

She had never realized that a few spoken words could have the solid substance of a physical object: that they could be a fence rail that hit you over the head . . . a sharp knife that penetrated deep into your bosom.

Did she love Andrew Jackson?

A hundred images of him raced through her mind. She could see Andrew standing at the front door on the first day of his arrival, looking lonely and forlorn, as though he had no home place; Andrew at the courthouse facing the bully and his gun, with "Shoot!" in his eyes; Andrew dancing at a party, indefatigable as a windmill, and similar in style. He was a man among men, she knew that: strong, reliable, teeming with energy and ambition.

261

But as for love . . . How could she love anyone when she had been so badly hurt by love?

She turned her back on Robards.

"Please go now, Lewis."

"You are my wife and I'm going to stay right here until you are ready to return to Harrodsburg. Colonel Hays would never put me out."

LEWIS was right: Colonel Hays refused her entreaties to ask Lewis to leave.

"I can't do that, my dear. He is still a member of our family."

"Then would you be so kind as to ride me over to Mother's?"

"No, Rachel. I think that's just as wrong as putting Lewis out. In a few days Lewis will become discouraged and leave of his own accord. In the meantime you are perfectly safe here with us."

She spent the next days in the house with Jane, spinning and embroidering, going out in the evening for a breath of cool air under the thick-leaved oak trees.

"I'm uneasy about your berrypicking party tomorrow," she told her sister as they sat brushing their hair before retiring.

262

"You and Robert invited Mr. Jackson, remember?"

"I'm sure we can rely on Mr. Jackson," said Jane soothingly, braiding her hair into two thick blond plaits. "And you'll come, too," she added doggedly. "You always loved to eat the berries right off the bush, with the hot sun on them."

But in the morning their mother arrived for a visit, and instead of going to the berrypicking, Rachel remained in the cool log house to tell her what had happened at Harrodsburg.

"It's really the end then," said Mrs. Donelson with a sigh of finality. "But how are you going to get free of Lewis?"

"I am free of him. In my mind, I mean, and that's the most important place. He can never hurt me again."

"Yes, my dear, but life consists of something more than not being hurt."

At that moment they heard a clatter of hoofs. Rachel ran to the window and saw Robert Hays jump off his horse with unaccustomed haste, toss the reins to a yard boy and storm into the house. Samuel, who had ridden in with him, remained in the yard, mopping his fore-

head with a big muslin handkerchief.

Colonel Hays was white-faced. "Your way would have been the lesser of two evils, Rachel."

"Then it's Lewis. What has he done?"

"Made some nasty remarks about you . . . and Andrew Jackson, loud enough for the whole party to hear. I've come to the end of my patience. He'll have to be gone from here before dark."

Mrs. Donelson had moved past her daughter and son-in-law, and was gazing out the front door of the house.

"If they don't bury him in the blackberry patch first," she interjected with a grim smile. "There goes Andrew to find him; he's just been talking to Samuel."

By nightfall Lewis was gone, leaving the countryside in an uproar. . . . Rachel tried to put the story together from garbled and conflicting reports: a young girl who had been berrypicking related that Andrew Jackson had said to Lewis, "If you ever connect my name with Mrs. Robards in that way again, I will cut your ears off— and I am tempted to do it anyhow!" One of the more excitable boys said that Lewis had ridden to the nearest magistrate, secured a peace warrant against Andrew and had it served by two deputies. Still another version was that Lewis had run into the cane, with Jackson in pursuit.

She did not see Andrew Jackson after the quarrel, but she knew that in any event he would have refused to discuss the matter with her. The whole affair had degenerated into a distasteful farce.

It was her youngest brother who really upset her. He caught her alone in the yard, under the oak tree.

"I have a word for you from your husband. Lewis said, 'You can tell Rachel for me that I shall haunt her.'"

CHAPTER 5

THERE was no direct word from Lewis during the fall months, only news that came indirectly as a result of unguarded conversations around Harrodsburg. At first the threats did not disturb her: the talk about legal rights, that he would come to Nashville and claim her. But one day she found Overton alone in his office.

"John," she said, "I'd feel so much better if I were completely free. Isn't there any possibility of a court action or a divorce?"

"Practically none, Rachel. Our law here derives from the English law, and even in London a man has to get an act through Parliament before he can have what's known as a legal separation. Each state makes its own laws about divorce. New York, for instance, does not allow court action for a divorce at all, and in Virginia the legislature has to grant each divorce separately. Anyway, you're a woman. To the best of my knowledge it is impossible for a woman to secure a divorce in this country. In fact, it's almost impossible for her to get into a law court at all, except as a spectator."

"Then there's nothing I can do to make sure Lewis will have no right to disturb me again?"

"Well, there is one possible way: you might be able to secure a separation down

266

in the Spanish territory, say at New Orleans or Natchez. But that would never be considered legal up here; if you should ever marry again locally, you would be considered guilty of bigamy. And if you had children . . ."

The hope drained out of her face. "I see," she said.

SHORTLY before Thanksgiving a letter reached Rachel informing her that Lewis had convinced a segment of the Harrodsburg folk that the Donelsons were keeping his wife away from him against her will. He was organizing a band of his cronies to take her back to Harrodsburg by force.

"Can he really do this?" Rachel asked the lawyers.

"He can try," Jackson said. "There is always the chance."

Tears came into her eyes. "I must go away, far away."

"But where would you go, Rachel?" her mother asked.

"It doesn't matter, Mother, just so long as there are thousands of miles between Lewis Robards and me."

"Colonel Stark is leaving for Natchez soon," said Samuel. "I've seen him outfitting his boat. Perhaps he would take Rachel along. She could stay there with Tom or Abner Green's family."

"Yes, you would be welcome there," said Mrs. Donelson with excited relief. "The Green boys have been asking us to come down and see the beautiful estates they've built."

"That's a mighty dangerous voyage," commented Jackson; "almost 2000 miles down the Cumberland, the Ohio and the Mississippi rivers, through lands inhabited by hostile Indians. And Colonel Stark is an elderly man. Unless there are experienced Indian fighters along . . . "

Rachel stood with her shoulders thrown back.

"I'm going!"

SHE and Samuel found Colonel Stark at the landing, supervising the loading of salt, cotton and whisky onto his boat. It was a 20-foot-wide, 100-foot-long, broadbottomed structure, some two thirds of which was covered by a round roof. Two other flatboats were also loading, as

268

part of the flotilla. The river was muddy, but a sharp current kept it covered with whitecaps.

Colonel Stark stopped his labors to speak to the young people.

"Now, Miss Rachel," he said, "you know I'd do anything for you I could. But I simply can't shoulder the responsibility."

"Colonel, we'll take full responsibility," said Samuel. "Rachel's simply got to get away."

"Tell you what I'll do, Miss Rachel: there's a young fellow in this town who's a real Indian fighter. He can smell an Indian a hundred miles away with the wind blowing in the wrong direction. I'm referring to Andy Jackson, of course."

"Colonel, that's out of the question! Mr. Jackson has his law practice, he's an officer of the court. John Overton says that he is going to appear in 50 cases here in Nashville in the next few months alone."

"He's young; he'll have thousands of law cases."

"No, Colonel," said Rachel, "I simply could not ask him. I will sell my possessions and hire a couple of good militiamen."

TWO DAYS LATER, having made inquiries about engaging the riflemen to make the trip under Colonel Stark's command, Rachel went back to the dock. She was surprised to have the Colonel greet her with a broad smile.

"It's all arranged, Miss Rachel. When you left here I went down to the court-house and put the proposition up to Andy Jackson."

"You didn't!"

"Certainly did. Told him I wouldn't take you unless he came along. He seemed mighty upset. Said he'd need a couple days to mull it over. Wasn't more than an hour ago that he told me he'd come along, and when did we leave?"

Arriving home late in the afternoon, Rachel made straight for the law cabin. John Overton was alone.

"John, do you know what Andrew Jackson has done?"

"Yes, he's turned all his cases over to me and he's going down to Natchez with Colonel Stark."

"From your tone of voice, it would seem that you approve."

"Yes, I must say I do. Andrew paced

this cabin for two days and nights. He told me that he was the unhappiest of men, that he believed you to be the finest woman he had ever known, and that he had unintentionally been the cause of your troubles for the past two years. He feels that he must get you safely out of Nashville and installed with your friends in Natchez, and then he will have done everything he could and should."

She cried, "But the family would never approve of his going."

"I think they will. I think your mother, Samuel and Jane, at least, are now convinced that you and Andrew Jackson belong together."

She dropped onto the log bench. It was true. She loved Andrew Jackson, loved him with all her heart. She knew that now. But did he love her?

She looked up at John, wondering how much she could tell him. If Andrew did not share her love, then she must never embarrass him by an expression of it. John's back was to her, as though he wished to afford her the opportunity of thinking in private. Now he turned, sensing that she was ready to continue.

"Have no fears, my dear Rachel," he said softly, "nor any misgivings. Andrew loves you, too. He has told me so."

THE morning of January 20, 1791, was leaden-skied. Samuel took her to the landing with her two heavy portmanteaus strapped on a packhorse. She picked up her skirts as she walked along the muddy bank, then across a plank and onto the boxlike boat. She stood irresolutely for a moment in the boat's cabin until Andrew, stooping low, came through the door. He greeted her with a pleasant smile, picked up her two cases, and led her toward the prow.

She found herself in the front portion of the cabin where Mrs. Stark, in a huge leather apron over her cotton dress, was directing her serving couple in the preparation of the noonday dinner. She turned to Rachel with an open-armed gesture; she was a big, shapeless, bustling woman who moved about with astonishing speed in a pair of floppy buffalo moccasins.

She took Rachel by the arm, leading her through the middle compartment of the flatboat in which were stored bales of cotton and barrels of salt and smoked venison, into the rear third of the cabin, which constituted the sleeping quarters. There were two bunks fastened to the log wall with leather hinges. A thick curtain of buffalo hide was pegged to the rafters; it fell heavily over the doorway.

"You and I will live here, child; it will give us good privacy."

THERE were three boats in the little flotilla. The rain and cold continued for a full week, and Rachel rarely left her quarters, spending her time reading, sewing, helping Mrs. Stark make a pair of bedcovers. In addition to the Starks and Andrew there were five traders on board the flatboat. When they went ashore at various settlements, Rachel and Andrew sat at the scrubbed cabin table in front of a blazing log fire, Andrew's red hair plastered down from the many hours under a heavy wool cap. He spent his leisure studying his briefs and the lawbooks which John Overton had loaned him. The Andrew Jackson she had known, the man with the teeming energy, the sparkling eyes and the deeply emotional nature, had remained in Nashville; the uncommunicative young man sitting opposite her needed but a pair of silver-rimmed spectacles to be John Overton. These periods of quiet, almost of solitude, were their only moments alone together.

It took them ten days to navigate the Cumberland and Ohio rivers. On the eleventh morning she awakened to find that their tiny flotilla was already several miles along the Mississippi, with the sun shining brightly overhead.

THEY were attacked twice by Indians, once from a high bluff when they had steered too close to the bank and another time from an island thicket which had looked innocent enough as they approached. There were a number of bullet holes in the superstructure, but only one man had been injured, slightly, by an already spent bullet.

Then late one February afternoon they became separated from the other two boats and were obliged to tie up to an abandoned landing at the foot of a dense forest. Andrew pointed out to Colonel Stark how close the cypress trees came down to the shore, how the bank made a lagoon so that the Indians could surround them on three sides and subject them to a murderous crossfire. However, the Colonel was unwilling to risk the river currents in the darkness. Andrew took the youngest of the traders and went onshore. Colonel Stark tried to dissuade them from going.

"I want every man to remain on board so we have our fullest fighting strength."

"You've got to have advance warning, Colonel, and the only way you can get it is for us to go ashore."

He picked up his rifle, summoned his companion, and the two men slipped noiselessly onto the old timbers of the landing, leaving orders for one of the traders to remain awake with an axe in hand, ready to cut the tie rope at the first sound of a shot.

Rachel watched Andrew until he had disappeared into the darkness, then went to the cabin, pulled her bunk from the wall and lay down fully clothed. After a time Mrs. Stark came in, undressed, pushed her own bunk down on its supporting legs. She got under the covers and began to talk, quietly and pleasantly, of other trips, other alarms. Rachel listened with only one ear, for the other was listening for sounds on the outside.

Then, in the middle of one of her own sentences, Mrs. Stark fell fast asleep. Rachel rose quietly and went out on deck to find the sky still black, with no vestige of a moon. The guard was asleep. She stood peering into the darkness. Then she saw the flash of a gun on the beach, followed by a burst of fire. The traders, sleeping on the deck, were awake at once. The guard grabbed the axe, but Rachel was waiting and seized his arm.

"Don't touch that rope."

"But Jackson gave orders. . . ."

"I don't care what orders he gave. Here, give me that axe. I'll cut this rope when those two men are on board, and not an instant before."

He stared at her. Then he shrugged, handed her the axe and picked up his rifle. Two more shots were fired. She saw Andrew and his companion come swiftly up the plank and drop onto the deck, and she brought the axe down sharply on the rope. The flatboat edged out into the river.

She and Andrew stood at the prow

watching the currents, with Colonel Stark steering as best he could. She heard Andrew chuckling to himself.

"Tell me the joke," she said.

Without turning his head, he replied, "So you refused to let them cut that tie line, eh? Don't you know you could have been massacred?"

"But how could we have left you on the beach and pulled away to safety?"

"From the evidence before this court, I would say you couldn't."

He put his arm about her in a slow encircling movement, holding her with his long sinewy fingers, crushing her shoulder to him in a momentary grip of avowal. Then, almost before she knew it had happened, he moved away.

THOMAS Green's home, Springfield, was the most luxurious Rachel had ever seen, bringing to mind the stories her father had told her about George Washington's Mount Vernon. It was a sturdy structure of red brick with six majestic pillars across the front and deep shade galleries hung with vines to ensure coolness. It stood high above the murky swamps, framed at the end of a row of magnificent oaks.

The Greens quickly assembled all the Americans in the neighborhood for a welcoming dinner party. Mrs. Green loaned Rachel a lace-trimmed pale-blue satin dress with a delicate lace cap. When she walked into the dining room on old Colonel Thomas Green's arm, she found a hundred candles in the chandelier throwing a glow of light on the silver, crystal goblets and polished wood.

"You've transplanted the very best of Virginia down here," she exclaimed.

"Too bad your father didn't live to see it, Rachel," said the old colonel, proudly. "He would have moved down here and built a house just like it."

Young Tom Green, at the head of the long mahogany table, said: "Since we can't have Colonel Donelson, perhaps we can have his daughter. How about it, Rachel?"

His wife nodded her agreement. "We feel as though we have scored a victory every time another American family joins us."

The elder Green lifted a goblet of Spanish Madeira. "You're staying this time, aren't you, Jackson? That's a fine piece of land you have over at Bayou Pierre. We'd like to have you with us when there's trouble with the Spaniards."

Rachel was disturbed by the implication that she and Andrew might remain in Natchez together, to establish another American family. Just how much were the Greens assuming?

Actually, Rachel saw little of Andrew while she stayed with the Greens, for he spent a number of days on business in Natchez, some 30 miles downriver from Springfield. After that one fleeting moment at the prow of the boat, in the seclusion of the dark Mississippi night, there had been no intimate word or gesture between them.

Then early on a bright, fragrant Sunday morning she rode with Andrew the two miles to Bayou Pierre to see his tract of land on the bluff overlooking the river. They stood before the door of the small log cabin he had built there, looking over the wide, slow-moving waters and the vast forest of cypress and oak rolling horizonward to merge with the pastel sky. It was a beautiful spot, almost too beautiful; it gave her a poignant feeling of nostalgia.

"You will have to be going back soon, won't you, Andrew?"

"Yes. The spring court in Nashville opens on April twelfth. There's a group of boatmen starting back at midweek. I'll travel with them."

His voice fell off; he stood gazing over the river for a moment. When he turned, his eyes were unguarded and full of his love for her. He untied the strings of her bonnet, took it off her head and ran his fingers through her hair.

"Rachel, I don't have to go back at all. We can stay right here together, the two of us. You could get an annulment in Natchez, from the Spanish authorities. It would be legal."

"Not really legal, Andrew, just a way around the law. You took your oath to the United States Government when they installed you as attorney general of the territory; I can't let you go back on your word. And you have the biggest law practice there. Even John says so."

"I couldn't be a lawyer, perhaps. I couldn't hold public office, and I'd have to become a Spanish subject, but I can do well down here."

Now there was a tiny edge to his voice. "Look about you. I had this whole Bayou Pierre plantation staked out before I even knew you." He rushed on, not wanting to give her a chance to answer. "The main house was to be over on the edge of the bluff; straight across I was going to build stables. One day we'd have a plantation as lovely as Springfield."

She slipped into his embrace, held herself against him.

"But how could you ever be happy as a subject of Spain? You'd have no voice here, no vote. You're an independent man. . . ."

"It wouldn't be for long; this country will be American. I wouldn't mind helping the Greens bring it into the Union."

"No, Andrew, I can't take the responsibility. If you ever became unhappy down here, or if somehow we failed . . . one morning you might wake up to find you had wasted your life in Louisiana. I can't put this burden on our marriage. Our love is right and good; our marriage must be right and good, too."

"But what are we going to do?" he cried, as though the volume of his voice could knock down the walls which enclosed them. "We are caught. We are helpless. Robards holds all the weapons."

She cupped his face in her hands, kissing him on one cheek and then the other. "No, Andrew, we have a weapon, too: we have our love."

He held her close to him. "Rachel dear, I am not a fickle man. I have never loved before, and I'll not love again. Only you. Always you." He kissed her full on the mouth.

"We will have to believe in miracles," he murmured.

AFTER six weeks with the Colonel and the Tom Greens, Rachel was invited to visit the Abner Greens, downriver at Villa Gayoso.

There was no word from Andrew, who had returned North, nor from any of the Donelsons; with the coming of summer, travel up and down the Mississippi ceased. The weeks passed and in the serene beauty of her surroundings Rachel felt her strength and sense of joy in life return in full measure. As the slow, lazy days of summer drifted by, her eyes became bright and luminous, her step buoyant.

She was sitting one day at the window of her bedroom when she heard hoofbeats on the main road. Horsemen came and went all day, but only one horseman rode like this: headlong, almost cyclonic, but always knowing his destination.

She picked up the skirts of her crisp white cotton dress and ran down the winding staircase. There stood Andrew in the doorway, hot, disheveled, in wrinkled buckskins, and wearing a three weeks' beard. She led him to the dark oak-paneled library, with its windows open to the pungent fragrance of the tropical garden.

He closed the door behind him, and they met in the center of the room. She felt his lips, dry and cracked from the long days on the trail, bruising her own. He held her securely for several moments, then blurted out:

"There's news."

"About . . . Lewis?"

"Yes, he has divorced you."

She gasped, felt a sharp pain in her chest.

"Divorced me? But how?"

"The Virginia legislature. He persuaded his brother-in-law there to introduce a bill. The legislature passed it."

"But on what grounds?"

" . . . well . . . desertion."

"And what else, Andrew? The Virginia laws don't allow divorce merely for desertion. Tell me the rest. I must know."

" . . . *adultery.* "

She felt as though she had been struck across the face. The only voice she could muster was so faint that she imagined she was saying the words inside her own head.

"Adultery! But . . . with whom . . . ?"

He enveloped her in his long arms and held her rigidly as though fearing she might fall.

"With me."

" . . . you . . . but when . . . ?"

"When we . . . 'eloped' . . . the bill calls it. From the Robards' home."

"Eloped? But the family sent you. When Lewis tried to persuade me to go home with him, he said there had been nothing wrong in your coming for me. He never would have come for me if he had believed for a single instant . . ."

She burst into tears, hot scalding tears,

while he stroked her hair and kissed her temples and spoke soft words to comfort her. After a time she looked up, her eyes wet, the tears still on her cheeks.

"I had expected he would try to kill me. This is worse."

"But don't you see, dearest—this is the end of our troubles. A bitter end, I grant you that, but it means that we can have our life together. We can have a home and children and never be separated again."

There was a constriction about her heart which she thought must burst it. "John Overton—what does *he* think of this?"

"When I first heard the news, I wanted to go out and shoot Robards. John stopped me. He said, 'Let's look at these facts calmly, as lawyers should. The divorce on these terms is Robards' final act of indignity. Forget the bad part of it and think only that you and Rachel can begin your lives together.' "

Her anger was spent now. She sighed deeply. "John is right; he's always right." She hesitated for a moment. "How did you learn all this? Was it published in a paper?"

"No, I think not. It reached the Cumberland the way most news does, by word of mouth. Your family heard about it first. Probably half a dozen men brought in word from Richmond."

"Then everybody . . . knows . . . in Nashville . . . ?"

It was his turn to be angry now; the harshness in his voice brought her head up abruptly.

"Everyone knows that Robards has secured his divorce. But there's not a soul in the Cumberland Valley who could believe you guilty. Everyone also knows that I came down here for our wedding. We are going to have a fine home and a fine life together, Rachel, and that will be the last we will ever hear of this wretched affair."

She lifted her face to his, kissed him. "I will always love you, Andrew."

"Then that is all we need. We will honeymoon here in my cabin at Bayou Pierre. Tom Green will provide anything we need, and we can be utterly alone. Perhaps more alone than we will ever be again in our lives."

They stood together, silent in the dark

room, holding tightly to each other.

This we will always have, she thought: our love. But Andrew, my dearest, you are wrong when you say this is the end of our troubles.

CHAPTER 6

THE marriage ceremony was held in Tom Green's drawing room under the heavy cut-glass chandelier. They danced cotillions for hours, then slipped away and rode over to Bayou Pierre. After a languorous two months there, they set out on the thousand-mile trip up the dangerous Natchez Trace, reaching Nashville on the first of October. They had been back there only a few days when Andrew came home to greet Rachel in a fever of excitement.

"Rachel, what do you suppose has happened? I've been elected a trustee of Davidson Academy."

She kissed him soundly. "Congratulations, my darling."

Even while she held her lips to his, a number of tensions suddenly relaxed. She had not been sure how their marriage would be received in Nashville. Hers had been the first divorce in the Cumberland

288

Valley. Several nights on the Natchez Trace she had lain awake, wondering whether Andrew's swift flight to Natchez and their immediate marriage might not be held against them. Now the most important men in the territory, all of them trustees of the Academy, had made it known that Andrew was one of theirs.

She had imagined that her husband's pleasure derived from the same source as her own. To her astonishment, his exultation was on an entirely different level.

"Forgive me if I gloat, my dear, but that's the last position I would have imagined I would ever be elected to. One of the heads of the Academy! Do you know how much formal schooling I've had? A month or two at Queen's Museum at Charlotte and a few years at a country school in the Waxhaws. All I've learned I've had to hew out of the few books I stumbled across. I'm going to pitch in and help make Davidson Academy one of the best schools this side of the Blue Ridge Mountains. Then our youngsters will be able to get themselves a real education."

"Amen," said Rachel under her breath.

THE AFFECTION OF the Donelson family for Andrew served as a cohesive which brought the brothers and sisters together at every possible opportunity. Jane's husband, Robert Hays, formed a partnership with him on a land deal; Samuel read law with him and had been promised a partnership; Stockly, another brother, was selling much of the goods which Andrew received in lieu of cash for his services. They had fun together on the snowy winter afternoons and evenings, convoking mock court around the blazing fire, Judges Jackson and Hays appointing neophyte Samuel as Lord Chief Joker and General Humbugger of North America.

On the first of May, Rachel and Andrew moved into Poplar Grove, a snug and fertile peninsula of 330 acres planted with tobacco and corn, bounded on the three sides by the slow-moving green Cumberland and across the river from the Widow Donelson's station. Rachel took from home the walnut secretary her father had willed her; her mother promised her the big Donelson clock. Her sisters and sisters-in-law had been weaving and spinning a good part of the winter and now presented her with quilts, pillows, mattresses and rugs. Andrew sent to Philadelphia for the largest canopied bed he could find; it completely filled their room. They stood in the center of the dark cabin, holding hands.

"It's our first home, and I love it," said Rachel emphatically.

He kissed her anxious mouth.

"You are a sentimentalist, and I love you for it."

RACHEL remarked the arrival of new seasons not so much by the changing weather as by the fact that during January, April, July and October Andrew attended court sessions in Nashville. While he was riding to the quarter sessions at Jonesboro, Gallatin and Clarksville, her sisters visited frequently with their children.

One day, as she went about the endless tasks of a self-sustaining plantation, her sister Jane commented:

"You're happy now, Rachel, aren't you?"

"Yes, completely. Or I will be, when I have children."

"No hope yet?"

"None. Is there a special prayer?"

"Not that I know of. For some women they come a little too fast, and for others a little too slow, but we Donelsons all seem to get our share."

"I keep remembering that."

Time went quickly; she and Andrew had been married a full year. They were sitting on the front porch watching the moon arch upward across the stars. Andrew turned to her with a touch of amusement in his eyes.

"Well, my dear, I've brought you home a first-anniversary present. You are now married to the judge advocate for our county militia. Last year I sent a plan to Governor Blount for the organization of our militia system; he liked it so well he forwarded it to the Secretary of War. I guess that's why they gave me the appointment. Anyway, I am now a Captain."

"May I kiss you, Captain Jackson?"

"I'll take that kiss, thank you, ma'am, but you can leave off the title. I'll use the Captain when I've earned it, fighting the Indians and the British."

WITH Andrew away so much of the time on legal business, the responsibility of running the plantation was largely Rachel's. In June there was the corn to be cultivated, the flax to be pulled, the hemp sowed; in July the wheat and timothy had to be harvested, the turnips planted; August was the best month for preserving. In the early fall, all buildings had to be repaired and chinked against the winter, meat had to be butchered and stored; there was the winter supply of candles to be made from the fats that had accumulated over the summer.

The presence of Moll was a comfort to Rachel. No one knew how old Moll was, least of all Moll herself. In spite of her white hair, she went about her duties tirelessly, humming spirituals under her breath, knowing the tunes to dozens of these hymns but not one complete line from any of them. She was an inexhaustible mine of information: she knew the recipe for making red dye out of logwood; the exact moment when the lye was strong enough for making soap; the right combination of woods and the degree of warmth for the smokehouse; how to make bayberry candles which burned slowly and gave off a pleasant scent.

Each day Rachel loved Andrew so deeply that she felt there could be no going beyond it. Yet always the next day was infinitely sweeter, their love heightened and more complete: for did not each new morning promise still another day of wonderful memories to feed and grow upon?

THE law practice of Andrew Jackson and John Overton was growing so fast that in the spring of 1793, with 155 cases docketed in Nashville, Andrew had been retained as counsel on 72 cases, while John had a considerable portion of the remainder.

"Rachel, why don't we build a guest cabin for John?" Andrew suggested one day. "We could set it up as an alternate office with a supply of lawbooks, and then I'd be home more."

"Good. I'll build it while you're away on the court circuit."

Rachel and the Donelsons set to work at once to make the necessary bedframe, desk and chairs. As her own contribution Rachel loomed a bed coverlet of indigo-dyed wool in the intricate design known as

Bachelor's Fancy. She asked her brother Samuel to stay with her for the two months that the men would be away.

Andrew had been gone only a week when there began a series of Indian attacks the like of which Rachel could not remember. The son of Colonel Isaac Bledsoe and a friend were killed opposite Nashville. Five days later two sons of Colonel Saunders were scalped; a couple of days after, Captain Samuel Hays, brother of Robert, was killed near the front door of John Donelson's new house. The militia commander issued orders that every home, stockade and group of men working in a clearing were to keep night and day guard.

Rachel was caught in a dilemma: she could not go to her mother's and leave her field hands at the mercy of the Indians, but if she took them with her, the Indians would burn the station to the ground.

"I'm not letting my husband come home to a mess of charred embers," she declared.

"No," said Samuel, "but you can't let him come home to a scalped wife, either. Maybe Mother can spare us two of the boys for the night watch."

Andrew and John returned home on April 9, the day Colonel Bledsoe himself was killed while working in the fields. Andrew's relief at seeing Rachel safe found its outlet in a torrential denunciation of all Indians. When he finally exhausted himself, John said in his driest legal tone:

"Surely you will admit that the Indians have a case, too?"

"Sure, a case of whisky from the British and a case of rifles from the Spanish."

John said, "Pun me no puns," then added, "Bad as the Creeks and Cherokees have behaved, they can't hold a candle to us. We have bribed them, corrupted them and broken practically every treaty."

Andrew jumped up from his chair, shouting:

"By the Eternal, John, I'll not have you taking the side of the Indians against me in my own house! Furthermore, I just heard that the federal government wants everybody to celebrate the Fourth of July this year. What are we supposed to bottom our celebration on?"

"On our independence," replied John. "The thing you got that scar for, remember?"

296

"What independence!" cried Andrew belligerently. "Do we in this territory have a vote? Do we have representation in Congress? Does the government build us roads or provide us with troops to police the frontier?"

This was the Jackson temper she had heard about. She went to Andrew, put her hand on his arm. He gazed at her for a moment and dropped heavily into his chair.

"I think it's a wonderful idea," she said. "We will have a big party here: an outdoor dinner for the Fourth of July."

MORE than a hundred adults and uncountable swarms of children came to their Independence Day party. In the cool of the morning they went berrypicking in the woods and when the sun got hot the youngsters splashed in the river. On the north side of the house, where the grass was the coolest, three fiddlers provided untiring music for the contra dance and the jig.

Rachel made her way from group to group, every once in a while looking for Andrew. A local planter, John Rains, sat in the shade of the doorstep and gathered listeners. The year before, he had raised a bumper crop of tobacco, built a flatboat and carried his cargo down to New Orleans where tobacco prices were high, but the Spaniards had confiscated not only his crop but his boat; and he had had to walk all the way up the Natchez Trace, empty-handed.

"Sometimes it beats me why we bother to stay here at all," Rains said. "Certainly those white-wigged New Englanders don't want us to be part of the United States. It was our own government gave the Spanish control of that Mississippi."

Looking about her, Rachel saw that every one of these men had fought against the British. Andrew spoke for them when he said:

"Our Congress says we're too young and too weak to quarrel with the Spaniards, and the mouth of the Mississippi isn't important anyway, so they give Spain control over the navigation on the Mississippi for twenty years. The English are still occupying forts in the Northwest that they agreed to get out of ten years ago. Does our government force them out? No, we watch them incite the Indians against the settlers. We're going to have to fight that war for independence all over again. But next time we'll make it stick!"

John Overton sighed, then said, "Now, Andrew, it's going to take years for us to grow strong enough to put the British out of those northern forts. We can't risk brawling with every nation that wants to quarrel with us."

"No wonder everybody despises us," growled Andrew.

When the blazing hot July sun finally settled itself onto the western horizon the guests started home.

"Was my party a success?" asked Rachel when they were alone. "People become so angry when they get involved in politics."

Andrew was astonished. "Why, darling, everyone had a wonderful time! Political arguments are one of the treats."

Rachel glanced at her husband quizzically. Maybe so. For herself, she had liked the way people had called her Mrs. Jackson, ma'am. She liked the feel of the name, and the attitude of the guests that this Jackson marriage and this Jackson home were permanent.

IT WAS a melancholy gray-black day the next fall when Rachel, standing at the door, saw Andrew coming heavily homeward. He slid off his horse, unsmiling, did not speak or kiss her, but held his cheek against hers so that she could not see his eyes.

They made their way into the house. Andrew slumped into his chair; she sat herself at his feet.

"What has gone wrong, my dear?"

He stared at her almost blankly for a moment.

"It's what you might expect. Robards."

"Lewis? But what could he do? We're safe, we're married. . . ."

She stopped short, her body frozen. Could it be possible? Had Andrew shaken his head?

"Andrew, what are you trying to say? That we're not—?"

"No, no!"

He pulled himself out of the chair and sank to his knees in front of her, his long arms clasped passionately about her.

"We're married. We always have been. We always will be."

In a hoarse voice she said, "He's challenged our marriage in Natchez?"

"No, it's not that. I only wish it was. He is only now starting a suit for a divorce! The report that he got a divorce from the Virginia legislature was not true. They refused his petition. When I rode down the Trace to bring you the news and we were married . . . "

She pulled back, gazing at him with terror-stricken eyes.

"I was still married to Lewis Robards!"

Her head began to spin. She thought, at last Lewis Robards has had his way. He has made me an adulteress.

RACHEL walked into the Donelson dining room and found her whole family assembled in their ritualistic places around the long table. She dropped into her regular seat and Andrew sat beside her. Now the council of war could begin.

Her brother Stockly spoke first.

"For heaven's sake, Andrew, what has happened? We can't make it out."

Andrew nodded toward John Overton.

"I guess we'd better let John tell us about this. He's the one found out about it."

All eyes traveled down the long table to Overton.

"When Andrew and I started for Jonesboro, I learned that the divorce was scheduled to be heard at the Court of Quarter Sessions at Harrodsburg."

Everyone sat waiting quietly. Then Stockly asked:

"What was the matter with the divorce granted by the Virginia legislature?"

"We were misinformed. The legislature refused Robards' petition for a divorce. What they actually passed was what we call an enabling act, which merely gave Robards the right to plead his case before a judge and jury."

"But he didn't do it at that time?"

"No, he waited until April of this year. The court wouldn't hear his case then, and it was put over until this September."

Robert Hays leaned forward across the table. "How could we have believed there was a divorce in the spring of 1791? Who was responsible for spreading that report?"

"I heard it myself from three or four

different sources," said Samuel, "men who came from Harrodsburg and Richmond."

"We accepted rumor as truth," replied Andrew bitterly.

"There was more substance than word-of-mouth, Andrew," said Overton. "While you were in Natchez I stopped with the Robards family for several days. It was the assumption of everyone in that family that Lewis and Rachel were divorced. Mrs. Robards told me she was happy Rachel was free. So did her daughter."

"Then how can all this be?" burst out Rachel.

John Overton answered:

"Perhaps it's because the whole subject of divorce is so new. Lewis's petition for a divorce was only the second that had come before the Virginia legislature. When the legislature passed the Enabling Act, I think only lawyers knew what it really meant; everyone else appears to have assumed that the bill actually granted the divorce, instead of merely the right to go into court to prove the charges."

There was a silence which Andrew broke, his voice hoarse with self-reproach.

"The fault is mine. I'm supposed to be a lawyer. What right had I to accept the report of the divorce, regardless of how many people repeated it? My first duty to Rachel was to get a copy of the Virginia bill. I should never have gone to Natchez without it."

"Now, Andrew," said Stockly, "I used to be a lawyer, too, and it never occurred to me that there could be anything wrong."

"And we were the first to tell you that the divorce had been granted," broke in Mrs. Donelson.

Jane Hays had been listening carefully.

"I don't think these soul-searchings are going to help us a bit. John, why is Robards trying for a divorce now?"

Overton replied, "Early this year Lewis Robards met a woman he wants to marry. Apparently, when he went for a marriage license he found he couldn't get one, because he was not truly divorced."

"On what grounds will he seek his divorce?" persisted Jane.

"Through fraud!" It was Andrew who had answered, his face blazing. "His petition to the legislature charged that Rachel had eloped with me from his home in July of 1790, and that we had lived together thereafter. He lied, and he knew he lied, because he followed us to your home and begged Rachel to come back with him."

"Robards is no longer bringing that Harrodsburg trip into the case," said John. "The new divorce papers state that he will introduce evidence that Rachel and Andrew lived as a married couple a year later, on the way up the Natchez Trace in September of 1791."

"But that was after we were married!" Rachel was aghast.

"He can't do that!" cried Stockly.

"You are right, Stockly," Overton said. "His original petition to the Virginia legislature charged that Rachel had eloped with Andrew from his home in July of 1790, and it is on that basis that the legislature gave him permission to sue for a divorce. It is that charge he must prove. We can go into that court in Harrodsburg and demonstrate that the divorce would be fraudulently secured; but the more effectively we defend ourselves in Harrodsburg, the more surely we throw out Rachel's marriage to Andrew."

There were gasps around the table.

"We've got to stay out of the case," snapped Jane.

Rachel buried her head in her arms, her body shaking convulsively. If she did not defend herself in Harrodsburg, was that not proof, eternal and indisputable, that she admitted her guilt?

"But it's unfair," cried Samuel. "We've *got* to defend Rachel. We can prove fraud against Robards, and falsehood as well."

John Overton turned to Rachel, his eyes deeply sympathetic.

"No. We must not defend you against those charges in the Harrodsburg court, Rachel. If Lewis can't get a divorce to marry again, neither will you be able to marry Andrew!"

He put a hand on Andrew's shoulder. "Andrew, you have no choice; you must keep out of the divorce case, get a Nashville license and be married according to the American law."

Rachel stood before him supplicatingly.

"John is right. We must be married again."

Andrew stood staring wildly into the fire, talking into the flames: "You are wrong, both of you. Terribly wrong. Don't

306

you see what this means? We publicly admit that we have not been married these two years, we plead guilty to the charges thrown against us in that Harrodsburg court, and be forever exposed to any scoundrel who wants to plague us with the record."

WHEN they went back to their own cabin later, Andrew gazed for a moment into the dark night, then turned to Rachel. The anger had drained from his face; in its place came hurt pride.

"In our own eyes we are married, and so are we in the eyes of our family and friends. No one else matters. No purpose is served by going through a second ceremony."

Rachel put her finger lightly across his lips, then said:

"Andrew, no price is too great if we can spend our lives together. Do this for me, my darling. Do it because you love me and because . . . when our children come . . . there must be no question. No man must ever be able to hurt them because of something we refused to do before they were born."

He took her in his arms and she felt his tears damp on her cheek, sensed his whole horror of this trial, the frustration of not being able to contest it.

"Yes, Rachel," he said at last. "I'll do it—for you."

CHAPTER 7

THE bleating had turned from the plaintive to the urgent; Rachel and Andrew quickened their steps, leaning forward against the wind which swept the big flakes thickly over Poplar Grove.

"How did it get out of the barn?" She turned her face full to Andrew in order that the wind would not carry away the words.

"I don't know. George and I locked everything secure last night."

A leafless poplar loomed up ahead. At the base, in trampled snow, they found one of their ewes, licking the moisture off a newly born lamb. Even as Rachel and Andrew reached her side the ewe weakened, began to stiffen in the snow.

"Is the little one still alive?" Rachel dropped to the ground, pushing the wool hood back off her head so she could see better.

308

"Just barely."

"Then let's get it up to the house quickly."

Andrew stripped off the long leather coat which he wore over a buckskin shirt and spread it on the snow, lifting the lamb onto its thick warmth.

Rachel ran ahead to the house, her black-leather boots making holes in the snow. She cried out to Moll to bring in warm milk, and spread a plaid wool blanket before the blazing log fire. Moll came quickly with a tumbler of milk.

"Should we put in a drop of whisky?" asked Andrew. He was brushing snow off his hunting shirt, making damp spots on the floor.

"Yes, in you. Moll, please get Mr. Jackson a hot toddy."

They sat in silence, Andrew in his big chair. Rachel was on the edge of the hearth, her full wool skirt crushed under her as she concentrated on getting the warm milk between the lamb's lips.

Andrew lit his pipe while Rachel finished feeding the milk and started to stroke the lamb's curly white wool. When his pipe was half ash, he said quietly:

"Rachel, I'm thinking of opening a store."

She looked up at him in astonishment.

"But, Andrew, why? You are attorney general for the territory, the most popular young lawyer . . ."

"Because I want cash money!" His voice sounded doubly loud because he rarely interrupted. "As a lawyer I'm still getting paid in land and livestock, but people will pay cash for what they buy in a store, three times what I can buy the merchandise for in Philadelphia."

The lamb stirred; she moved it gently so that she could nestle its head between her breasts.

"Andrew, how long before we'll know whether it will live?"

"If it's on its feet by nightfall. Now what I'd like to do is gather up all our lands, go to Philadelphia, sell them for cash and use that cash to buy stock for the store. Then, when we take our cash profits from the store, we can buy even bigger tracts of land. Rachel, this is going to become the greatest trading center of the West. The man who opens a trading post here will become the richest man on the frontier."

310

Andrew walked to the window to stare out into the snow. His red hair shone in the brilliant firelight. Though it was not yet four in the afternoon, darkness had fallen.

"I've got it all figured out: our land has cost us about ten cents an acre; I can get a dollar in Philadelphia. There's a cabin on the main road I can buy cheap; it can be the store."

He was pacing the cabin now.

"But what about your cases, and your work as attorney general?"

"John will handle the cases on circuit, Sam can do the paperwork in the office. It'll only be a matter of a few years, Rachel, and then we can have the great plantation I've always dreamed of. We'll be at the top. No one will ever be able to climb up high enough to attack us."

She lowered her head until her chin nestled on the softness of the lamb's head. For a full year now, since they had been remarried, she had known that he was determined to have wealth and power. The higher he rises in the world, she thought, the more untouchable he thinks we will be.

She raised her head. Her voice was clear.

"I'm sure the store will be a success, Andrew. And I'll help all I can."

She felt a slow movement against her bosom. It was the lamb raising its head, the slim legs twitching.

"You can set him on his own feet now, my dear," said Andrew. "He wants to walk."

She put the lamb down. He stood a moment weakly, looking about the room, backed away in fright from the fire, then suddenly raced straight-legged down to the end of the cabin and back to Rachel.

AFTER Andrew went off to Philadelphia to sell his land, Rachel rarely left Poplar Grove, even for a brief trip into Nashville. She had developed a sixth sense about people and could tell at the first piercing glance if her story was close to the top of their minds. She feared the probing glances, the guarded talk. She flinched from meeting strangers, even when she knew them to be friends of her family. In her own home, on her own grounds, she had a lulling sense of security.

312

While she waited for Andrew, she lived in a suspended world in which she filled every hour with tasks. The Nickajack Expedition of the militia had driven away the hostile Indians and for the first time since coming to the Cumberland she could walk her fields without fear of attack. She kept the lamb by her side as a pet.

In the first bright April sunshine, she directed the field hands in the plowing and planting of the crops, striding across the furrows in her high boots and long skirt of heavy cotton twill, a large straw hat shading her face. By mid-May the rows were showing fresh green lines, and the ewes and cows and horses began dropping their young. She, too, felt young and vital again.

She had need of her strength and calm, for the messages from Andrew were disturbing. A depression had settled over the East and the arrangements he had made by correspondence had fallen through by the time he reached Philadelphia. The land he had planned to sell at one dollar an acre he had brought down to twenty cents, and still no takers. "The dam'st situation ever man was placed in," Andrew

313

wrote her. "I would not undertake the same business again for all the lands. . . ."

SHE was prepared to find Andrew disgruntled and upset when he finally got home, but there had been no way to prepare herself for the sight she encountered when she came up from the barn in the heat of the scorching June day to find him sitting slumped in the saddle in front of their cabin. His eyes were sunk in their sockets and his cheeks were gray and hollow. The wrinkled brown clothes hung on his body as though he were made of crosssticks.

She led him into the house, got him into a clean white linen sleeping gown and tucked him into bed, where he fell into a sleep of exhaustion. When he awakened he wanted to get up at once.

"Right now I'm stronger than you are," she replied resolutely. She stood with her hands on her hips, her apron berry-stained from making preserves, her brown eyes reflecting her happiness at having him home. "You are going to stay in bed for several days."

When they took their first walk across

the fields to the river he was delighted with everything he saw.

"You're a wonderful manager, darling; you do a better job than I do."

They slid down the bank to the water's edge. Rachel took off her moccasins and waded at the edge of the shore, while Andrew told her what had happened in Philadelphia. He had been on the verge of leaving the city without a sale of any of the land, but rather than admit defeat had sold their holdings to David Allison, a former Nashville lawyer who had gone east.

"Only trouble was I had to take Allison's personal notes to get the money to buy my merchandise," he concluded.

His greatest excitement seemed to center about the packet of books he had toted all the way from Philadelphia: Comte Maurice de Saxe's *Reveries on the Art of War,* Frederick William von Steuben's *Regulations for the Order and Discipline of the Troops of the United States. . . .*

"My love, I don't think I've ever told you," he said casually, when he had described them to her. "I intend to become a Major General of our militia."

Rachel threw back her head, laughed

315

heartily, shook loose her long black hair that had been held up by only one small comb. She put her arms about his neck and made him pull her up until their lips were on a level.

"Do I detect a note of disbelief in that laughter?"

"No, General Jackson; it was pure joy. Now I know you are well again."

ON THE Fourth of July, before the heat rose, they walked their horses to the old log cabin Andrew had purchased as his store. The interior was saturated with dust, cobwebs, ashes and grease.

Rachel grimaced. "I'll bring a boy over this afternoon with a bucket of lye water. Who's going to sell your goods? Surely you're not planning to stand behind the counter?"

"I wouldn't mind. But I've got to ride the circuit again in September, and if Governor Blount's count of our population goes over 60,000 we'll have a Constitutional Convention and form ourselves into a state."

She caught the eagerness in his voice. "Apparently you think we are going to

316

have 60,000 people. And even more apparently, you intend to go to the Convention. I thought you weren't interested in politics?"

He smiled. "I certainly do hope to be elected to that Convention. Governor Blount told me in Knoxville that he's going to put my name in nomination. I've got a lot of ideas about how this new state should be set up. As far as population is concerned . . . " He chuckled. "There's not a citizen of this territory so mean-spirited that he wouldn't step up and be counted at least three times."

On August 1, Samuel, who had brought Andrew's merchandise by flatboat from Limestone, Kentucky, arrived in Nashville. Three weeks later a trader brought Andrew a letter from Philadelphia. It was marked IMPORTANT.

It was a short message, but from the way the blood drained out of Andrew's face Rachel could see that it was too long.

He looked up, his eyes dazed.

"It's from Philadelphia. David Allison is in trouble. I'm going to have to meet his notes myself."

Rachel stood still. This meant that

317

Andrew's working capital was wiped out. She was saddened, not by the loss of the money, but by the blow to Andrew's pride. To what new ends would he drive himself to reach that state of affluence which appeared now to be his primary need?

ONE sunny day that fall, Rachel and Andrew took a picnic lunch and rode up the winding path that led to the top of Hunter's Hill, the highest eminence in the countryside, overlooking the Cumberland and Stone rivers. They reached the crest at about noon. Andrew spread a blanket on the lee side of the hill; they could hear the wind above them blowing away the few remaining autumnal leaves.

After lunch they stretched out side by side in the center of the blanket, her head nestled comfortably on his shoulder. He wrapped the rest of the blanket around them, then began speaking in a light, jocular tone.

"I brought you up here under false pretenses. I really wasn't so anxious for the picnic I dunned you into. I have a story to tell you and I thought you would like to

318

be sitting on top of the world when you heard it."

"Wherever you are is the top of the world."

"Thank you, my dear." He paused. "I've sold the store."

"For enough to meet the note you owe?"

"No, there's no one with cash who'll buy; Elijah Robertson's paying me with 33,000 acres of good land worth a quarter an acre. The Philadelphia people will give me time to sell. I don't like failure—no man does. But I've learned a lot; I'll not make those mistakes next time."

He lay quietly, looking down at her and stroking the hair back from her forehead, tracing the high arch of her brows with his fingers. Then he said, "Governor Blount sent me word yesterday that the population count is finished. He wants me to help write the new Constitution."

She thought: This is what he really came up here to tell me.

"Good work, Andrew. How I'd like to see you at the Convention speaking to all those men!"

She rose from the blanket, walked a little distance and gazed below her at the groves of trees, the creeks shining in the sun. She did not hear him come up behind her.

"It's a magnificent view, isn't it?" he asked.

"The finest I've ever seen."

"Could you be happy here?"

"Oh, yes. One would live above so much of the struggle that goes on below."

"I'm mighty relieved to hear you say that."

She turned about swiftly.

"Andrew, what do you mean?"

"My dear, you've been picnicking on your own land. I've bought Hunter's Hill."

"But . . . "

"I'm going to build you the finest home in the whole new state, Rachel. It's going to be the first house of cut lumber in the Cumberland Valley. I brought nails and glass back from Philadelphia and have kept them hidden away. And wait until you see the furniture: brocade settees, walnut tables. We'll have French wallpapers—"

"With what, darling? We've just failed

in our first business venture. The new land from Robertson is worth twenty-five cents an acre, but you may only get ten cents, or five."

. In his excitement he was towering over her.

"Ah, my dear, that's the time you must dare to pull yourself up to the heights, when you have failed and everyone thinks you are on the road down. When people see us at the top of Hunter's Hill in a magnificent home, they'll look up to us. Rachel, the whole world will come to your door."

She slipped her hand into his. "Whatever you want, Andrew, I know you can do."

WITH Poplar Grove up for sale and Andrew at the Constitutional Convention, Rachel moved back to her mother's house. There was no regular mail service from Knoxville but a steady flow of travelers brought her news of the Convention each day. Andrew and Judge McNairy had been selected as the two local delegates to help design the state government, and Andrew was working 14 hours a day to create what he called a "Jeffersonian Constitution": two legislative houses instead of one; the right of all men to vote after six months' residence; only a two-hundred-acre ownership necessary for election to the legislature. Rachel read the newspaper report of Andrew's speech when proposals had been offered to name the new state after Washington or Franklin:

> Georgia was named after a King; the Carolinas, Virginia and Maryland after Queens; Pennsylvania after a colonial proprietor; Delaware after a Lord; and New York after a Royal Duke. Since Independence, there is no reason for copying anything from England in our new geography. We should adopt for our new state the Indian name of The Great Crooked River, Tennessee, a word that has as sweet a flavor on the tongue as hot corncakes and honey.

The day Andrew was due back, Rachel returned to Poplar Grove and invited John Overton to spend the evening.

"I suppose I'll be calling you Congressman pretty soon now?" John asked Andrew.

"Congressman! I'm not interested in politics."

322

"Then you can put those military books away because you're evidently not interested in the militia, either. Your army is going to evaporate unless Congress repays the thousands of dollars our Tennessee militiamen spent for the Nickajack Expedition."

Andrew shook his head in despair.

"Now there's a choice assignment! The War Department forbade us to go out on that expedition against the Indians. The federal government has declared the whole expedition illegal—and now you want me to go to Washington and get Congress to pay for it!"

RACHEL found that Andrew's prophecy about Hunter's Hill proved sound: he no sooner started construction of the house, which attracted visitors from all over the Cumberland, than people began to speak of his tremendous success.

They finally moved into the place on a Tuesday; it was the day of the week on which Andrew liked to begin new ventures. The house seemed enormous to Rachel, with its parlor and dining room on either side of the entrance hall, and Moll's kitchen to the left beyond a porte cochere. The furniture Andrew had selected in Philadelphia was installed in the parlor—a settee and upholstered chairs covered in double damask—and on the floor a 16th-century Tabriz animal carpet.

Upstairs there were four bedrooms, but only their own bedroom had furniture in it. The half-empty rooms gave Rachel a sense of hollowness. The small cabin at Poplar Grove had seemed to hold her close, to protect her; the vast areas of Hunter's Hill seemed to expose her on all sides. Her husband might find the eminence of Hunter's Hill dominating and powerful; she felt it only made them more vulnerable.

That summer Andrew worked in the fields to raise the small crop that had been planted in the spring. On July 30 the Tennessee legislature voted him five years' back pay owed him as attorney general. He used part of the money to build a road up the hill to the front door, while Rachel supervised the erection of plantation buildings.

"We've come to the end of our troubles," Andrew declared with satisfaction.

"If I could get back to Philadelphia . . . "

She hated the thought of another separation, but keeping all emotion out of her voice she said, "You'd really like to be our first Congressman, wouldn't you?"

"There's so much I could do. John was right about the money for the Nickajack Expedition. If I could get Congress to appropriate that fund—and collect some of my own money from Allison, enough to buy merchandise for another store . . ."

Her heart sank, but she managed a smile.

"Andrew, you're going to be the busiest Representative in Philadelphia!"

THAT year was the first since their marriage that she and Andrew were separated at Christmas, for he had been elected to Congress, and left for Philadelphia in November. All the dictates of logic and expediency had made her agree that Andrew should go to Philadelphia; but she could not help worrying when she realized that the more past business he settled there, the freer he would be to set up future investments. One afternoon she learned that the paper for which he had traded 33,000 acres of his land had become practically worthless because the Bank of England had suspended its specie payments. From his letter, Rachel could not tell whether Andrew was maddest at having lost his money or at learning that America was still controlled by the Bank of England.

In his next letter Andrew told her that the moment he had reached Philadelphia, he had ordered a black coat and breeches to be made by a tailor.

> They fit me quite well, and I thought I presented a handsome figure. But when I got to the Congress, I found myself the only one with a queue down my back tied with an eelskin. From the expression of the more elegant nabobs, I could see that they thought me an uncouth-looking personage with the manners of a backwoodsman.

In addition, Andrew's very first act in Congress had antagonized not only most of his fellow legislators, but Tennessee as well. This news she learned when she went on a Sunday to her mother's home for dinner; as she came into the big room, sentences were left dangling in midair like the wool threads of an unfinished coverlet. She said in an impersonal voice:

"Very well, my husband has done something you don't like. Let's get it over with and not spoil Mother's Sunday dinner."

"Let's don't," replied Jane. "You're not responsible for your husband's political ideas."

"My dear Jane, the newspapers will reach me tomorrow."

Samuel spoke. "You remember President Washington's farewell speech to the Congress? The House drew up a eulogy to make in return. Andrew voted against it. He said it was a blanket approval and that some of Mr. Washington's acts sorely needed criticizing."

Robert Hays pulled a letter from Andrew out of his pocket:

> "Every day's paper proves the fact that the British are daily Capturing our vessels, impressing our seamen and Treating them with the utmost severity and brutality, but from the president's speech it would seem that the British were doing us no injury."

"I suppose it's all right for him to hate England so intensely," commented Severn, "but he has no right to make it appear that that's the way everybody in Tennessee feels. If he's not careful he'll get us into a war with the British."

Jane took the letter from her husband's hand and gave it to Rachel, murmuring, "The last paragraph is for you."

Rachel's eyes went quickly to the bottom of the page:

I make one request: that you attend to my Dear Little Rachel and soothe her in my absence. If she should want anything get it for her if you can and you shall be amply rewarded.

She returned the paper, a smile on her lips.

CHAPTER 8

DURING the latter weeks of January, the cold intensified until one morning Rachel found ice on the ground and her plants and young shade trees frozen. Moll was missing at breakfast. Rachel went to her cabin and put a hand to Moll's forehead.

"You've got fever." She made a quick tour of the other cabins: the grippe was of epidemic proportions; only one family had escaped. She dispatched one of the younger boys to Nashville for the doctor, while she herself went into the kitchen to brew the bitter tea of herbs and marshmallow root which her own mother used to fight the grippe. She carried the steaming pot from cabin to cabin, plying the sick ones with the liquid.

For the next week she nursed her people night and day. And no sooner had she been able to leave off making night rounds among her sick than she was awakened one midnight by the sound of a horse coming heavily up the road, and by someone pounding on the front door. She opened the window and called:

"Who's there?"

"Mrs. Jackson, ma'am, it's Tim Bentley, from over beyond Willow Spring."

"What can I do for you, Mr. Bentley?"

The man's words came in a frenzied jumble. "It's the wife, Sarah, and the baby. . . . It just won't get itself borned. I think Sarah's going to die, ma'am, the baby and she both. . . ."

"Go around the side to the kitchen

house and wake George; tell him to saddle me a horse."

In a matter of minutes she was racing downstairs. In the yellow glow of the porch lamp she saw the face of Tim Bentley, a weak-looking, sallow-skinned youth who did not seem far out of his teens. She told George to saddle another horse and to bring along soap, blankets, sheets, towels, candles and food, and they soon set off.

It required little light to indicate the ramshackle nature of the Bentley cabin. One end of the roof had begun to sag; inside, the floor logs showed gaps of cold damp earth beneath, while the one window had been pasted over with successive layers of brown paper drenched in bear's oil. A young girl lay on the wooden bed, covered by a ragged blanket. The only preparation for the expected baby appeared to be a crude cradle on which rested a linen christening gown they had apparently brought from the East.

Rachel said, "Hello, Mrs. Bentley. I'm your neighbor, Mrs. Jackson, from up on the hill. I'm going to stay with you until your baby is born. Why didn't you call someone before?"

"We was hopin' to see it through by ourselves. But it's lasted so long. . . . The minute I heard your horses, I felt better." She hesitated. "Are you *the* Mrs. Jackson, ma'am?"

"Who is *the* Mrs. Jackson?"

"The one they talk about so much? But you don't look at all like that kind. That Mrs. Jackson wouldn't come help me."

Rachel stroked the girl's hair soothingly.

"I want very much to help you. I've never had the good fortune to have a baby myself, but my sisters have, dozens of them, and I've helped them. So you see, everything *is* going to be all right. . . ."

While speaking, she had slowly lifted the blanket. She recognized it as a breech birth, and she made herself speak to the girl with considerably more calm than she was feeling herself.

"Your baby is beginning to show itself, Sarah. Before another hour you will be holding it in your arms."

She wiped the girl's face with a cold cloth, and had the father build up the spindly fire until there was a good blaze.

When George arrived with the supplies she washed her hands with hot water and soap, then fixed a basin of water for use at the bedside.

"You're doing fine," she encouraged the young woman.

After she was able to take a deep breath, Mrs. Bentley replied, "I can tell I am."

With the next pain Rachel grew tense. Mrs. Bentley grabbed the sides of the bed, making a strong effort. A minute passed, then two. Nothing was happening. Rachel placed her hand on Mrs. Bentley's abdomen and threw her whole weight on it. The mother let out a scream—and the baby was born. It was a girl.

Rachel sponged the infant and put her in the cradle. She washed Mrs. Bentley with warm water, put her in one of her own white gowns, covered her with the blankets from Hunter's Hill, gave her a cup of coffee and some of Moll's apple cake.

It was some 40 hours later when she finally reached home. She went into the parlor and sank into a chair in front of the cold hearth. She knew that she should be cold and exhausted; but she wasn't feeling cold at all. Or tired. Or alone. She had not been able to bear a child of her own, but that baby would have been dead without her help. This, too, was a way of creating life. She could feel the infant in her arms, its blood racing against her blood, warming it, warming away the dull ache that had settled in her when she had heard, "Are you *the* Mrs. Jackson?"

As LONG and severe as the winter had been, just so quickly was it gone. Andrew was still in Philadelphia when the hickories began to show their fine leaves and the pelicans came flying in long trains, lighting on the surface of the river below. Hunter's Hill had the makings of a rich plantation. If they farmed it diligently it would not be long before Andrew could build his longed-for racecourse and train Thoroughbreds.

Rachel was out in the fields as usual, in a short-sleeved cotton dress, her hair piled in a knot under the wide-brimmed straw hat, when John Overton brought her the news that Andrew had persuaded Congress to legitimatize the Nickajack Expedition and pay back every dollar that the

Tennessee militiamen had invested out of their own pockets. Rachel was delighted; this meant that Andrew would soon be home.

She had Hunter's Hill fully planted by the time he finally reached the plantation on April 1. He had not enjoyed his session in the Congress, but as far as Rachel could make out, his feeling was more of bafflement than disappointment.

"I just don't feel comfortable in Philadelphia, Rachel. Those Federalist nabobs! I think they've never stopped regretting they admitted us as a state. Anyway, the House is for men of a certain temperament, men who like to work with large groups, with plenty of debate and compromise. I'm not good at that kind of thing. Just between you and me and the front hitching post, I'd still like to master one field. . . ."

"The state militia?"

He grinned. "Yes, the militia. But I'll take this plantation off your hands now, darling. From the look of it we're going to be rich come next November."

He put his arms about her waist, which was as slim as when he had met her, and

334

held her lightly, studying her face. Despite the wide straw hat she wore in the fields her skin was tanned almost as deep as the brown of her eyes.

"You're going to have your husband home for good," he said. "No more politics, no more circuit riding, no more stores, no more debts. From now on, I'm going to be a domesticated animal."

The house that had been so empty these many months was now crowded with visitors from all over the state; militiamen who had received their long-due pay came to express their thanks to Congressman Jackson, and remained for serious discussions of what was needed to revitalize the state troops. They came as friends, enthusiasts, admirers, their loyalty to Andrew discernible in every word and gesture. Rachel welcomed them all; and strangers who came for an hour, diffidently, knew by the heartiness of their reception that they could stay as long as they liked. What they did not know was that a considerable part of her emotion was gratitude, for here at last was a circle she need not question or doubt, friends who would be her staunch defenders.

New boxes of military books arrived for Andrew: books on military engineering, military discipline, fortifications. But the studies Andrew seemed to enjoy most were the ones on the Revolutionary War. When Rachel saw him reading these volumes with such intentness and relish, she let him see her distress. War meant people killing each other; she hated every aspect of it.

"My dear, I wouldn't take a first step to encourage war with England or Spain," Andrew said. "But if you could be in the Congress for a while and see how close we actually are . . ."

He paced the floor and made a wide gesture with his arm to include every new military volume in the room.

"Only the strong, the prepared, can keep out of war or, if dragged in, end it quickly and without great loss. The weak are set upon and attacked by every passing bully."

"You make it sound very logical. But do you mind if I pray for peace—among my other prayers. . . ?" Suddenly, she burst into tears. "Oh, husband, how I have prayed that we had a child!"

336

He took her in his arms.

"Darling, God knows what to give, what to withhold."

"Somewhere in the back of my mind I had given myself until my 30th birthday. . . ."

" . . . and that's tomorrow, June 30th!" He released her, strode to the door and began bellowing for George. "Wait here, no matter what commotion you hear in the hall."

She sat in Andrew's work chair, her hands folded in her lap. After a considerable amount of hammering he came back to the room, his coat off, a smudge across his forehead and his shirt ripped just inside the elbow.

"Come along, but close your eyes." He led her through the hall, then released her hand. "All right, you can open them now."

In the center of the formerly empty music room was a shiny black pianoforte, standing on four delicately carved legs in front and two at the rear. She went to it, breathlessly ran her fingers over the keys.

"Oh, Andrew, it's beautiful."

She played a few chords. From behind

her she heard strange sounds. She whirled about in astonishment.

"Why, it's a flute! You never told me you could play a flute."

He lowered his arms, gazing raptly at the ebony instrument.

"I couldn't. There was a man at my boardinghouse in Philadelphia who used to practice in the parlor every night. He offered to teach me. I thought how pleasant it would be if we could play duets."

She jumped off the little bench and flung her arms impetuously about his neck.

"Andrew Jackson, you are the strangest and most improbable creature God ever created! And I am the luckiest of wives."

She had never seen his joy at being home or working in his own fields so great. Watching him run the big plantation, she knew that he was really a first-rate farmer. If he read of a new tool or an improved seed, he would send away for it; if he learned of a breeder who was raising a higher-quality stock, he would study his methods in the hope of improving his own breed. He said that most men farmed by intuition, but that farming could someday become a science if a man would take the trouble to make himself expert at it.

In the early evenings, after supper, Rachel ran scales for him while he practiced on his flute; then they would try the songs they had learned together. Afterward they would go into his office, where he worked on his military books, drawing up his own battle maps. They retired late, yet frequently when she was awakened by the first rays of the sun, she would find Andrew reading by candlelight at the little mosaic table under the window.

"Andrew, you should try to sleep until dawn."

"Sleep? It's pure waste, when you're as happy as I am."

ONE afternoon that spring, Rachel saw a carriage with two women in it coming up their road. When they alighted at the front door she recognized them as Mrs. Somerset Phariss, president of the newly formed Nashville Culture Club, and Miss Daisy Deson, its secretary. The group was composed solely of Nashville ladies.

She took a quick look in her dressing mirror, and went down the stairs.

Mrs. Phariss was the cultural leader of

Nashville. Married to the son of an English peer, and a graduate of one of the best academies in Boston, she was still using her New England accent to express her opinion of everything she found uncouth or provincial on the frontier. She was a big woman, modishly dressed. Her companion, Daisy Deson, was a slim, attractive young woman who came from one of the best-liked families in the Cumberland. She had charm and talent, but in the midst of being sweet and delightful could suddenly lash out with remarks of such penetrating cruelty that everyone in the room would wither under the blow. She had been losing prospective husbands by this method for years.

The two women accepted Rachel's offer of a cold drink with hearty thanks. Mrs. Phariss then went about inspecting the house.

"What an interesting room. This is a double Belfast damask; you can tell by the precise way the flower figures stand out. But perhaps you wonder why we drove out?"

"I think it was most friendly of you," Rachel said politely.

"Mrs. Jackson," said Mrs. Phariss, "it's my feeling that town society should join forces with country society. By working together, we can throw off the primitive aspect of our backwoods life. We would like you to join our Culture Club, and attend our meetings every Tuesday. Each week there will be a different attraction: a literary reading, a musicale, an inspirational talk . . . Our membership already totals 30."

Rachel blanched at the thought of walking into a room filled with 30 strange women.

"But I never go out. . . . I'm not at all social."

"Come now, Mrs. Jackson, you're being too modest," said Miss Deson, glancing about the large, elaborately furnished parlor. "We've heard about the dinner parties you've given here at Hunter's Hill for the young militia officers, and Mr. Jackson's political friends from Philadelphia—"

"No, no," Rachel interrupted, "people just drop in, that's all. And everybody who comes is welcome."

"Well, I know you will want to join the

Culture Club," said Mrs. Phariss firmly as she rose from the settee. "After all, the wife of our Congressman has a public obligation."

After the women had bid her adieu, telling her they expected her to join them the following Tuesday, Rachel felt a warm glow creep over her. It was kind of Mrs. Phariss and Miss Deson to invite her to join the Culture Club, even though the invitation had sounded more like an order; it was an act of espousal.

Tuesday morning she rose early and set out the new costume she had prepared to wear to the meeting. The skirt needed a bit of adjusting, but Sarah Bentley, who was now a popular seamstress, would take care of that when she came by.

Sarah arrived while Rachel was at breakfast and went quickly to the sewing room. When Rachel joined her she saw that the girl's eyes were red, the lids damp and swollen. The new skirt lay across her lap but she had given up all pretense of sewing. Rachel stared for an instant, then put a hand on Sarah's shoulder.

"What's wrong, Sarah? Are you ill?"

"No, Mrs. Jackson, ma'am, unless it's

my heart is sick. I can't sew on your skirt today, because I can't let you go to that meetin'. They don't want you, really. All day yesterday I sewed at Mrs. Phariss's house; about ten of the ladies was there, and they was fighting over you something awful."

Rachel took the skirt from Sarah and handed the girl her own linen handkerchief.

"Oh, Mrs. Jackson. We love you here in the country; you don't belong with them . . . city folk. They say you are a bad woman."

The blood drained from Rachel's face; her fingertips felt like ice.

"Go on, Sarah."

"One lady, she said she knew you when your husband sent you home to your mother for misbehavin'. Another said she heard all about you in Harrodsburg, and the trial where they accused you of wrongdoin', and she was surprised at Mrs. Phariss to suggest you come into the club. Then Mrs. Phariss said her husband thinks Mr. Jackson is going to be a very important man in Tennessee, maybe even governor someday, and that it's important for a club to have the wives of men in politics; and besides your house would be elegant for big balls. When I left Mrs. Phariss's at four o'clock they was still arguin' and fightin'. Oh, Mrs. Jackson, ma'am, you can't go to that meetin' with those ladies who think you're sinful."

She looked up at Rachel pleadingly. Rachel would have liked to comfort her; but what good to explain the long, painful story to this child? Out of the bedroom window she saw George bringing her carriage up the drive. He had spent hours shining and polishing it. She lifted Sarah from the chair.

"You go home, Sarah; we won't do any sewing today. And when you get downstairs, tell George I shan't need the carriage."

She took the unfinished skirt, folded it and set it in her big cedar chest. Then she pulled the cord to summon Moll. Perhaps some hot coffee would dissipate the chill.

CHAPTER 9

DESPITE Andrew's dissatisfaction with his first term in Congress, there had always been the chance that when the moment came he might change his mind and go back. But the only politics that seemed to interest him during the summer were the troubles of his friend and sponsor, Senator Blount, who had been expelled from the Senate for conspiring with the English to drive the Spaniards out of Louisiana and Florida. He rejected the overtures of Blount's friends who arrived from Knoxville to inform him that he was the unanimous choice to finish out Blount's unexpired term.

But by October most of the crops had been brought in; the market was good and the crops sold for high prices. Andrew became restless. Rachel recognized the symptoms. When the Blount forces again urged him to reconsider the senatorial post, she saw that he was carrying their offer around in his pocket.

"Actually it's not so bad an idea as it seemed at first," he said one day, tentatively. "I think I might like the Senate better than I did the House. I might be able to arrange a new Indian conference, and get back the land Tennessee lost under the Holston Treaty. Besides, if I went up to

Philadelphia, I could buy the merchandise for a new store. . . ."

AGAIN, Rachel was alone. Andrew left for the Senate on a Friday that fall, in the midst of a torrential downpour, complaining that it was the wrong day to start a journey. Rachel went to bed as soon as he left and slept long and deeply. When she awoke, her mouth and lips were dry, and the heat she felt could not be the warmth of the room on this raw autumn day.

"You all right, Miz Rachel?" asked Moll with a troubled face. "I'll bring some coffee."

Rachel knew what was wrong. As so often happened when she was alone, her despair at remaining childless had returned to grip her. Women had children after they were 30, but these were generally added to a long line. Her line seemed to have ended before it began.

She closed the curtains around her bed. Her mind went back to something Andrew had said back at the Donelson stockade: "I think the greatest thing a man can have is a family." Of how much was she depriving her husband by remaining

346

childless? The politics in which he professed not to be interested, the numerous business affairs, could these be substitutes rather than real desires? This was her failure, that she could not perpetuate his name.

She grew thin and pale and, after a time, unwilling to distinguish between the gray darkness of night and the gray darkness of day. She did not keep track of how long she lay abed torturing herself with self-reproaches, the victim of twisted and poisoned images, but at length the cycle wore itself out. She awakened one morning to find a warm November sun flooding into her bedroom. She groped at the head of the bed for the bellpull, shocked at the pallor of her hands. When Moll came running she managed a little smile; Moll stopped short in her tracks, clasped her hands and exclaimed:

"The Lawd be praised, Miz Rachel's come home again!"

Moll helped her to dress, and Rachel sat on the front porch with her face in the sun. In those long days of illness she had made a discovery. Before, she had thought that her love for Andrew was as great and

347

full as it was possible for a woman to know. Now she realized that she had been cheating him, hoarding, holding back the love and devotion she was reserving for children.

It would be different now, she vowed. There were no reservations in her mind, no more locked compartments.

FEW visitors came to Hunter's Hill that winter of 1797 while Andrew was away. To the people of the neighborhood who had learned that she was available no matter what the nature of the illness or adversity, she became Aunt Jackson. There was not a cabin for miles around where she had not tended the sick and comforted the afflicted. She became a familiar sight riding alone through the fields and woods, bringing medicines and a rapidly growing knowledge of the illnesses of the Cumberland.

From Andrew's letters, she gathered that the Senators were doing little but sitting in their big red chairs with their spyglasses trained on the war between England and France. Andrew had ordered a handsome brown outfit with a velvet collar and vest, and had had his hair cut short. He was staying in a comfortable hostelry where he had attended a dinner party given by former Senator Aaron Burr.

By the end of January, when both Houses and President Adams had consented to the new Indian treaty Andrew wanted, the signs of his restlessness began to multiply: he sent home specifications for a store he wanted her to build, and told her that he had bought $6000 worth of stock.

RACHEL was sleeping soundly one soft spring night when she awakened to find Andrew standing above her. Too impatient to wait for the Senate to adjourn, he had left Philadelphia on April 12 and accompanied his stock of goods to the Ohio Falls, riding the last hundred and eighty miles in three days and nights. He was completely done in.

"I've been drenched by rain every day for a week, and some of the cabins I stopped at were the poorest I've ever seen. Once I woke up to find a snake in my bed."

"Serves you right. You should stay home with your wife."

She was rewarded with a smile. She put on a robe and went to her mirror to comb her hair. After a moment Andrew came and knelt behind her, gazing at his own countenance.

"You send me away looking fat and sleek and see how I come back to you! I look twice my 30 years. Good thing you didn't marry me for my beauty."

She turned, cupped his bearded face in her hands and replied in a gentle voice, "You never looked better to me than you do this very instant."

He put his arms about her and kissed her on the lips.

"Oh, Andrew," she whispered, holding her cheek against his, "to maintain one's love amongst the difficulties of living . . ."

". . . is like maintaining one's life in the midst of a war."

His mind once more on his own affairs, Andrew became a whirlwind of activity. The new store proved successful, and he built a landing and flatboat to serve as a ferry. He bought a newfangled cotton gin he had seen in Philadelphia, and rode over the countryside explaining to the planters how fast the gin worked, offering to process their cotton on a percentage basis. While in Philadelphia he had bought an extensive law library, and he was again riding into Nashville to handle a few of the matters that old clients were urging him to take.

Rachel's hours with him were sweeter than they had ever been: this was what she had; this was what she would always have. Sometimes, watching him carry on the tasks of half a dozen men, she realized that he was not only her child but a whole brood of children; and that to keep him fit and happy would require all of her strength and devotion.

Life with Andrew, she realized, would always be a series of surprises. One evening late in the fall John Overton rode out from Nashville with him. Both men were deep in talk as they entered the house.

"What is it, Andrew?" Rachel asked.

"Well, there's a vacancy coming up for the state Superior Court. The legislature has to elect a new man in December. Mr. Blount and Governor Sevier both think my name should be put up."

"I agree with them," she exclaimed heartily. "Tell me more about it."

"The appointment is for six years, pays six hundred a year . . . in cash. It's an independent office, outside of political factions and quarrels."

Rachel smiled broadly. This is good, she thought. Judges are above . . . gossip; no one would ever dare talk against a judge— or his wife.

BUT contrary to Rachel's expectations, Andrew's elevation to the Bench did not put their private lives beyond petty gossip. In fact, his becoming a judge had caused the disparagement to be directed against him as well. For the next ten years they would live their lives in the poisoned atmosphere of rumor.

As a judge Andrew soon won praise throughout the state: he got rid of weak and crooked sheriffs and instilled respect for the Bench wherever he sat. Yet there were those in Nashville—many of them women of the Culture Club—who set out to prove that Mrs. Jackson was a backwoodswoman who was at home only among the poor and ignorant, and that

Mr. Jackson did not have the dignity or decorum required of a judge.

Finally Rachel learned that her husband was spending much of his time suppressing a whispering campaign against her. She sought him in his study.

"Andrew, I can't let you waste your time and energy trying to fight gossip. Not all the combined armies in the world can stop these women from talking."

"But why should they want to hurt us?"

"The fault has been mine. I did not obey Mrs. Phariss's demand that I join her group. I'm going to become a member of the Culture Club, go to their meetings. . . ."

The declaration took all her strength. She sought shelter in his arms. He sat on a corner of his desk and held her close.

"Rachel, you mustn't do it. If they can conquer you with these methods, you will not only be their slave but you will be at the mercy of every last person who stoops to slander to gain his ends. We have staunch and loving friends all over Tennessee. In Knoxville and Jonesboro, I have been asked again and again, 'Won't you bring Mrs. Jackson with you the next time you come?' By the Eternal, Rachel, this time you are going with me!"

It was her first trip with Andrew since they had come up the Natchez Trace. In Knoxville, Governor Sevier gave them an official banquet, and the Blount family had a magnificent ball. At Hartsville they were the guests of honor for the opening of the racing season. She had not realized how many families she had entertained at Hunter's Hill; every stop on the circuit was the occasion for a gala party. Rachel's natural buoyancy and gaiety rose as she found herself surrounded by old friends from early morning until she and Andrew could escape to their bed late at night. Lying by her husband's side she would close her eyes and think of the gratifying picture she would take back to Hunter's Hill: Andrew presiding over the Knoxville court, handsome in his black gown, his tall lean figure towering over the courtroom, treated with vast respect by officers, lawyers and clients alike.

From Jane, via Tennessee's new mail service, she learned that the reports of the many banquets and balls with which she

354

was being honored had had the effect of silencing her Nashville detractors.

AT THE the end of the summer, Mrs. Donelson died, and was buried on her own plantation, as she had requested. Saddened though they were by her passing, Rachel and Andrew had much to be thankful for that fall: Hunter's Hill and the stores were running at a profit at last. "It's a good thing," grumbled Andrew. "I've been working for the county, territory, state and nation for 12 years now and I've yet to make my first dollar over expenses. You can't get rich working for the Government."

"You're not supposed to, Andrew. But they did name that new district, 'Jackson County,' after you."

To add to their blessings, the Jacksons made a new friend, John Coffee, a flatboat owner and captain in the militia who was to remain close to them the rest of their lives. Powerfully built and sunburned from his outdoor life, Coffee was gentle as the lamb Rachel had raised at Poplar Grove, and so enormous he filled any room he entered. Andrew said to him one day:

"Jax, I try to tell the truth most of the time but it seems to me that I frequently miss by a fraction. How do you manage to drive the center every shot?"

"I'm not clever enough to distinguish between the various kinds of truth," Coffee replied. "They all look alike to me."

AT THE turn of the century, practically everyone in Tennessee voted the Republican ticket for the election of Thomas Jefferson and Aaron Burr, both of whom were sympathetic to the western states. When, by a technicality, Burr received the same number of electoral votes as Jefferson, the election was thrown into the House, where the defeated and disgruntled Federalists, who hated Jefferson as a revolutionist, did everything in their power to put Burr into the Presidency. Aaron Burr was loved in Tennessee because he had been one of the leaders in the fight to have the state admitted to the Union, but even the Tennesseans wondered why he did not step up to the dais of the House and make the simple declaration that he had run for the Vice-Presidency, an act of forthright honesty that

356

would have put an immediate end to the paralyzing controversy.

IN SPITE of his judgeship, Andrew was plunged into state politics again. Governor John Sevier, having served three consecutive terms, was obliged by the constitution to step aside for one session. Up to this time, Tennessee politics had been controlled by the Blount family and Sevier on a friendly basis; now the Blount faction, to which Andrew belonged, decided to form its own party and elect its own governor.

At a caucus in Blount's home early in the new year, they selected Andrew's friend and colleague Judge Archibald Roane. But Andrew resisted the pressure the caucus put on him to stand for the Congress again.

"I don't want to leave the state right now," he confided to Rachel. "Major General Conway is in poor health. Within a year, I think, our militia is going to need a new commanding officer. And you know how long I have hoped for a chance to serve there."

As Andrew foresaw, Major General Conway died soon after. An election was posted for a new commanding officer. John Sevier immediately announced his candidacy; just as promptly Andrew was nominated by a group of militiamen.

Among the officers of the militia, 17 cast their votes for Sevier, 17 cast their votes for Andrew. According to the state constitution the deciding vote had then to be cast by the newly elected Governor Roane. Former Governor Sevier, chagrined at the tie, sent a message to Andrew requesting that he withdraw. Andrew replied that he would not walk out on the men who had supported him, and that he thought the properly constituted authority should make the decision.

Governor Roane cast the deciding vote for Andrew, leaving the Sevier forces angry and critical. Andrew, however, was jubilant.

"The state of Tennessee is going to know they've got a new commanding officer," he said. "I'll never rest until our militia is a first-class fighting force."

For his first general muster in Nashville in May, Andrew had a uniform made, the first he had ever owned. The collar was high, coming up just under his ears, with a long double-breasted coat, a row of buttons down either side, gold-braid epaulets and a broad brightly colored sash.

THE muster was the grand event of the year for Nashville. All officers were dressed in their gayest trappings, the soldiers in fringed hunting shirts. It was Andrew's duty to supervise the inspection of the foot soldiers, making sure every commissioned officer had sidearms, that every private was provided with either a musket, a cartouche box with nine charges of powder and ball, or a rifle, powder horn, shot pouch and spare flint. With the horse troop he had to ascertain that every soldier had a good mount with a serviceable saddle, bridle, pistol and sword. The men received no pay and provided their own horses, uniforms, guns and ammunition—a situation which Andrew was determined to remedy as soon as he could get funds out of the state legislature.

Andrew had ridden his fastest horse to the muster, but bad news reached Rachel at Hunter's Hill ahead of the returning General. Captain John Coffee brought it,

his usually amiable face set in grim lines as he explained:

"The reason I'm here, Mrs. Jackson, is I'm afraid Mr. Jackson will do something rash. You must calm him. It seems there was a young fellow at the muster, Charles Dickinson, a friend of ex-Governor Sevier's. They say he's the most brilliant young lawyer in Nashville. Dickinson was standing with a group of friends when the general rode onto the parade ground. Someone asked:

" 'What great military exploit has Mr. Jackson performed that entitles him to such exalted rank?'

"Dickinson had been drinking; he replied in a voice loud enough for everyone to hear:

" 'Why, gentlemen, he has done a most daring exploit. He has captured another man's wife!' "

Rachel placed her weight against the mantel, trembling.

"Dickinson has a reputation as the best shot in the whole Cumberland Valley, ma'am," continued Coffee. "Andrew's a great commanding officer, but I can out-shoot him ten to one. Don't let him challenge Dickinson to a duel; if there's going to be shooting, I want to be at the other end."

Rachel thanked Coffee for his offer. Then she ran up to her room and threw herself face downward on her bed. Andrew and she had been married a full ten years now. Would people never forget? Charles Dickinson's remark would be repeated all over Tennessee.

Then her head cleared: bad as Dickinson's remark had been, it had merely intimated that Andrew had won her away from her first husband. She would have to make Andrew accept this and allow the affair to pass over. Not that he would forget; but he must not provide the community with further fuel to keep alive the fires of scandal.

When he came home, Andrew reluctantly agreed with her. He knew that for Rachel's sake, he must swallow his own furious anger.

THE unfortunate incident proved to be the start of a series of disturbances. Some of Andrew's decisions as a judge were criticized, and what had appeared to be a friendly break with John Sevier now began to look like a political fight to the finish. When Sevier announced that he would seek another term as governor, Andrew publicly charged that Sevier was no longer fit to serve.

"I can prove that he was deeply involved in the Glasgow land-fraud case," Andrew told Rachel. "Why, he and his friends have stolen almost a sixth of the state of Tennessee."

Rachel was shocked, but she found herself unprepared for the clamor caused by Andrew's accusing letter in the *Tennessee Gazette* of July 27, 1803. Everyone in the state read it, or had it read to him. The contest was no longer between two candidates for governor; people now asked, "Who are you siding with, Sevier or Jackson?" Feelings were inflamed and bitter. When Andrew held court in Jonesboro, a mob of Sevierites threatened to tar and feather him. Andrew stood with both pistols cocked. The crowd saw "Shoot!" in his eyes; it melted away. But a few weeks later, Tennessee elected Sevier by a full one-third majority.

ON SATURDAY, October 1, 1803, after the adjournment of his Knoxville court, Andrew made his way toward the front door of the courthouse. In the sunshine he saw John Sevier standing on the top step with a crowd below him. Before he could turn away he heard Sevier say:

"Judge Jackson is an abandoned rascal, a man whom the people have made a judge and thereby promoted to the unmerited status of a gentleman. I'm glad to remember that I was the man who won independence for this state. I drove out the Indians, I formed your first government. . . ."

Andrew strode over to Sevier and stood face to face with him.

"I do not contest your past services to the state of Tennessee, Governor. But I believe that I have performed public services, too, and most of them have met with the approval of my fellow citizens."

"Services?" cried Sevier in a voice which carried to the other end of the public square. "I know of no great service you have rendered to the country except taking a trip to Natchez with another man's wife!"

364

Murder sprang into Andrew's eyes.

"Great God! Do you dare to mention *her?*"

Sevier drew his sword. Andrew swung his heavy walking stick, and shots were fired in the crowd. Friends intervened, carrying Andrew off in one direction and Sevier in another.

Andrew instantly challenged Sevier to a duel. The remark made by Charles Dickinson had been uttered by an irresponsible young man who had been drinking and who later had denied having made it. But this charge by Governor Sevier in a public square could never be denied or retracted. For Sevier had accused them before the world of wanton, deliberate adultery, and John Sevier was the best-known and most influential man in Tennessee.

Travelers and friends came in from Knoxville to Hunter's Hill, bringing Rachel news. Sevier had ignored Andrew's first challenges, confiding to his friends that his advanced years and large family should make it unnecessary for him to satisfy Jackson's demand. But when Sevier failed to answer his challenge, Andrew placed an advertisement in the *Gazette*.

To all who shall see these presents, Greetings. Know ye that I, Andrew Jackson, do pronounce and declare to the world, that His Excellency John Sevier . . . is a base coward and poltroon. He will basely insult but has not courage to repair.

Andrew Jackson

For five days Andrew awaited Sevier's reaction . . . and for five days, out at Hunter's Hill, Rachel plodded through her tasks, dreading the news.

At last word came to her: Sevier had finally sought Jackson out with a party of his friends. In the melee that followed, Andrew drew his pistols and so did Sevier. But members of both parties intervened, and though the principals damned each other volubly, they put up their arms.

IT WAS the end of the duel. But not of the strife.

On November 5, Governor Sevier pushed two bills through the legislature, the first of which split the Tennessee militia into two districts; the other bill provided for a second Major General, to have equal status with General Jackson. The next morning Governor Sevier appointed a former Senator, William Cocke, head of the Eastern Division of the militia, and dispatched him to Natchez with 500 militiamen to make sure that Spain did not interfere with the transfer of the Louisiana Purchase, which France had just sold to the United States. Major General Jackson and his carefully trained men had been left twiddling their thumbs at home.

When the news came, Rachel walked into Andrew's study. She found him slumped in his chair, his face ashen. She had seen him through all manner of adversity, but she had never seen him so completely beaten.

The final victory had been Sevier's; the ultimate defeat Andrew's—and hers.

CHAPTER 10

ON NEW Year's Day of 1804, Rachel and Andrew sat alone in their big room, before a banked fire. It took no complicated profit-and-loss system or surrounding pile of ledgers for them to know where they stood after their years at Hunter's Hill. They had extended considerable credit, but a drive to collect the money owed them had been fruitless. Most of the cotton crop in the Cumberland Valley had failed, and Andrew's personal notes were piling up in New Orleans and Philadelphia. In addition, he had lost considerable prestige through the setback to his militia and his feud with Sevier: though he still held the title of Major General, his command had virtually disappeared. It was obvious that he would have to resign his judgeship and devote himself to his financial affairs. They both knew that they would have to sell Hunter's Hill and everything else, for whatever price they could get.

"Where are we going to live, Andrew?" asked Rachel.

"I don't know. There are one or two tracts we might save; that Hermitage land, for instance, across the river. It's a fine tract, gently rolling, with abundant springs. There are beautiful trees, one cleared field."

"Is there a house on it?"

"No, just an old blockhouse and a couple of smaller cabins close by."

"Could we go see it?"

He ran his hand through his hair, and laid his palms across his troubled eyes. "I

368

can't move you there. A crude, half-decayed cabin on a wild piece of land—just as though we were poor settlers! How low I've brought you!"

Rachel laid a hand on his arm.

"Please, Andrew, ask George to saddle our horses."

They rode for two miles. When they took a trail that curved around a burnt summer meadow, Andrew told her she was now on the Hermitage land. They walked their horses through a cool stand of hickory, coming upon a bubbling spring and a brook which ran into the adjoining woods. Close by were a group of four log cabins, shaded by catalpa trees. They dismounted.

Andrew lifted the heavy leather latch of the two-story blockhouse and stood aside for her to enter. She walked in, the sun streaming over her shoulder. The downstairs was a single room, 24 feet wide and 26 feet long with a smooth-log floor. The logs had been fitted with a master mechanic's skill, and the passage of the years had polished them to a high sheen, a luminous silver-gray. She walked to the fieldstone fireplace; the stones, selected with care, shared the silver-gray luminosity of the rest of the room. She stood before the fireplace, deeply moved.

"Andrew, it's beautiful."

"It's just a log cabin, like all the others. . . ."

"Oh no, my dear, it's not like any of the others. That name—Hermitage—doesn't it mean a place of refuge?"

AFTER August 1804, when they moved to the Hermitage, their expenses and responsibilities were cut to a minimum. An old acquaintance had advanced $5000 on Hunter's Hill which enabled Andrew to meet his most pressing debts. And as his fortunes slowly improved, he became easygoing again, full of laughter and goodwill. He avoided the more rabid Sevier clique in Nashville, in particular young Charles Dickinson, but recaptured many of the friends he had alienated during the late quarrels. His chief pleasure was fixing up the Hermitage as Rachel wanted it, putting in big window lights in the main house and guest cabins and building a springhouse and a buttery.

To Rachel it seemed as though ten heavy years had fallen off Andrew's shoulders; and when he had the opportunity to buy a racehorse he had long admired, Indian Queen, and won his first race with her for a $100 side bet, he looked once again like the 22-year-old boy she remembered standing at the front door of the Donelsons', asking if he might be taken in.

"I'm going to build a stable of horses around Indian Queen," he told her. "I've already picked a site where they will have good grazing and plenty of water. And by the way—I hear that the Anderson brothers don't have enough money to finish their racecourse in Clover Bottom."

She caught the note of excitement in his voice. "And we do!"

"Are you encouraging me to buy? You're supposed to be the conservative member of our family."

"I'm only conservative when it comes to making money. When it comes to making fun, I'm as radical as any man who signed the Declaration."

He gathered her up and kissed her quickly, delighted with her approval.

SHORTLY THEREAFTER Andrew officially bought a two-thirds interest in the Clover Bottom racecourse—John Coffee taking the other third. The spring races that year had already been scheduled for Hartsville, but by the fall they were to inaugurate Clover Bottom. At the end of April, Indian Queen was scheduled to run against Greyhound, Lazarus Cotton's champion gelding. Andrew bet $1000 in notes on Indian Queen to win.

The Jacksons found a large crowd gathered at Hartsville for the races. Rachel bet everything she had on Indian Queen, then wagered a pair of gloves against the walking stick of Greyhound's owner. Theirs was not the important race of the day; the big one came later when Greyhound was to race against Truxton, one of the most famous horses out of Virginia. Nevertheless, interest was high in the Jackson entry. Suddenly, seeing their rather small mare against the famous Greyhound, Rachel had her first doubts.

"Are you sure Indian Queen can win?"

"Now, don't worry," said Andrew. "All Greyhound is going to see of that Queen is dust coming up from her hind hoofs."

But it was Indian Queen who ate dust the first time around the track; and if the second time around she ate no dust, it was because it had already settled.

"Think of the fun we've had training her," Rachel said consolingly as she saw Andrew's disappointment. "It was worth every cent we lost."

It was Greyhound's day; the big gelding went on to beat Truxton as handily as he had Indian Queen. In the din she heard Andrew saying against her ear:

"Let's go round to the stables."

Truxton was an enormous bay stallion with white feet. Andrew put his arms up slowly, bringing the horse's head down onto his shoulder. "This is the greatest horse I've ever seen on a racecourse. He should have beaten Greyhound."

"Why didn't he?"

"Because he was poorly trained. If I could take him home to the Hermitage with us for one month, he would beat Greyhound by ten lengths."

"But, Andrew, he's not our horse. . . ."

"You wouldn't like to place a small bet on that, would you, Mrs. Jackson? There's his owner coming toward us now.

Have you ever seen an unhappier man?"

Mr. Verell approached his horse with reluctance. "I had everything I owned on him, and quite a lot of money I didn't have. They'll be seizing Truxton for debt, twelve hundred dollars' worth."

"I'll make you a fair offer, Mr. Verell: I'll assume that debt and pay you three geldings in addition, worth over three hundred dollars. If Truxton wins an important race for me this year, I'll pay you two geldings as a bonus."

"That is indeed a fair offer, Mr. Jackson. I'll take it."

Andrew's eyes sparkled with excitement. Rachel saw him snap his head as he made a fast decision. To Lazarus Cotton, Greyhound's owner, he said:

"Mr. Cotton, I've just bought Truxton. I have five thousand dollars' side money says he can beat your Greyhound one month from today on this same course."

Rachel gasped; five thousand dollars! In paper, of course, like the land sales; but even so it was a lot of money. She heard Mr. Cotton say:

"Done! June twelfth, right here. Five thousand, side bet!"

374

The month that intervened was the most hectic the Jacksons had ever known. There was considerable plowing and seeding to be done at the Hermitage, but the better part of their time was spent at Clover Bottom, working with Truxton. The horse had power and speed; the one thing he lacked was stamina.

"That's because they treated him too delicately," Andrew explained. "They were afraid to work him hard for fear of exhausting him. We'll get him trimmed down until there's nothing left but pure fighting horse."

Rachel turned to her nephew Andy Donelson, who was visiting them.

"Truxton doesn't know it yet," she said, "but your uncle Andrew has just inducted him into the militia."

Toward the end of May, Andrew rode into Nashville to preside over a dinner being given for Aaron Burr, whose term as Vice-President of the United States had recently been concluded, and to bring him back to visit at the Hermitage. Rachel went about preparing the largest of her three guest cabins. She knew that Colonel

375

Burr would be considered the most important visitor, socially, to have come to Nashville. What if she were to give a dinner party for him the following Sunday? It might even be a good idea to include Mr. and Mrs. Somerset Phariss, and Miss Daisy Deson. . . .

In the midafternoon she went out to gather dogwood, forsythia and violets for the cabin; as she walked among the blossoms she thought of the strange career of the man who would shortly be her guest. Colonel Burr had been a resourceful commanding officer in the Revolutionary War; Andrew was not disturbed by the fact that he had been dismissed from General Washington's staff and was frequently in conflict with his superior officers. He had been a brilliant and prosperous lawyer in New York, then United States Senator during the time Andrew had been in the House, rising from comparative obscurity to become Thomas Jefferson's running mate in the 1800 election. The previous July he had shot and killed Alexander Hamilton, first Secretary of the Treasury, in a duel in Weehawken, been indicted by the state of New Jersey for murder, and obliged to flee south. However, he had returned to Washington at the beginning of the year to finish out his term as presiding officer of the Senate. The chief topic of conversation in the days preceding his arrival had been:

"What is Aaron Burr doing in Nashville?"

Andrew and the Colonel reached home at dusk, both delighted with her plan for a party on Sunday. Though Burr was a small man, Rachel thought him handsome, with dramatically curved eyebrows, all-consuming jet-black eyes, a sensuous mouth. His full sideburns had a fringe of pure white, making him seem older than his 49 years.

Sunday dawned clear and warm. By one o'clock when the first guests began arriving, a refreshing breeze stirred the branches of the catalpa trees. Rachel wore a filmy pale-pink batiste and her eyes glowed with excitement; both Mrs. Phariss and Daisy Deson had considered her invitation an important one: they were richly gowned in silk and lace, with brilliant fans and very large hats.

The guests had barely finished their

appetizers when Rachel knew that this was going to be the most successful dinner party she would ever give. She watched Colonel Burr with the gratitude of a hostess who senses that her guest of honor has the entire table entranced, for Aaron Burr's magnetism reached out to capture everyone.

The most important part of Colonel Burr's talk concerned the Spanish in Florida and Texas: Andrew and his guest agreed that they must be ejected. Rachel assumed that this was the answer to Colonel Burr's future: he was heading south to prepare the way for the American occupation of Florida. However, as Burr talked to various people around the dinner table she became a bit confused: to Mr. Phariss, who was interested in new settlements in the South, he intimated that the purpose of his present trip was to recruit settlers for a colony on the Ouachita River in Louisiana; to John Overton he dropped a hint that one of the purposes of his trip was to prepare for the invasion of Texas.

Whatever Burr's real plans might be, Andrew was enjoying himself thoroughly. He was particularly pleased when Colonel

Burr assured him his wines were as fine as any he himself had served. For Rachel, the day was successful simply because the Culture Club ladies had been enchanted with the Colonel.

It's so easy to get on with them this way, she thought. Why didn't I do it before?

AFTER Colonel Burr left, the Jacksons set off, one hot June morning, for the Hartsville course and the great race between Truxton and Greyhound. In a dozen other carriages were their friends from the neighborhood who had wagered everything they could on Truxton. Andrew himself plunged deeper and deeper; he bet the equivalent of fifteen hundred dollars in wearing apparel, and a number of his best tracts of land.

When Truxton and Greyhound were led to the starting line, Andrew's face was pale under the bushy red-orange hair, his eyes the deepest blue she had ever remembered them.

"I just had a brief talk with Truxton."

"And what is his latest statement?"

"He says not to worry about his being overtrained."

380

"I think it's us who are overtrained: if we lose we are going to have to walk home. Never mind. I'm happy." She folded her hands in her lap and looked up at him serenely from under her beribboned bonnet.

"I like to win because it's more fun that way, but if we lose we don't lose anything important."

The crowd suddenly went still; then the starter gave the signal. Greyhound took an immediate lead, setting a killing pace. Rachel turned to Andrew questioningly. Andrew, who was sitting tense but quiet, said:

"We're letting Greyhound set the pace. Wait till they round the curve."

The horses began the long straightaway opposite the spectators. Truxton seemed literally to shoot through the air, his flying hoofs making a continuous white blur against the landscape. He finished a full 20 lengths ahead of a thoroughly tired Greyhound.

"Too bad the race wasn't three times around the track," gloated Andrew. "That poor overtrained nag of ours would have passed Greyhound a second time."

She said impulsively, "Now, Andrew, be charitable in your victory."

"Oh, I'll be charitable," he cried; "in fact I'm even going to give Lazarus Cotton a chance to recoup his losses by selling me Greyhound. He can be had mighty cheap right now."

Greyhound was bought for only a portion of their day's winnings—which were sufficient to pay off the remainder of their indebtedness. Andrew set out triumphantly to travel the state, looking for more horses to add to his stable.

When Andrew got home from his expedition, he found a challenge. Captain Joseph Erwin, who owned two of the fastest racers in the West, Tanner and Ploughboy, had served notice that he would run Tanner against any horse in the world at the opening meet of the Clover Bottom course for a $5000 side bet. Andrew accepted the challenge for Greyhound. Rachel heard about it with regret, for Captain Erwin was Charles Dickinson's father-in-law, and Mr. Dickinson had half his father-in-law's bet.

At the meet, Greyhound beat Tanner in

three straight one-mile heats. It was a gala day for the Jacksons, and to Rachel's intense relief Captain Erwin took his defeat gracefully. He made only one request, that Andrew give him a return match at the end of November, this time with Ploughboy. The side bet was to be $2000, and $800 in forfeit money was to be paid if either withdrew from the race. Andrew accepted the match. Charles Dickinson again had half his father-in-law's bet—and also was half owner of Ploughboy.

But when post time arrived, Captain Erwin suddenly announced that Plough-boy had gone lame and that he would pay the $800. Rachel waited in her carriage while Andrew went to collect the forfeit. Considerable time elapsed before he returned, his face an angry red.

"Why, Andrew, what's happened?"

"Well, you know we agreed on a list of promissory notes to be used for payment, all notes due and payable on demand. However, Captain Erwin offered me paper that's not due until next January. I told him I had to have half the forfeiture in notes I could cash at once, as I had agreed to give that much to the trainer, who is leaving Nashville."

"But you settled everything amicably?" Her voice was anxious.

Andrew hesitated for a moment, then spoke:

"Charles Dickinson stepped in and offered his own due notes for $400. Erwin and I agreed on another race between Ploughboy and Truxton in the spring."

Two days after the forfeit, John Overton's brother Thomas came riding up to the Hermitage at breakneck speed. Rachel and Andrew came to the door of the springhouse where they were turning their cloth-wrapped cheeses.

Thomas flung himself out of the saddle to the ground. Then he hesitated a moment before he said:

"John thinks you should know something that was said at Clover Bottom the other day. Charles Dickinson was hanging around the tavern after the forfeit. He's a loose talker, you know, when he's imbibed too much."

"Was it something about the forfeit notes?" asked Andrew.

384

"No, it was something Mrs. Jackson said."

Rachel was startled. "Something I said? But I never laid eyes on Mr. Dickinson."

"It was when Captain Erwin announced Ploughboy couldn't run. Seems you turned to your nephew Andy, and said, 'It's just as well, for our horse would have left Ploughboy out of sight.' One of Mr. Dickinson's friends heard what you said and repeated it to him. Dickinson shouted, 'Yes, about as far out of sight as Mrs. Jackson left her first husband when she ran away with the General.' Begging your pardon, Mrs. Jackson, ma'am . . . "

Rachel flashed Andrew a look of despair.

"Oh, Andrew, this time the fault is mine. I struck at Mr. Dickinson with my bragging words; and now he's struck back at me."

"Struck back is right: with a weapon of war."

"But I can't understand: what injury have we ever done him?"

"Dickinson wants to become the political leader of Nashville, and he thinks I stand in his way. He thinks I'm bad for Tennessee, too: that I'm a crude, ignorant backwoodsman who might have been all right in the days of the Indian raids, but who has to be put out of the way now in order for Tennessee to become respected in Washington."

"He has actually said these things about you?" she asked, incredulous.

"Yes. But he has a perfect right to attack me politically."

She linked her arm through his.

"I'm proud of you, Andrew, for not challenging him."

"Well, I'm not so proud of myself. I've kept the peace, but the only result seems to be that Mr. Dickinson is beginning to think me a coward. I wonder how many lives he thinks he has?"

The whole timbre of his voice had changed. She searched his face and saw that it was dark, his lips set firmly.

"Andrew, you won't fight him?"

He smoothed the worried lines in her forehead.

"No. I'm going to Captain Erwin's tonight and ask him to use his influence over his son-in-law."

She took his hand and held it against her cheek.

To RACHEL's relief, Captain Erwin *did* bring his fiery son-in-law—a handsome, poised young man of 27—out to the Hermitage, and Dickinson proffered a half-hearted, grudging apology, which the Jacksons accepted. Soon after, they heard that he had left Tennessee for Natchez.

With rising spirits, Rachel thought the whole affair could be forgotten. But worse was to come. In Dickinson's absence, a friend of his published an attack on Andrew in the Nashville *Impartial Review*, and Andrew was forced to reply. The dispute was now public property; it could no longer be kept quiet. All through February and March, charge and countercharge were printed. The only person who seemed to enjoy the row was the *Impartial Review* editor who charged for all the statements at his regular advertising rates.

Spring came at last. Dickinson was still away, and Andrew returned to Clover Bottom to train Truxton for the big race against Ploughboy. It was overcast the morning of the race, but the somber grays of the outdoors could not match Andrew's mood; two days earlier Truxton had injured his thigh and the swelling would not yield to massage or liniment.

The two horses were led to the starting line amid gloom among the Jackson backers; they had bet extraordinarily heavily on Truxton. The word was given, and the horses shot forward. Truxton took a slight lead. Then as they came into the stretch, Truxton forged steadily ahead. He won the first heat easily; but he was limping badly. One of his front legs had also gone lame, and there was one more heat to go. Captain Erwin's supporters were shouting that the race was over. But Jackson surprised them.

"Truxton's going to run," he announced. "If he can beat Ploughboy with one bad leg . . . he can do it with two."

And Truxton did, by a full sixty yards, in a sudden heavy rain, running the two miles in one second short of four minutes. Andrew and his friends had won $10,000; Captain Erwin and his supporters were utterly crushed. It was the most humiliating defeat in the history of Western racing.

388

Rachel's heart pounded as she left the course.

ANDREW'S victories with his racehorses had now established him as the top turfman of Tennessee. Captain Erwin paid his debt, congratulating Andrew on having infused a great fighting spirit into his horse; and though reports came that Charles Dickinson had engaged in considerable pistol practice on his way down the Mississippi, Rachel dismissed this as no more than gossip.

But one night toward the end of May, Andrew came home from his store upset. Shortly after sundown, Thomas Overton reached the Hermitage, and Rachel, working on the small loom in her bedroom, heard the men's voices talking downstairs. Soon Andrew came upstairs and told her he had to go into town for a day or two on urgent business. She searched his face for some clue to the matter, but he kissed her, completely preoccupied, and left the room.

Around noon, two days later, George brought her a Nashville paper. In it was a statement by Charles Dickinson; she had not even known that he had returned to Nashville. She read:

> I declare Andrew Jackson to be a worth-
> less scoundrel and a coward. A man who,
> by frivolous and evasive pretexts, avoided
> giving the satisfaction, which was his due
> to a gentleman whom he had injured.

She sat on a hard dining chair, unable to move or even think until she heard Andrew's horse coming across the field. Then she ran to the open door, shading her eyes from the midday sun. He alighted in the yard, gathered her in his arms for a moment and, glancing at the newspaper she still held, murmured:

"Bad news travels fast, because it has so many helping hands."

He led her into the house. Moll was cooking supper. She took a quick look at Rachel's face, then left soundlessly.

"Andrew, you won't challenge!"

He took her hand in his.

"I have to."

"Darling, you're not going to let this hotheaded boy shatter our lives?"

He walked away from her.

"I have no choice."

390

"This is not going to be like other duels, is it? You are both going to shoot to—"

"Yes. If Dickinson had made the remark to me privately, then perhaps I might have found some way to answer him privately. But I'm still a Major General of the militia, and there are hundreds of militiamen who will read this challenge and know instantly that I must fight Dickinson. If I fail to do so, the whole militia stands in disgrace. If their leader is a coward, so are they. I fight, or I resign. I fight, or I lose everything."

She went to him, took his hands in hers.

"Dickinson's the best shot in this part of the country. He can hit a coin in the air before it falls, sever a string at 20 yards."

"He's gone to great pains to have these stories circulated."

"Then . . . he can . . . miss you?"

"Not totally. But I promise you I'll not miss him, either."

"Oh, Andrew, I don't want you to be guilty of killing a man. Think of his wife—and their baby son."

He stood staring at her for a moment, then turned away, went to the door and called out:

"Moll, would you be so good as to serve dinner now?"

SHE had expected to find some change in Andrew's routine in the days that preceded his departure for the dueling site at Harrison's Mill, perhaps some final preparations he would make or instructions he would leave, papers he might straighten out, accounts he might balance. But he did none of these things. He went about his day's work in the fields and exercised the horses, and he never again alluded to the oncoming duel.

He was to leave Thursday morning at five. They went to bed early the night before and awoke at four. As they breakfasted together, there was much she wanted to tell him: how much she loved him, how fine their years together had been, and how dear their love; yet she realized she could not utter one word, that she must not indicate by a single gesture that she feared she might never see him again. Instead, when it was time to go, she said:

"Don't ride too hard; but come home as quickly as you can. I'll be waiting for you. I'll have a whisky ready, and a hot supper on the fire."

There was gray light in the east by now. She stood at the doorway waving as he went across the fields. Then she turned back into the house. It was dark and still.

Rachel went about her chores for the day, feeling suspended in both time and space. Jane arrived at about midday with a small portmanteau. She said nothing about the duel or Andrew's absence: she was simply there as she always had been when Rachel was in trouble.

Jane slept with her that night. Several times Rachel fell into a nightmare, and was racked by throttled screams. Then she felt Jane's arm about her, comforting her.

At the first sign of the sun, Rachel got out of bed quietly, and left the house. She walked a very long time, having no way of telling precisely when the shots would be fired. But she felt in her heart that if anything serious were to happen to Andrew she would sense it.

It was ten o'clock when she returned to her cabin. Jane was sitting out in front knitting. She looked up, made a swift appraisal of Rachel's face, then said:

"For a time there I thought you'd gone to Harrison's Mill to fight the duel for him."

"There's been no news, Jane?"

"No. How could there be? It's still a number of hours before Andrew could reach home, no matter how fast he rode." Jane rose, linked her arm through her sister's. "You need rest."

"I believe I *could* sleep . . . for an hour or two."

She fell into a bottomless slumber. It was late afternoon by the time she awoke, and even as she descended the stairs she heard the noise of fast-moving horses. By the time she reached the door she saw Andrew coming down the trail flanked on either side by Thomas Overton and a Nashville surgeon, Dr. May. She was at his side as he lifted himself gingerly off his horse.

"Thank God, darling! Are you all right?"

"Oh, he pinked me."

"And Mr. Dickinson? How is he?"

"Well, I don't know precisely. He was hit."

The men followed Rachel into the

house and to the bedroom upstairs where they helped Andrew off with his coat and shirt. His chest was bandaged, but the blood had soaked through.

"How bad is it?" Rachel asked.

"Painful," Dr. May said, "but not dangerous: the ball broke a rib or two and raked his breastbone."

She sat beside him, holding his hand while the surgeon cleaned the wound and redressed it. Andrew gritted his teeth, saying to her between gasps:

"Mr. Dickinson's aim was perfect. He shot for exactly where he supposed my heart was beating. But you know how loosely that blue frock coat fits me? Standing sideways, as we did, it billowed out in front of me. It actually saved my life."

Dr. May took a handkerchief out of his pocket and wiped the perspiration from his face. "Right now I think we all could do with a good strong whisky. Mr. Jackson will have his in bed."

The men accompanied Rachel downstairs. Thomas Overton plunged into a recital of the duel.

"On our ride out to the dueling grounds, Dickinson's second and I dis-

cussed how the duel should be fought. As
you know, the pistols were to be held
downward until the word was given, then
each man was to fire as soon as he
pleased: the one who was the quickest

might end the duel with one shot. Should we try to get the first shot, or should we permit Dickinson to have it? We agreed that Dickinson would be sure to get the first fire. . . ."

" . . . please, Mr. Overton. . . ."

"I'm telling it as fast as I can, Mrs. Jackson. Well, when I gave the word 'Fire!' Dickinson raised his pistol like lightning and fired. I saw a puff of dust fly from the breast of the General's coat, watched him raise his left arm and place it tightly across his breast. Dickinson fell back a pace or two, saying in a faltering tone, 'Great God, have I missed him?' 'Back to the mark, sir,' I cried. The General took aim at Mr. Dickinson and pulled the trigger. The gun neither snapped nor went off; it stopped at half cock. The General drew the trigger back, took second aim and fired. He did not miss, I assure you. That will be an end to Mr. Dickinson's challenging men he is positive he can kill at 24 paces."

When Robert Hays came for Jane, Overton and Dr. May left with them. Rachel climbed into bed gently, not wanting to wake Andrew. She slept only intermittently, knowing she could not rest until she had had reassuring news about Charles Dickinson.

The news came the next morning, by messenger, from Nashville: Charles Dickinson had died at nine o'clock the evening of the duel.

Rachel fell to her knees on the floor. "Oh, God, have pity on the poor wife," she prayed. "Pity the babe in her arms . . . and have pity on us, too."

CHAPTER 11

RACHEL brooded over the death of Charles Dickinson. She watched with anxiety as the Cumberland Valley people reversed the roles of the duelists: somehow in their grief Andrew Jackson had become the invincible marskman who had mercilessly killed a less experienced opponent. Mrs. Somerset Phariss even charged Rachel with having egged her husband on because of Dickinson's two attacks on her, insinuating that Charles Dickinson's blood was on her hands.

It was no longer necessary for Rachel to set her table for 20; they ate alone. The throng of admirers who had once come from all over the state to counsel, make land deals or swap horses vanished like morning frost. Only Andrew's young aides in the militia of West Tennessee remained loyal; and despite Rachel's unceasing efforts to bring him back to health, Andrew remained thin to the point of emaciation all that summer. After a few trips to his store, Andrew stopped going and Rachel did not need to ask why; she knew the store was empty of customers.

One night toward the end of September, they heard a rider come up the trail. Andrew went to the window and exclaimed:

"Why, it's Colonel Burr."

Burr's face lit up with an affectionate smile when they opened the door to him.

"How wonderful to see you and the General again, Mrs. Jackson. I've been looking forward to it for days. That is the only excuse I can offer for intruding upon you at this late hour."

"Indeed, Colonel, I would have been deeply hurt if you had not."

Rachel went to the springhouse to get the men a cold fried chicken, a loaf of Moll's bread, some chilled butter and a bottle of white wine. When she came back, she found them deep in a discussion of the hostilities with Spain. Andrew's face, so drained of life all summer, had never seemed more intensely alive. Only now did she realize how terribly he had missed being at the center of political and military events. She heard Colonel Burr report that Spain's armed forces, operating inside American territory, had imprisoned five United States citizens and had cut down an American flag flying over a friendly Indian nation.

"By the Eternal," Andrew exclaimed, "it looks as though our moment has come!"

"I have purchased a tract of 200,000 acres on the Ouachita," continued Burr, "and several hundred young fighting men have already signed to settle there with me. When the war breaks with Spain we'll be a self-constituted army, ready to move on Texas and Mexico."

"All of Nashville will be glad to hear your news, Colonel," said Andrew. He turned to Rachel. "My dear, I want you to invite to dinner all who were at our first dinner for Colonel Burr."

Rachel shrank as the two men looked toward her. Would anyone come? Should she risk rejection for this chance to bridge the gap of coolness and hostility that had sprung up since the duel? John Overton was in close contact with Nashville society; she decided to speak to him first.

John was one of the managers of the Nashville Dancing Assembly, whose first ball was to be held that Saturday night; Rachel asked if the Assembly would like to invite Colonel Burr as its guest of honor. John decided this would lend social importance to the occasion, and sent announcements to all the Assembly subscribers. The next afternoon he visited Rachel.

"Seems I acted without my usual judicial calm in inviting Colonel Burr for Saturday night. Several men have come to my office to say they do not think we should honor him. It seems he is charged with engaging in a number of questionable activities."

"Such as?" Rachel asked uneasily.

"Such as: the Federal Court at Frankfort is arraigning the Colonel on charges of planning to injure a power with which the United States is at peace."

"Oh, you mean his preparations for a war against the Spanish. Andrew approves—"

"Such as: at Cannonsburg, Ohio, he

told Colonel Morgan that the Union would not last, that a separation of the states could not be more than four or five years off; and that with two hundred men he could drive Congress, with the President at its head, into the Potomac."

"But that's treason!" Rachel exclaimed. She was dumbfounded. "Do they have any proof of these charges?" she asked.

"No proof. All bottomed on rumor. . . . In any event we've reached a compromise: Colonel Burr will be there, but he's not to be our guest of honor. . . . And of course you and Andrew will attend the ball."

Saturday night, at the Assembly, she had a moment of uneasiness when Andrew entered the ballroom with Burr; but to her relief they were received cordially. For the most part, Burr's efforts to instigate a war against Spain were looked upon with favor in Nashville. Rachel followed Andrew with her eyes; it was wonderful to see him talking and laughing with friends whom he had not seen since the duel.

BURR continued south, and at the beginning of November Andrew received from him a packet of $3000 in Kentucky banknotes, with an order to build five flatboats and to outfit them. Andrew turned the money over to Jax Coffee with instructions to start building the boats.

A few days later a handsome, blond young man knocked at the door, and introduced himself as Captain Fort, a friend of Colonel Burr. He was invited to stay for dinner. After dinner, while the two men were smoking their pipes in front of the fire, the conversation took a strange turn. Though Andrew had not moved, Rachel had seen his back stiffen and felt his intense concentration upon the glowing bowl of tobacco.

"This separatist movement is the best thing that could have happened," Captain Fort was saying smoothly. "It will give the Western states a focus and a capital."

"And where is this new capital to be?"

"New Orleans. We will seize the port, then move on to conquer Mexico, with General Wilkinson, now commanding at New Orleans, at our head."

Andrew knocked out the gray pipe ash on the hearth, straightened up and looked fiercely at Fort.

"Is Colonel Burr in on this scheme?"

"My information comes from a high officer who is well acquainted with Colonel Burr."

All doubt had fled from the Jacksons' minds at the identical instant. There was a betrayed look on Andrew's face. He controlled himself with a determined effort, dismissing Captain Fort curtly. When he was gone, Andrew closed the door and bolted it. He was trembling.

"My God, is Burr really a traitor? I gave him military lists! Jax is building boats for him and buying provisions. Do you know what can happen if what Fort says is true?"

"Not altogether."

"Aaron Burr has put me in a position where I too can be charged with treason!"

THE news came by courier from Frankfort that Aaron Burr had been arraigned in Federal Court and released again for lack of witnesses to testify against him. Soon after, he arrived at the Hermitage, his smile warm and charming. Rachel planted herself squarely on the threshold.

405

"I'm sorry, Colonel Burr, but General Jackson is not at home."

"I'm indeed sorry to have missed him. Could you perhaps give me some information about the five boats I ordered from him?"

"I can give you no information."

Burr flinched. "If you are concerned about those absurd charges, Mrs. Jackson, I think I should tell you that I was completely exonerated in the Kentucky court."

"Colonel Burr, there is nothing I can do. Might I suggest the tavern at Clover Bottom? I am sure they can make you comfortable."

Burr pulled himself up to his full five feet four, bowed in imperious fashion, turned, mounted his horse and disappeared across the fields.

When Andrew returned he rounded up John Coffee and Thomas Overton and rode over to the Clover Bottom Tavern for a final accounting with Burr. He came back several hours later and dropped into a chair. Rachel asked:

"What happened, Andrew?"

"Frankly, I don't know. He very nearly convinced me that those charges were pure nonsense. Do you know what he has in his possession? A blank commission, signed by President Jefferson." He looked down between his widespread knees, studying the carpet pattern. "Anyway, we gave him back his money and told him he could take delivery of the two flatboats we have already finished. I don't know how far he can get in them, without provisions."

Burr departed with his two boats at dawn on December 22. Five days later the explosion came in the form of a proclamation from President Jefferson warning that an illegal conspiracy against Spain had been set in motion; all military and civil officials were ordered to seize the conspirators. The Dickinson clique wrote to Governor Sevier demanding Andrew's removal as a General of the militia, and when Aaron Burr was burned in effigy in the public square, the figure looked more like gangling Andrew Jackson than it did the short-statured Burr.

Then the insurrection collapsed. Burr surrendered to the authorities just above Natchez and was returned north as a prisoner. At the beginning of May, when they were in the midst of planting Indian corn, a subpoena arrived from the Federal Court in Richmond, summoning Andrew Jackson to appear and testify in the trial of the *United States* versus *Aaron Burr.*

AGAIN Rachel was left to manage the plantation alone. Andrew had the energy to run a dozen farms as big as the Hermitage, but somehow there was always something to keep him from it. The constant, penetrating sun in which Rachel had to work was burning her face deeply red, and despite her sunbonnet, her hair was baked dry. She was 40; her figure was beginning to thicken at the waist. She sent in to Nashville for the new French creams, rubbed oil through her dry hair, ordered field gloves in which to work.

Their separation served no good purpose. During the solid month that Andrew spent in Richmond the case had not even come to trial. He returned disgruntled.

"The first 20 days we sat there doing nothing because General Wilkinson refused to obey his summons to appear. Then Chief Justice Marshall tried to get President Jefferson to testify, and Jefferson refused to come. There we sat, trying to convict Burr of treason because he put together a few flatboats, while only a few miles away the English warship *Leopard* raked our ship the *Chesapeake*, killing and wounding 21 of our seamen on the flimsy pretext that we had a couple of English seamen aboard. Does Jefferson protest to the British? Does he threaten to blow their own ships out of the water? No! I made an hour's speech on the courthouse steps, best darn speech I ever made in my whole life. 'Mr. Jefferson has plenty of courage to seize peaceable Americans and persecute them for political purposes,' says I, 'but he is too cowardly to resent foreign outrage on the Republic. Millions to persecute an American,' I told that crowd, 'but not a cent to resist England.'"

Rachel shook her head at him in amused despair. "My, my, that's going to make you popular with the Administration."

SHE had never seen Andrew as irascible and depressed as he was that year. Though Burr had finally been acquitted in the Richmond court, most of the Cumberland felt he had committed no treason only because his conspiracy had been discovered in time. Andrew incurred additional disfavor by defending Burr locally. Enlistments in his militia ceased altogether; not enough soldiers assembled on drill days to warrant a review. When the presidential election of 1808 rolled around, Andrew canvassed the countryside for James Monroe in an effort to defeat Secretary of State James Madison, whom Jefferson wanted as his successor. Andrew's effort, which did not succeed, earned him a renewed vote of hostility from the Administration.

And now, after 17 years of marriage, a strangeness fell between them; Andrew went about his chores silently, glumly. He glowered when she made little jokes and, when she suggested that they try a few duets, put her off with a wave of the hand. He began going into town to spend his afternoons at the Nashville Inn. Word seeped back to the Hermitage that he was drinking too much, pounding his fists on the table and getting red of face.

In her need, Rachel found company and friendship with her brother Severn, who

410

had built a cabin near the Hermitage. Rachel had never been close to Severn: his illness had made him shy and he had kept himself apart from the family. Now she learned that Severn always read in the Bible for an hour upon awakening and before going to sleep at night. Perhaps that is the source of the tranquil sense in him, she thought; anyone who grows up hand in hand with death must have a feeling of intimacy with God. To Rachel, God had been the all-powerful ruler of the universe, a terrifying force. Now, after talking to Severn, she felt God's presence in her own house; she was able to pray for Andrew with more devoutness and humility than she had ever known. In her confused and frightened frame of mind, she had found someone whose very nature fitted her need.

In return, she was able to help Severn's wife, Elizabeth, who was increasingly unable to cope with their brood. She had borne five children in the eight years of their marriage, and had had a bad period after the birth of each child. During Andrew's frequent absences, which now extended to several days at a time, Rachel walked over to Severn's, bringing a lunch basket and sweets; sometimes she took the four older youngsters back home with her. When Elizabeth was with child again, she cried to Rachel:

"It isn't that I don't love them, but I just don't have the strength to bear them and nurse them and keep them out from under my feet."

Rachel thought, Oh, Liz, if you could know how terribly I have wished that God would bless me with just one. She recalled Jane's saying shortly after she had moved into Poplar Grove: "For some women they come a little too fast, for others a little slow, but we Donelsons all seem to get our share." Jane, how wrong you were!

ANDREW had been away for a week when Rachel came back from Severn's cabin to find word that he was on his way home. She heated a tub of water for a bath, then dressed in a soft brown muslin with the full skirt, which she preferred to the newly fashionable narrow ones. She had the large candelabrum polished and put it in the center of the white hucka-back-linen board cover. The papaws were

412

ripening, and she piled some in a pewter bowl on the sideboard next to Andrew's decanters. When he arrived home shortly before dark and saw the special preparations, he asked:

"Party?"

"For two."

"I see." Then with a wry smile, "Welcoming home the prodigal husband? I guess you could call me that; and it would be the kindest thing that has been said of me in quite a while."

"You should stay home more often and listen to your wife. I can think of all sorts of nice things to say if I thought you were interested."

"I'm always interested in anything you have to say, Mrs. Jackson."

"Not for the past few months you haven't been, Mr. Jackson."

Slowly, almost apologetically, he moved toward her, took her in his arms and kissed her.

"Darling, you haven't kissed me for so very long."

"I know, I've been too unhappy. When you hate yourself and the whole world around you . . . "

"But, Andrew, you've always been so strong, so sure of yourself."

"I don't know. Everything seems to—"

"Could one of the reasons be that you are quarreling so constantly with Mr. Jefferson and President Madison? What would you do if you were in their shoes? Each section of the country has its special problems and demands. With the war still going on in Europe each foreign country has its demands, too."

"I'll admit poor Mr. Madison is beset by everyone . . . including me." He grinned, the first sign that the good soil of Andrew Jackson was sprouting life again. "God help anyone who has to be President! But by the Eternal, I'd be tougher with the British. I'd kick them out of those forts in the North."

Soon a political event brought them great pleasure: the election of their old friend Willie Blount as governor.

WHEN Severn's wife, Elizabeth, was ready to be delivered, Rachel hired the best midwife in the neighborhood and went herself to assist. The child got itself born without difficulty, but there was a complication which resolved in the form of a second child, a twin boy. Elizabeth burst into tears.

"Why does it have to be two when I have barely the strength to nurse one?"

One of the twins began to cry. Rachel took the baby, wrapped him in a soft blanket and put him on her shoulder with his head nestled against her neck. She was standing this way when Severn and Andrew came into the room. Andrew stood above her, gazing down at the infant in her arms, sensing how her heart ached with the need to keep this newborn babe right where he was. Then, suddenly, Elizabeth called from the bed:

"Keep that boy, Rachel. We only expected one. We wouldn't be losing anything. We know how you've longed for a child, and he'll be well off."

Weak with expectancy, Rachel sank into a chair, still holding the child.

"You can't be serious, Liz. Wait until you recover your strength before you make such an important decision."

"If we could bring some happiness to you," said Severn, "and at the same time help Liz and the boy . . ."

Andrew's expression left her little doubt about how he felt.

Elizabeth asked: "Do you have a woman at home who can wet-nurse him?"

"Yes. Moll's daughter has a little one."

"Then take him right this instant. Andrew, you go into Nashville tomorrow and file adoption papers."

They named him Andrew Jackson, Junior. Andrew brought Rachel the adoption papers, signed and approved by the court, to put into her strongbox. Andrew was a long lean baby, with a thatch of black hair and blue eyes; he cried little except in the early morning when he was hungry.

The baby at once had an inspiriting effect on Rachel. A new buoyancy permeated her outlook and her actions. She felt light on her feet, running the hundreds of errands needed for the child. She was happy and grateful; she no longer turned inward, wondering what people knew or thought about her. Indeed, she met strangers as easily as she did friends.

Andrew, too, had seemed to develop a renewed faith in himself. With $1000 won on a young racing mare he had picked up,

he decided to buy arms for his depleted militia, to spark them back into life. "I'm going to talk to every militiaman who ever served under me," he told Rachel. "If I can't persuade them back into the ranks, convince them that we'll be training for the war I see coming, I'll simply bribe them back with whatever they need—a horse, a sword or a gun."

Within a year, as a result of his new fighting spirit, Sunday was once again open house day at the Hermitage. When the weather was warm, Rachel spread long tables under the catalpa trees; when it turned cool she served inside, using her cherrywood dining table as a buffet, with some 30 men standing in groups eating and discussing military problems. Andrew, Jr., learning to walk, made the adventuresome journey from one military leg to another as though he were wandering through a forest of young trees.

For the militia's first master muster the following spring, Rachel rode in her carriage to the drill grounds. There formerly had been some 2000 members of the militia; there were not more than 200 assembled now. Yet even to Rachel's experienced eye it was clear that there were many new guns in evidence, as well as fine horses and considerable of what Andrew called accoutrements. Andrew was pleased.

"Wait till word gets around about the new spirit and the new muskets," he told her. "The volunteers will start drifting back of their own accord."

It seemed only a few months before a visiting officer declared General Jackson's militia the finest of its kind in the United States.

ANDREW's preparations were proved justified when the United States declared war on Great Britain. The war he had first predicted at the Donelson stockade, 20 years before, started on June 21, 1812.

The next few months passed in a fever. Again, Rachel began supervising the work in their fields, releasing Andrew for the thousand tasks involved in getting his troops trained. "If President Madison approves," he said, "I can move to Canada in 90 days and take Quebec. The British forces there are still feeble."

But months went by while Andrew and his militia were passed over for service by the War Department, though news of the war in the North was catastrophic. General Hull, who commanded the largest part of the American troops in Canada, had surrendered Detroit and his entire army. Andrew paced the Hermitage, unable to sleep.

Then, in November, Governor Blount bypassed the unwilling War Department and gave Andrew a commission as a Major General of volunteers assigned to New Orleans—to a subordinate position under General Wilkinson. Andrew would have to, as he put it bitterly, "sneak into the war through the back door."

CHAPTER 12

THE first reports from Andrew that filtered back to Rachel were good; John Coffee's cavalry and Andrew's militia were making excellent progress toward New Orleans. It was the news from the North that continued to be disastrous: Brigadier General Winchester, captured by the British in Canada, had given up his two regiments, and most of the Kentuckians with him had then been massacred by Indians fighting alongside the British.

Then, less than a month after Andrew had left Tennessee, a new Secretary of War, John Armstrong, took office. Almost instantly upon sitting down to his desk he wrote a dispatch to Major General Jackson:

> War Department, February 5, 1813
> Sir,
> The causes for marching to New Orleans the Corps under your command having ceased to exist, you will on receipt of this letter, consider it as dismissed. . . . You will accept for yourself and the Corps the thanks of the President of the United States.

The War Department had not wanted Jackson in the Army in the first place. Now they had succeeded in booting him out.

Six weeks later, summoned by a courier,

Rachel rode her fastest horse into Nashville to find Andrew's troops, back from the South, drawn up in the square. The men were gaunt and threadbare after their monthlong trip up the Trace. Remembering the crowds that had turned out to bid them farewell, she was saddened to see that there were only a handful of onlookers.

She had not seen Andrew himself so fleshless since his first return from Philadelphia in 1795. But there was nothing thin about his spirit; he kissed her on the mouth, hard, the sharp bones of his body hurting her wherever they touched. As he stood there, his arm fiercely about her, watching his discouraged men leave the square, his emotion was not one of hurt pride, but of sheer grim determination that the War Department must not dismiss these fighting troops.

A few days later they made a trip from the Hermitage into Nashville. Their carriage had no sooner entered Market Street than several people cried out, "There's General Jackson!" When Andrew had tied the horses in front of the Nashville Inn they were quickly surrounded by a group of young men. Someone called:

"Three cheers for Old Hickory!"

"Would this Old Hickory be you?" Rachel demanded.

"Might . . . Let's go inside and find out why I've changed into a hero overnight."

In the lobby of the inn she heard half a dozen stories at once: how Andrew had walked all the way home from Natchez, his mounts being used to carry the sick; how he had nursed the boys and walked alongside the wagons, sometimes holding their hands—and bringing every last one home alive.

"He ate less than anybody, walked further, worked harder and slept the least," one of the soldiers said. "He's so tough we started calling him Old Hickory. We was proud to be serving under him."

HOME again at the Hermitage, Andrew waited in enforced idleness, riding and fishing with little Andrew and fretting while the war news went from bad to worse. One day, Rachel returned from a visit to Severn to find Andrew closeted with his brigade inspector, Major William Carroll, who, it seemed, had been challenged to a duel by a hotheaded young officer, Jesse Benton. And Jesse's older brother, Thomas Hart Benton, was a good friend of Andrew's—and far away, in Washington, where he could not reason with his younger brother.

Rachel exclaimed: "Andrew, surely you are not going to let those two young men fight?"

Andrew replied quietly:

"I'll do everything in my power to stop them."

But when he returned home the next day she learned that his efforts had been ineffective. Jesse Benton had decided that he must fight if he were to continue to live in Tennessee; while Carroll insisted that his commanding officer serve as his second.

"I just couldn't find any way of saying no to him, Rachel. He's such a poor shot with a pistol, and Jesse Benton is a good one. I've got to serve."

Monday morning, when Andrew came home from the duel, he was wearing a broad smile.

"Young Benton wheeled so fast he couldn't aim, and only hit Carroll in the thumb. Then he suddenly doubled up at the waist and exposed the broadest part of his anatomy to Carroll. And that's precisely where he got shot. He'll have to eat his meals standing up for a week or two."

Rachel's relief at this news was short-lived. When Thomas Hart Benton returned from Washington, he charged that Andrew had conducted the duel in a "savage, unequal, unfair and base manner." Friends brought word to the Hermitage that he was about to challenge General Jackson.

Rachel was operating the churn in the shade of the catalpas one day, with young Andrew helping her, when Robert Hays appeared in view, his horse breathing hard.

"There's been a ruckus in town, Rachel; Andrew's got himself hurt. I think you best come in with me."

As they drove off, Robert linked his arm through hers, telling her what had happened: Tom and Jesse Benton had run into Andrew and John Coffee at the City Hotel in Nashville. Tom Benton went into his breast pocket for his pistol; Andrew snatched his own pistol out of his back pocket, pressing it against Benton's chest and backing him down a long hall. Jesse Benton suddenly appeared behind them and fired, hitting Andrew in the shoulder.

Robert Hays led her quickly through the lobby of the Nashville Inn and up the stairs to Andrew's room, where several doctors were clustered about his bed.

Andrew's face was lifeless, his lids closed tight over his eyes; he hardly seemed to be breathing. His left shoulder was heavily bandaged but soaked through with blood.

Dr. May came to her side.

"I'm sorry, Mrs. Jackson, but the General is badly wounded: one bullet broke a bone in his shoulder, the second is lodged against his arm bone. We've agreed that the arm cannot be saved; if we do not amputate, gangrene . . ."

The room went black. She heard Andrew say hoarsely:

"Thank you, gentlemen, but I'll keep my arm!"

The youngest of the doctors present, Felix Robertson, said:

"With all due apologies to my fellows in

medicine, Mrs. Jackson, I don't think the arm needs to be amputated. I've applied strong pressure to stop the bleeding, and put poultices of slippery elm on the wounds."

By now she had regained control of herself. She thanked the doctors, dismissed them all except young Robertson, who bent Andrew's elbow and fixed his forearm to his chest with bandages. By the end of the second day, Andrew was able to take small quantities of solid food. Robert Hays came to report that Nashville was in an uproar, that the Bentons nearly had been murdered by some of Andrew's former soldiers, and had left town hastily, promising never to return.

"On the strength of that good news," said Andrew, "I think I'll go home."

When they returned to the Hermitage, two field hands carried Andrew into the house and up the stairs, his arm still tightly bound, his smashed shoulder useless. Dr. Robertson informed her that it might be months before he could be up and around, or have the use of his left side.

She was able to keep him quietly in

bed for precisely 24 hours, for the very next day news reached Nashville that the Creek Indians had attacked Fort Mims, in Mississippi Territory, massacring 400 men, women and children. A delegation including Governor Blount and John Coffee arrived at the Hermitage to inform General Jackson that the state militia was disconsolate because he could not take command. Rachel waylaid them downstairs.

"Governor Blount, you know the General hasn't the strength to stand on his feet, let alone ride a horse for hundreds of miles and fight a war."

No one answered her, for all eyes had turned toward the stairs. There, coming down slowly, his good right arm holding his shattered left one, was Andrew, his lips set, his eyes bright as hot coals. When he reached the bottom of the stairs he walked across the room, put his arm about Rachel's waist. "Gentlemen, a patriot cannot be sick when his country needs his services. We'll be ready to march in a few days. I shall command in person."

She helped him into his uniform, took

his hand, holding it against her cheek for a moment. How could he fight a war when he had to be helped into his saddle?

IT WAS not long after he left that Rachel received the magnificent news: Andrew had forded the Coosa River and taken the Creeks by surprise at dawn. Three hundred of the Indians were killed.

The victory-starved nation, defeated and humiliated so often in the past year and a half, was singing General Jackson's praises. After eleven years of preparation, this was his first actual battle; and he had emerged triumphant.

But in spite of the exultation of the press, Andrew's militia was left in the wilderness with almost no supplies. Officers and soldiers who had been existing on squirrels, and then on acorns, now threatened to go home. General Jackson lined the road with loyal men, promising to fire on all deserters. When fifteen hundred fresh troops arrived, Andrew dismissed the mutinous regiment, only to learn that the new arrivals had but ten days further to serve before their enlistment expired. Soon his command was reduced to a hundred and thirty cold, starved and ragged men.

He himself was suffering excruciating pain from his unhealed arm. In addition, he was stricken with diarrhea because he had no food but acorns and nuts. Sometimes for hours on end he could retain consciousness only by remaining on his feet, his arms dangling over a tree limb to hold him up. But reinforced by 800 recruits delivered to him in person by Colonel Robert Hays, he won another victory over the Creeks at Emuckfau, leading his scant and greatly outnumbered reserves into action himself.

Once again a beaten Administration and a starved press hailed the victory, calling it the greatest ever enjoyed against the Indians. Andrew Jackson became the most exalted commander in the field, and 5000 volunteers poured into the Indian country to report to him.

Buoyed by the presence of a company of U.S. regulars, Andrew attacked the Creek bastion at Horseshoe Bend. In a ferocious hand-to-hand encounter he lost 49 men, but by the end of the day only a handful of the Creeks survived, their leader surrendered, and all their British guns were captured. The Creek war was ended. The British would have to find themselves new allies in the South.

EARLY in May, with the sun warm overhead and the peach trees a mass of delicate blooms, a courier brought a note from Andrew asking Rachel to meet him the following noon, five miles out on the road to Nashville. It was ten o'clock when her carriage reached the designated spot, having passed hundreds of Cumberland Valley folk who were lining the road waiting for a sight of General Jackson. She heard a rushing clatter and her carriage was surrounded by a dozen mounted men. Before she could distinguish their faces, her carriage door was flung open and Andrew was by her side, crushing her to him. She had time for only one swift look at his face, but even in that fleeting instant she saw that his eyes were more truly alive and fulfilled than she had ever seen them before.

A WEEK at the Hermitage saw the grayness disappear from Andrew's face. There

430

were many guests during the day; the dining table was crowded with friends and admirers. In East Tennessee and Kentucky some people were already booming him for governor.

Rachel and he had a month's honeymoon. They were never apart, riding out for the day into the cooler hill country, picnicking on cold chicken and buttermilk, gazing down on the river valley and the flatlands while they talked.

Then one morning a courier arrived from the War Department with sealed dispatches. Andrew took the envelope and broke the seal.

"I take back everything I ever said about the Secretary of War," he cried. "He is a man of infinite wisdom. Listen to this:

" 'War Department, May 28, 1814
Sir,
Major General Harrison has resigned his commission in the army, and thus is created a vacancy in that grade, which I hasten to fill with your name.
John Armstrong' "

They both held their breath for an instant, then Andrew exploded:

"By the Eternal! After all these years, they've finally taken me into the regular Army."

She reached her arms up about his neck. He lifted her until their lips were on a level and kissed her harder than she had been kissed in years. Then he set her down and stood with his head cocked to one side, smiling.

"I will have command of the Seventh Military District; that includes Tennessee, the territory of Mississippi and Louisiana. This means that you are not going to be left behind anymore. As soon as I go South and set up headquarters I'll send for you."

A FEW days later, news reached the Hermitage that the British were in Paris, and that Napoleon had fallen. The long war in Europe was over. A thousand British vessels and numerous regiments of untrained troops would now be free to descend upon the United States. Jackson left for his command in the South at once.

Soon Rachel, waiting at the Hermitage, heard that three British ships had arrived at the Spanish town of Pensacola with land forces and large supplies of arms. Fourteen more warships and transports were already in Bermuda with Lord Wellington's army. Andrew confided to her in a short note:

> Before one month the British and Spanish expect to be in possession of Mobile and all surrounding country. There will be bloody noses before this happens.

The army that had smashed Napoleon was advancing rapidly on the shores of America, and Andrew Jackson was promising to bloody their noses! It would be Andrew's will to win pitted against the might of the British army—the army that had just captured Washington, burned the Capitol, shelled Baltimore, occupied the state of Maine. Nashville papers reported that Andrew had sped to Fort Bowyer, on Mobile Bay, setting up his cannon just as the British fleet attacked. Two British ships were destroyed, and the rest of the fleet fled to sea. It was Andrew's first victory against the British.

The next word told Rachel that Andrew had stormed Pensacola in the face of heavy guns and British warships, capturing the city and forcing the British to blow up Fort Barrancas and once again put to sea. He had then moved into New Orleans.

That there was a gigantic struggle pending near New Orleans no one could doubt.

IT WAS at New Year's that Robert Hays and several of Rachel's brothers rushed to the Hermitage with news of the battle.

The British, with nine to ten thousand men, had landed at Lake Borgne, pushed through five miles of swamp and seized the Villere plantation, eight miles from New Orleans. Though he had only one thousand regulars and two thousand militiamen, Andrew cried:

"By the Eternal, they shall not sleep on our soil! We must fight them tonight."

Within two hours, he was leading his troops out of the city. At seven that night he surprised the British around their campfires. The British were disorganized and casualties were heavy; best of all, the British major who had burned the Capitol was captured. In the morning Andrew pulled his troops back of Rodriguez

434

Canal, then built his defenses with every shovel, musket and able-bodied man from New Orleans pressed into service: for the British before him were constantly being reinforced.

On the morning of January 8, the famous British General Pakenham fired a silver-blue rocket announcing the great attack. General Jackson was ready with his troops, deployed in a deep-dug defense arc. At seven in the morning a heavy fog lifted. Standing on the parapet above Rodriguez Canal, Andrew saw, little more than 600 yards away, British soldiers by the thousands, white belts across red tunics, muskets at the ready.

They charged. Andrew gave his order: the 12-pounders went off. Then the first rank of men fired, stooped to unload; the second rank fired, then the third. They were all woodsmen, dead shots; the close-packed British lines fell. But others came on; Andrew's men and cannon, protected by their defenses, poured in more fire.

Fewer than 100 English soldiers ever reached Rodriguez Canal. A few lived to scale the embankment—and died. After only an hour and a half of fighting, the

British withdrew, their morale shattered, their fighting force spent. Seven hundred British soldiers lay dead on the field; fourteen hundred more were wounded. Andrew had lost but seven men.

The British, beaten and broken, made their way back to their ships. Andrew chose not to pursue them. The next day he received a note from the British commanding officer, General Keane—Pakenham had been killed—offering remuneration for his beloved battle sword, lost on the plain before Rodriguez Canal.

"Did Andrew return the sword?" Rachel asked when she heard the story. "I hope he returned it. It could be a symbol for that other English sword that cut his head so cruelly when he was a boy."

"Oh yes, he returned it," said Robert Hays. "And sent with it a letter expressing his feeling for all the brave English soldiers who had fallen in battle."

Now his victory is complete, Rachel thought. Over the British . . . and over himself. She added, aloud: "Now little Andrew and I can go to him in New Orleans."

438

At sunrise the next morning, they boarded a riverboat for the long trip South.

CHAPTER 13

NEW Orleans was a phantasmagoria of band concerts, plays in the Théâtre d'Orléans, dinner parties in the sumptuous homes of the Creole families. Rachel became a close friend of the lovely Louise Livingston, queen of New Orleans society. But Andrew was having trouble keeping discipline in the restless city, tired of martial rule. The rains fell heavily, turning the country into a quagmire; provisions were difficult to get from the New Orleans merchants, and hundreds of soldiers came down with influenza, fever and dysentery. Andrew's portrait in the Exchange Coffee House was destroyed by an angry mob. The Hero of New Orleans had become the Villain of New Orleans, accused of being a dictator who was holding military control over the city for his own gratification.

Then on March 13, 1815, official news of the ratification of the peace treaty at long last reached New Orleans. The British fleet departed. Andrew lifted martial law and sent his troops home. The sun came out; the fickle throngs were in the street again shouting, "Jackson and peace."

A few days later, Rachel was fixing her hair before a mirror on a handsome Louis XIV chest in their quarters. Her glance fell on a letter on top of the chest where Andrew had put it. She recognized the signature of a cousin on her mother's side, John Stokely, who held an important Government position in Washington.

Suddenly, the words stood out before her startled eyes:

> We are entitled to a President from the West. Your activity and uniform success has rendered you very popular amongst the American people and I do conceive that you ought to fill the chair of the Chief Magistrate of this Union.

She sat down on the edge of a gilt-backed French chair, one hand clutched at her breast, her heart pounding in her throat. She was too stunned to think. If they had been plunged into a caldron of animosity when Andrew ran for modest

440

offices, if they had found themselves embroiled in scandal, feuds and killings, what in the dear God's name would happen to them if he should ever get involved in a campaign for the Presidency of the United States?

THEY left New Orleans for Tennessee at the end of the first week of April 1815. The streets and country roads were lined for miles by people crying out their gratitude and benedictions. Every hamlet along the way gave Jackson a tumultuous reception. Almost frenzied crowds took over their party at the Tennessee border and led them into Nashville as though they were a triumphal procession. It seemed as if every last soul in Tennessee had come to pay homage. To people humiliated by the Treaty of Ghent, signed with England after three years of military defeat, Jackson's triumphs had been electrifying. Rachel recalled that Louise Livingston's husband, Edward, had said:

"You know, General, the road north from New Orleans could lead directly to Washington."

The air at the Hermitage was filled with presidential talk: the Federalist party, which had declared for surrender in the war, was now passing from existence. Whoever the Republicans nominated was certain to be elected. The Virginian James Monroe was the favorite, yet there were many who felt that another man was wanted, an outsider with a fresh face and a strong will and new ideas. Who better fitted these qualifications, people were asking, than the Hero of New Orleans?

Andrew's health was by no means good. He had suffered six months of the almost universal military dysentery. They had both assumed that all he needed was a regular routine and a lot of good solid food, but now, safely ensconced at home, he grew more rather than less ill. Rachel cut off the flow of visitors. She sat by his bedside feeding him chicken broth, accompanying each spoonful with a prayer that he would be able to keep it down.

"You have simply used up the energies of six years in the past six months, Andrew. You need a great deal of rest. We have absolutely nothing to worry about now. Cotton prices are soaring and we are going to have a bumper crop."

"I wanted to go to Washington to make my reports . . . participate in the reorganization of the Army . . . but it can wait."

"Of course it can. When the warm weather comes you must take your son fishing. And I must get you strong and handsome again because you have to have a painting made to send to Congress for that medal they are awarding you."

BY OCTOBER, after a lazy summer, Andrew became restless. He decided he must go to Washington at once: to designate the military posts that were needed in the wilderness; to explain why Indian opposition to the land treaty should be disregarded; to secure permission to move all Indian tribes west of the Mississippi so that they could not again be armed and used by a hostile European nation; and to urge the Government to drive out the Spanish, who still held Florida, and were thus in a position to allow enemy troops to

443

invade the United States. This time, Rachel accompanied Andrew; she had had enough of separations, and her fear of gossip, of strangers, had lightened with Andrew's success and her own wonderful stay in New Orleans.

The inns at which they stayed each night were comfortable, but she was glad when they neared Lynchburg and the home of a friend's parents, where they were to rest for a few days. As Rachel and Andrew were about to go down for supper the first night, their host came running up the stairs.

"General, there's a delegation downstairs from Lynchburg; the town is tendering you a formal banquet tomorrow. Thomas Jefferson is riding in from Monticello to preside!"

Rachel saw the flash of joy cross Andrew's face. She reached out a hand to him. He squeezed it hard. With his eyes brilliant he murmured:

"I've been a wasp stinging at Mr. Jefferson all these years; and yet he's so fine a gentleman as to ride almost 100 miles to be at a dinner for me."

Yes, thought Rachel, you can forgive

each other now that the war with Britain has been fought and won.

The following afternoon at three o'clock she entered the ballroom of the hotel, her hand lightly on Mr. Jefferson's arm. Their 300 hosts stood at attention while she and Andrew walked slowly down the center aisle of the ballroom on either side of Mr. Jefferson. She had only a fleeting impression through dinner of the succeeding courses as they were placed before her and taken away, for underneath the quiet talk she felt a submerged tension, as though everyone were expecting something of critical importance and no one was quite sure what it would be. At last, when the tables had been cleared, the chairman rose, gestured for silence and turned to Thomas Jefferson. Mr. Jefferson got up slowly from his chair, stood with a wine goblet raised, the white hair falling thickly over his ears, his face at 72 still patrician and beautiful. He extended his glass toward Andrew and in a low, yet carrying voice said:

"Honor and gratitude to those who have filled the measure of their country's honor."

445

The 300 men rose in their chairs, extended their glasses toward Andrew and drank to him. Rachel's head began to spin. Was Mr. Jefferson merely putting into words the thanks of the nation for Andrew's indestructible will to victory? Or was he putting his public seal of approval on Andrew Jackson as the next President of the United States?

Silence filled the room, silence fraught with the deepest drama. Everyone's eyes were fixed on Andrew: how would he respond to this toast? Would he use this banquet room as a political stump, making known his willingness to contest the presidency?

Andrew rose on the other side of Mr. Jefferson. His eyes were masked. After what seemed to her an intolerable time, he raised his glass, smiled down at Mr. Jefferson and made his own toast:

"James Monroe, late Secretary of War."

The great hall broke into bedlam. In those six short words, Andrew Jackson had bowed himself out of the presidential race of 1816, officially nominating James Monroe of Virginia. He had voluntarily given up this chance of becoming the

446

first man of his country. On Mr. Jefferson's face she caught a strange expression: was it, she asked herself, one of not too completely disguised relief? Had Mr. Jefferson taken a long gamble believing that Mr. Jackson would make the *beau geste* of acclaiming James Monroe? He had not wanted Jackson to be President; he had passionately wanted Monroe, his friend, neighbor, and protégé, in that office.

WASHINGTON was a frightful disappointment to Rachel, with its muddy streets and ugly brick houses standing unshaded amidst fields and swamps. This impression of rawness, almost of desolation, was heightened by the damage that had been caused by the British burning of the Capitol, the President's House, the Treasury and the Departments of State and War, only part of which had been repaired. However, the ugliness of the city was more than offset by the tremendous cordiality of its citizens; it seemed that every last family wanted to entertain for them. President Madison gave them a sumptuous dinner

447

at the Octagon House, with the entire diplomatic corps present, including members of the British Embassy. To Rachel's amusement Andrew and the British Ambassador had a long and cordial conversation.

One Sunday, they visited Mount Vernon with its superb panorama of the Virginia countryside. The Custis family received them with the utmost hospitality, showing them through the beautiful home. Later, Andrew and Rachel sat on the front porch overlooking the Potomac.

"Next to Bayou Pierre," Andrew murmured, "this must be the most beautiful prospect in the world."

"Yes, along with our own view from that knoll on the Hermitage."

He turned his face full to her, studying her meaning for a moment. Then he said, "My dear, we are no longer poor. We could build the equivalent of Mount Vernon in Tennessee: a lovely house and garden like this, overlooking the fields and forest, with the Cumberland and Stone rivers in the distance."

"Andrew, I had no such thought and

you know it! I am completely happy in our cabin. I don't ever want to move."

"You won't be so happy when we get back in January and you feel that north wind come through the logs."

"I've survived that north wind for 11 years now."

He did not reply. She saw by his sense of inner excitement that he had not been dissuaded.

BACK at the Hermitage, things went as well as they had in Washington. They sold their cotton crop that year for the highest price ever: thirty-eight cents a pound. For the first time in years they were out of debt, with more than twenty-two thousand dollars to their account in the Nashville bank. But they had been home less than three weeks when Andrew announced that he had to make a tour of the Indian country: the Creeks were complaining about the treaty Andrew had given them, and were rousing their neighbors, the Cherokees and Chickasaws.

"Do you really have to go?" Rachel asked. "Jax is surveying down there and would let you know if trouble were brewing."

"As long as I am on an Army salary," Andrew replied stubbornly, "I'm going to continue doing the best job I know how. I can't bear to report unfit for duty while eating the public bread."

No sooner had Andrew ridden down the trail to the Tennessee border than a virulent epidemic which the doctors called "cold plague" broke out, felling whole families. Once again Rachel became a familiar figure in the countryside, riding across the fields at night wrapped in a dark cape and hood, carrying provisions and medication and warm friendliness. Day after day she closed the eyes of friends and neighbors who died while she sat by their bedside, ignoring the doctor's warning that since six and seven members of a family were dying within hours of each other, the disease was highly contagious.

By the time spring came, and an end to the plague, almost a third of the population of the Cumberland had been wiped out. Rachel took to her bed, her own strength gone. Desperately as she missed

Andrew, she was glad that she would have a few weeks in which to recuperate.

HE WAS gone five months in all, and their happiness in his return was soon spoiled by a formal notification from the new Secretary of War, William Crawford, that Andrew's treaty with the Creeks had been set aside, and that vast tracts of land had been returned to the Cherokees. Andrew was wild with anger. He wrote the Secretary a blistering letter—one that did not endear him to the politically powerful Crawford—and began leading mass meetings of indignation.

President Madison named him as Commissioner, with instructions to return to the Indian country and buy from the Cherokees the lands which he had taken from them and that Secretary Crawford had given back. Once again, Rachel was left alone; and Andrew had hardly returned, months later, when he announced that he was going south again, at the head of a military expedition, to "send the Spanish Dons home from Florida."

And that was precisely what he did,

leaving her for a fourth long journey within the period of two years.

The Hermitage was in the hands of a capable overseer; she no longer had to go into the fields, to be exposed to the hard labor, to the drying heat of the sun. Yet it seemed that each day brought its own misfortune: her invalid brother, Severn, died; John Overton became so ill he had to resign his judgeship and retire. When Andrew returned from Florida after a half year's absence, his hands were shaking as though he had palsy and he had a cough as bad as the one that had killed Severn. He had a mysterious pain in his side which kept him from sleeping, and his left shoulder had stiffened so severely that he had no use of the arm.

Before a week was out she learned that her husband's seizure of Florida had caused an international scandal. Spain was demanding an immediate return of Pensacola, with indemnities. England was threatening war over his court-martial of two Britishers charged with spying and helping the enemy in Florida. Negotiations between Spain and the U.S. Government for the purchase of Florida, which had been progressing slowly, collapsed. There was a movement in Congress to impeach Andrew and relieve him of his military command.

Rachel had had Andrew sitting up in a chair for a few hours each day, but this fresh crisis put him back in bed again. There he remained for two solid months, neither his temper nor his health helped any by newly elected President Monroe's apologetic return of Pensacola and St. Marks to Spain, thus nullifying Andrew's conquest of Florida.

IT WAS characteristic of Andrew that he picked this discouraging moment to begin building the fine house he had promised Rachel. They went across the fields one hot August day, Andrew walking with slow steps. At the top of a slight rise overlooking their cabins, the spring and the deep woods beyond, he stopped, and with his stick began outlining the house he had in mind; it was to be a two-story brick building with a big hall downstairs, two good-sized rooms on either side, and four rooms upstairs directly over the four below.

The harvest season brought them another excellent crop, and when they found a limestone quarry on their own land, Rachel agreed that they should take several of their more skilled hands out of the fields to start the foundation work. They built their own kiln, experimenting with the fires in an effort to get the kind of brick they wanted, and rode through the forest, marking the best poplar trees for lumber.

Before actual building could start, Andrew was called away again, to visit the Indian country and arrange a treaty with the Chickasaws. From there, he went to Washington, where his enemies had started impeachment proceedings against him for his conduct in Florida.

Rachel filled her days with the completing of the big house, building a separate kitchen just across the porch from the dining room, sinking a deep well which brought up cool water by windlass and bucket, and staking out her first garden inside a low white picket fence. Young Andrew was in school in Nashville, yet Rachel could hardly say she was alone, for the air crackled with news about her husband. In Washington, the Speaker of the House, Henry Clay of Kentucky, had stepped down from the dais to attack the Creek Treaty and the conquest of Pensacola, charging Andrew Jackson with being a military chieftain who would one one day destroy the liberties of the American people.

Rachel rode over to see John Overton, whom she found puttering in his greenhouse amidst his young plants.

"I simply can't understand the ferocity of these attacks, John."

"Mr. Clay wants to be President," replied John. "He'd kill his own grandmother if he thought she stood in his way. The same applies to Secretary of War Crawford. Each gentleman thinks Andrew Jackson is standing in his way."

"But Andrew has said he doesn't want the Presidency."

"Messrs. Clay and Crawford remain unconvinced. But our side will have its turn. Let me give you some of these purple flags to take home; they'll grow wonderfully in your new garden."

For the next two weeks the Nashville papers were filled with the fiery defense set up by the Jacksons' friends. When the final vote was taken Andrew was vindicated. Philadelphia gave him a four-day celebration, New York a five-day reception. Rachel was convinced that if Andrew's military career had not been attacked he would have remained a general and a gentleman planter; but would he be content to remain so now with the ovations of Philadelphia and New York fresh in his ears?

She had the new Hermitage completed, with carpets in the bedrooms, draperies at the windows and her cherrywood table installed in the dining room by the time Andrew returned from Washington in mid-April. They had their first supper that night under the many candles of the crystal chandelier.

After dinner they walked outside to look at the house against the night sky; it had a simple grace and dignity that made them proud. Andrew brought forth a box from his waistcoat pocket, then leaned over to kiss her.

"It seems I'm forever leaving you home to finish something I started."

Rachel opened the box to find a set of beautiful mosaic jewelry—a necklace, earrings and belt clasp. She took the necklace from the case and Andrew stood behind her to fasten the catch, then kept his arms about her. He went away so often, yet he always returned to her completely, bringing his full love and desire. She turned in his arms, found herself clasped against him. He couldn't help seeking the heights; he was driven. He had great spirit, courage, leadership. Half the time she knew him to be physically more dead than alive; but the inner fire never went out.

At the beginning of June they received a visit from President Monroe, who had been touring Georgia. He proved to be the most undemanding of guests. A deep and abiding affection between the President and Andrew was apparent in their every word to each other as they lingered over a late supper. Mr. Monroe was to have only two or three free days before going into Nashville for a grand ball; Rachel saw to it that he had complete relaxation.

After Andrew left to make part of the return journey with the President, Rachel found that newspaper editors and politicos all over the country were asking: just what were the implications of President Monroe's visit to the Jacksons? Some said that General Jackson, in affording hospitality to Mr. Monroe, had taken this means of announcing to the country that he was supporting Mr. Monroe for re-election in 1820. Their own friends in Tennessee maintained that by going directly to the Hermitage before he visited Nashville, Mr. Monroe was announcing publicly that he favored the succession of General Jackson to the Presidency in 1824, when Monroe's second term would be over.

CHAPTER 14

SPAIN finally signed the treaty selling Florida to the United States, and Andrew received a letter from President Monroe offering him the governorship of Florida. After some hesitation, he accepted.

Rachel went with Andrew this time. They descended the Mississippi to New Orleans by steamboat in eight days, their freshly painted carriage securely lashed in the hold. It seemed to Rachel as though all of New Orleans had assembled at the pier to welcome them, with a full band playing martial music. That night they were conducted to the Grand Theatre by a guard of honor, and when they entered their box the audience rose to its feet, shouting: "Viva Jackson! Long live the Jacksons!" Later a delegation came into the box to place a crown of laurel on Andrew's head.

A few weeks later, in Pensacola, Rachel stood on her balcony watching the Spanish troops drawn up in the square, their flag still flying, the Americans in position opposite them. The Spanish flag was lowered halfway; she saw Andrew give a command and the American flag rose in its place. At long last, Andrew Jackson had made a bloodless and permanent conquest of Florida! The Spanish people below her burst into tears and walked disconsolately out of the square; her own exultation faded in the face of her sympathy for them.

But her sympathy soon veered to her husband, for while the Spanish residents were prospering under the influx of Americans, Andrew was encountering little but obstruction and aggravation from the Spanish officialdom. Because he was idle and frustrated, he got into a row over the archives with ex-Governor Callava: Andrew insisted that the records be handed to the new American government. Callava refused; Andrew had him arrested and seized the records in Callava's house. That night, closeted in their bedroom, he confessed:

"I should never have come. The whole thing's been a wild-goose chase."

"Not entirely," Rachel replied consolingly. "If you hadn't come you might always have had an unfinished feeling in your mind about Florida. But if your job is done, why don't we pack our trunks and go home?"

THEY returned to the Hermitage during the first week of November, after having been gone eight months, to find that a demand was already being made for a Congressional investigation of Governor Jackson's behavior in Florida, in particular his jailing of Callava and his seizing of the Spanish archives.

"It's Crawford and Clay again," declared Andrew. "They are still trying to eliminate me from presidential consideration. I'm going to write a letter saying that I shall support Secretary of State John Quincy Adams for the Presidency instead of running myself when Mr. Monroe retires. That will put an end to their hellish machinations."

He was right; the Congressional investigation was dropped.

With the coming of spring Andrew got out on the farm to supervise the planting. Rachel saw that he was in better health and spirits than at any time during the past ten years. Each week saw a group of excited friends at the Hermitage, showing letters from their friends indicating that if Andrew would run for the Presidency, Pennsylvania would go for Jackson; or New York would; or he need only appear in Boston to assure himself of Massachusetts. But if these presidential handicappers made any impression on Andrew, she could find no evidence of it. "I've never been happier than during this quiet year, being a gentleman planter," he told Rachel. To a niece in Alabama, Rachel wrote:

> I hope they will leave Mr. Jackson alone. He is not well and never will be unless they allow him to rest. He has done his share for the country. In this as in all else, I can only say, the Lord's will be done. But I hope he may not be called again to the strife and empty honors of public place.

IT WOULD have been difficult for Rachel to tell the exact moment at which Andrew began to grow restless again. Was it when the Tennessee legislature nominated their favorite son for the Presidency in July of 1822? Was it the information that Monroe was supporting Jackson's old enemy, Crawford? Was it the fact that Henry Clay was rapidly gaining adherents, the disconcerting news that the man Andrew was backing for the post, John Quincy Adams, was losing ground?

One fateful day, everything came to a head. John Overton rode out to the Hermitage posthaste to say that Jackson's can-

462

didate for Senator seemed certain to be defeated. Andrew himself must run for Senator if he were to take a leading role in the forthcoming presidential campaign. Listening to the words that would decide their future, Rachel found herself unable to breathe. Andrew seemed to sense her emotion; he turned to gaze at her. After a moment, he murmured, "Excuse me, I wish to talk to my wife."

He came to her side, put his hand under her arm and lifted her from the chair. They left Andrew's office, went through the hall and into the parlor. He closed the door behind them.

They stood in the center of the room facing each other, their eyes boring deep. Rachel knew that she must find out what, under the layers of wounds, ambitions, accomplishments and failures, Andrew really, deeply, wanted. He grinned at her sheepishly.

"It's not honor I seek in public office, my dear," he said, as if he read her thought. "I've had all of that any man could want. It's the chance for service that intrigues me. I'd like to fight for this country every minute of the day, just as hard as I fought at New Orleans."

"And just as well, too . . . If you are sure that is the thing you want, Andrew, then you must do everything in your power to achieve it."

He opened his arms to her and they clung to each other.

"And what of you, Rachel? What of the consequences?"

She left his side, walked over to the big front window, her head lowered. This could be the most important decision of her life, for the followers of Crawford and Clay would not hesitate to dig up the old, painful stories as a weapon against Andrew Jackson. The presidential campaign would be bitter indeed.

Our lives have come full circle, she thought. We have come through all these years and all this suffering only to be caught in the identical predicament at the end of our lives that we were in in the beginning.

She walked to her husband, who had been standing awkwardly in the center of the room, trying not to intrude upon her decision. She lifted up her face to be kissed, then said quietly:

"I will accept the consequences."

464

THE LONG SEPARATION after Andrew had been elected to the Senate and gone to Washington was not as dreary as earlier ones had been. The house was filled with Rachel's young nieces: there were seldom fewer than five or six of them visiting at one time and that meant their admirers and suitors as well. The evenings and weekends were gay with music and laughter. It seemed to Rachel that she was never alone; she did not discover until spring that this was no accident, but rather an express order from Andrew in Washington to his nephew, Andy Donelson: "Keep your aunt's spirits up."

After Christmas, Rachel was able to fulfill a wish she had been nurturing for several years: to have a little church right on the Hermitage, where their relatives and friends could come on Sunday mornings for services and one night a week for a good bout of preaching. The building of the church and the hiring of a pastor absorbed most of her energies over the winter.

One day late in March she perceived through a subtle change in the tone and manner of her family that something untoward had happened. She asked young Andy to tell her what it was.

"It is not important, Aunt Rachel: just an annoying thing that's happened. Uncle Andrew says that the people behind Crawford are growing desperate because they see his strength waning and so they are trying to arouse Uncle's anger." He hesitated, but there was no turning away from the command in her eyes. "John Overton has received a letter from Senator John Eaton asking for detailed information and proof about your marriage . . . so they can put an end to some of the rumors around Washington."

Rachel sat down on a nearby bench. This still had power to hurt; she seemed unable to get enough air into her lungs. And there was a sharp pain about her heart. Andy got her some water, self-reproaches tumbling from his lips.

"No, Andy; it's better that I should know. Could you help me upstairs?"

She remained in bed for two days, provoked with herself for feeling ill. Her troubles had always worked themselves out, given time enough. This one would, too.

ANDREW RETURNED IN mid-June with the news that they would go to Washington for the election. He looked well, his skin bronzed, his eyes clear and peaceable. Rachel was delighted to find that for the first time politics was agreeing with him.

"According to our best reports," he told Rachel, "the presidential vote is going to be split between Adams, Clay, Crawford and myself. I doubt if any one of us will get a majority of the electoral votes. The election will therefore be thrown into the House of Representatives for decision."

"What do you intend to do about the election?"

"Remain home and watch it. My advisers want me to attend musters and barbecues to 'meet the people.' They say it's a new form of campaigning, because this is the first time the President is going to be elected by the voters instead of the Congress. But I'm not going."

Each week brought its important development. John Calhoun decided to content himself with the Vice-Presidency, and threw his weight behind Andrew; William

467

Crawford suffered a paralytic stroke and some of his supporters were talking of shifting to Jackson. Andrew's friends had already moved them into the White House, including even the usually level-headed John Overton.

They left for Washington on November 7, 1824, accompanied by Rachel's niece Emily Donelson, and just one month later crossed the bridge which led into Washington from Virginia. They made their way up a dirt road called Pennsylvania Avenue. When they passed the White House Rachel said to Emily, "That's where Mr. and Mrs. Monroe live." Emily leaned out the window, gazing rapturously at the structure.

At their hotel, the Franklin House, Rachel and Andrew had a comfortable suite of bedroom and parlor. Their rooms were soon crowded with a host of neighbors from Tennessee, officers from the Creek and British wars, the ever-growing clique of President-makers and the many eastern friends Andrew had made since his first trip to Congress in 1796. But by the second afternoon, Rachel realized that their callers were men only. No

468

woman had so much as left her card. Though there was a written invitation from President and Mrs. Monroe to a reception at the White House, Washington society, dominated by the wives of the highest officials, was pointedly staying away.

That evening when Rachel went in to bid Emily good night she found her niece in tears. At her feet she saw a newspaper, obviously crumpled in anger. She picked it up and saw that it was from the Raleigh *Register*. The offending article read:

> I make a solemn appeal to the reflecting part of the community, and beg of them to ponder well before they place their ballots in the box, how they can justify it to themselves and posterity to place such a woman as Mrs. Jackson at the head of the female society of the United States.

Emily sought refuge in her aunt's arms. "Oh, Aunt Rachel, they're saying the most terrible things about us: that we are vulgar, ignorant and awkward frontierswomen without breeding or decorum. But they have never even met us!"

Rachel held Emily at arm's length.

"Wipe your eyes, child. This is all part of what your uncle would call the 'consequences of politics.' "

THE wives of two Senators finally called and at once took a liking to Rachel. That, and Elizabeth Monroe's party for them at the White House, broke the social ice. Soon Rachel and Andrew had to turn down hundreds of invitations, content to remain in their hotel sitting room before the fire, receiving a few intimates.

On December 16, the final election results reached Washington. Andrew had the largest popular vote, 152,901, with Adams coming in second, with 114,023; Clay was third, and Crawford fourth.

In the electoral votes by states Andrew had a decisive lead also: 99 to Adams' 84, with Crawford showing a surprising 41 to Clay's 34. Because no candidate had achieved a majority, the election would go into the House. There were rumors to the effect that Clay had offered to throw his votes to Adams in return for an appointment as Secretary of State. Andrew, however, did not take the rumors seriously.

470

"Mr. Adams is an honest man. He would not engage in a corrupt bargain. If he gets the majority of votes in the House, I will be content. He was my first choice, anyway."

On February 9, the day of decision in the House of Representatives, snow fell heavily. The first course of dinner had just been set on their parlor table when the news came in: Mr. Adams had been elected on the first count! By prodigious efforts and brilliant maneuvering Henry Clay, single-handed, had swung Kentucky, Ohio and Missouri behind Adams.

Then on February 14, President-elect Adams offered the post of Secretary of State to Henry Clay. All hell broke loose, in Washington and across the nation . . . and particularly in the Jacksons' two rooms in the Franklin House. People came and went continually, all passionately protesting against what now appeared to have been a swap of votes for office.

Every ounce of Andrew's calm and acceptance vanished. Rachel knew that nothing in his career had ever made him so utterly determined to avenge a wrong.

As he stood in the far corner of the room surrounded by his most ardent supporters, she heard him cry:

"So the Judas of the West has closed the contract and will receive the 30 pieces of silver? The end will be the same. Was there ever witnessed such a barefaced corruption before?"

As their carriage left Washington for Tennessee three weeks later, Rachel felt Andrew stiffen at her side. He turned in his seat, gazing long and hard at the Capitol. In his expression she saw the unshatterable resolve she knew so well.

He turned his face to hers.

"We'll be back."

CHAPTER 15

THEIR journey home was more like a triumphal procession than the return of a defeated candidate. The crowds that assembled in every town to greet Andrew were tremendous; at Louisville, in Clay's home state of Kentucky, they attended a banquet where toasts were drunk to General Jackson as the next President of the United States. The dominating passion was hatred of Adams and Clay, and the

conviction that the will of the people had been thwarted.

In October of 1825 the Tennessee legislature formally nominated Andrew Jackson for the Presidency in 1828. He persuaded Rachel to accompany him to the capital at Murfreesboro where he accepted the nomination and officially resigned his seat in the Senate. Then they swung west to visit Jane. The hurtleberries were still abundant in the swamps, and the sloes, serviceberries and grapes were heavy on the vines. Jane's figure was still trim, her hair had lost little of its blond light and her eyes were penetratingly clear. The two sisters sat before the fire talking nostalgically of the past, exclaiming at the vast extent of the Donelson clan throughout Tennessee, Kentucky, Mississippi and Louisiana.

But when the Jacksons passed through Nashville on the way home they found the town abuzz: a seedy little man by the name of Day had spent the past few days there asking endless questions about the Jackson marriage, and displaying a transcript of the Robards' divorce records from Harrodsburg. On their return to the Hermitage John Overton told them he believed the material would be used to make Andrew withdraw from the race.

Rachel went upstairs, undressed, got into bed and pulled the covers over her head. Here they were, still three years away from the election of 1828, and already some member of the opposition had sought her out as a potential weapon.

There was only one way to avoid the torment: go to Andrew and say, I've made a mistake. I thought I could take the consequences, but I can't. I haven't the moral strength. You must release me. I've been a good and faithful wife to you for nearly 40 years. We're going on 59. You know that I love you dearly. I know that you love me. Then, Andrew, sacrifice this last campaign. This is no longer an ordinary political contest; it is war. Surely if, to become

President, you had to place me on the battlefield, you would refuse?

But several hours later, when Andrew came up to bed, she said nothing. Hadn't they undergone countless attacks since their difficulties in 1793; and hadn't they always managed to survive them?

EVEN as admirers thronged the house, a pamphlet reached the Hermitage, printed in East Tennessee:

> Andrew Jackson spent the prime of his life in gambling; and to cap it all tore from a husband the wife of his bosom. . . .
>
> General Jackson has admitted that he boarded at old Mrs. Donelson's and that Robards became jealous of him, but he omits the cause of that jealousy . . . that Robards surprised Jackson and his wife exchanging most delicious kisses.

Rachel's first reaction was one of shame: shame that this vulgar assault should have sprung from her home state. But she was determined to be calm. She burned her copy of the scurrilous lines, resolutely putting them out of her mind. Andrew grew silent and grim; no word of the pamphlet passed between them. It would be allowed to die.

But they had underestimated the power of the printed word. Shortly after, the editor of a Cincinnati newspaper, emboldened by the fact that he now had a published precedent, wrote an article for his paper based on the East Tennessee pamphlet, adding to it the stories collected by Mr. Day. The clipping was sent to Rachel anonymously through the mail:

> If the President be a married man, his wife must share the distinction of the station he occupies. Her qualifications for the station, her character, and standing must all be drawn out, and made subjects of remark. If she be weak and vulgar she cannot escape becoming a theme for ridicule, a portion of which, and its consequent contempt, must attach to her husband.
>
> Wherever Jackson was known in years past public rumor circulated suspicions as to the correctness of his matrimonial alliance. . . . It was no case of possible indiscretion. On the contrary . . . it was an accusation of gross adultery, in which outrage upon the rights of the husband was urged against General Jackson, and deser-

476

tion from her husband to the arms of a paramour, was charged against the wife.

In September 1793, a jury, after hearing proof, declared . . . that Mrs. Robards was guilty of adultery. Ought a convicted adulteress, and her paramour husband, to be placed in the highest offices?

Rachel's arms fell wearily to her sides. The Cincinnati newspaper dropped to the floor. There it was at last, in print, the dread and awful word that had pursued her all of her married life, that had changed her from a gay and happy young woman into a wounded prisoner within her own walls:

Adulteress.

SHE did not hear Andrew come into the room and stand behind her. When his hand touched her shoulder she turned, saw that his face was ashen. He held in his hand a copy of the same publication.

"Do you know that this is the most difficult task of my life, to be forced to sit here, impotent, while they call you foul names, debase our love and our marriage? I've never wanted anything so much in my life as to go to Cincinnati and shoot that slimy creature in his tracks. When I realize that I let myself get into a position where, no matter what they say about you, I cannot rise up in your defense—"

He stopped, sat in silence for a moment, his misery hovering about him like a cloak. Then he drew a letter from his pocket. "This has just arrived from my campaign director. Listen to what he says: 'All you have to do is remain quietly at the Hermitage and the people will sweep you into office.' "

He rose, went to the window and stared out moodily, his back to her.

". . . sweep you into office." He turned around abruptly. "I saw it as a chance for service. There's so much I thought I could contribute to the growth of our country. But now that they're crucifying you . . . is it worth it?"

To herself she murmured, It's too late for this kind of questioning. We are committed, like soldiers, to this battle.

At least Rachel and Andrew did not stand alone now. Taking the Cincinnati attack on a Tennessee woman as a personal affront, the members of the Culture

Club, now the Nashville Ladies Club, went out of their way to express their vote of confidence. Many letters came to the Hermitage; three of the Club ladies came to call. By way of further buttressing their defenses a mass meeting was called by Andrew's closest friends at the Nashville courthouse. They pledged their support to the Jacksons, resolving:

"To detect and arrest falsehood and calumny by the publication of truth."

A committee of 18 of the most respected citizens of the state, headed by John Overton, was set up to examine all materials relative to the relationship and marriages of Rachel and Andrew Jackson.

The full report of the Overton committee was published in the *United States Telegraph* on June 22, 1827, and widely reproduced throughout the country. Reluctant as Rachel had been to expose the details of her marriages to the eyes of thousands of strangers who had known nothing about them before, she found that the report had an immediate and salutary effect. Letters came to the Hermitage from Washington, Philadelphia, New York and New Orleans offering congratulations "on the vindication of your innocence," and assuring her of continued friendship.

RACHEL found herself living in two worlds. The first was the normal routine of her everyday life. Most of it was pleasant: the dining table she had bought in New Orleans was always set for its full capacity of 30 dinner guests. All roads from all directions appeared to lead through the Hermitage now, and all faces there turned to Andrew in admiration and friendship. But there was a second world that engulfed her at times like a black cloud, a politicking world filled with hysteria and insanity, with which she found herself unable to cope. There was no tiny segment of her husband's life that was left unraked: he had tried to kill Governor Sevier in a public brawl, had murdered Charles Dickinson in cold blood, had conspired with Aaron Burr to destroy the Union, had fought the Battle of New Orleans stupidly, set himself up as a military dictator. . . .

There was no respite. Each week saw

deadlier charges hurled, and the deadliest came back to the same theme: Rachel Jackson. Andrew Jackson had "torn her from her nuptial couch and seduced her"; they had "indulged their unbridled appetites" while she was married to Robards; she had not gone downriver with Colonel Stark and his wife, but had followed in a second boat on which she and Andrew had lived alone. Her relations with Andrew had been a "standing jest for nearly 30 years"; she was even today an adulteress, for there never had been any marriage performed between Rachel and Andrew Jackson.

The attack was so virulent that the walls of the Hermitage were not thick enough to hold it out. It was mixed in the air she breathed and the food she ate; at night when she went upstairs while Andrew remained below at his desk frantically writing hundreds of letters of defense and justification during the dark hours, she lay rigidly in bed, every bone and muscle in her body aching, her eyes wide and staring, hearing the word reverberate hollowly about the room, encompassing her, possessing her.

Adulteress . . . Adulteress . . . ADUL-
TERESS . . .

The election approached; the tension
mounted. The pro-Adams press joined the
hunt, referring to her as "the woman they
call Mrs. Jackson." Crude caricatures
showed her as an ignorant backwoodswoman; ribald songs were chanted
about her in the streets of big cities;
obscene poems were printed by the
thousands.

When Rachel was the most soul-sick
she went for comfort to her little Hermitage chapel. She had been praying for a
cessation of the attacks; now her clergyman taught her that instead of praying for
herself she should be praying for her tra-
ducers, for they were the ones who would
need her prayers on Judgment Day. That
night she knelt by the side of the bed and
prayed:

"Forgive them, O Lord, for they know
not what they do."

SUMMER came on. Hundreds of test
ballots were taken throughout the land.
In most, Andrew emerged triumphant by
landslide proportions. Finally, on Novem-

ber 24, the governor of Tennessee rode up to the Hermitage in great excitement. Rachel received him in the parlor. His face was shining. He bowed, kissed Rachel's hand, exclaimed: "I would let no one else bring the news. I wanted to be the first to tell you. . . . Andrew Jackson has been elected President of the United States."

It was over. She had survived. They were safe at last. She stood before the governor in silence, hearing only the tremendous pounding of her own heart, which felt as though it would burst through her chest. When Andrew came into the room she put her arms about his neck and kissed him.

Nashville went wild with joy. A huge celebration banquet was planned for December 23. It seemed to Rachel as though the entire Cumberland Valley came to the front door of the Hermitage to shake Andrew's hand and then hers. The Nashville Ladies Club was having a beautiful inauguration wardrobe prepared for her. Yet she observed that there was not much of rejoicing or exultation in Andrew. He would become

Chief Executive of a torn, almost shattered country, with whole classes of its society loathing him, predicting that the day he took office would mark the end of the great American Republic. She found herself pitying Andrew for the terrifying task that lay ahead.

There was much work to be done before they moved to Washington. December was hectic; Rachel found herself growing increasingly tired and she called the family physician, who bled her, relieving the pressure. Several times when she was supposed to go to Nashville for fittings or to buy what they needed for their trip she could not summon the energy to get out of bed. The months of anguish had taken their toll.

On Monday, December 17, she received an urgent message from her old seamstress, Sarah Bentley, now in Nashville: if she did not come in at once for the final fitting on her inaugural dress she could not possibly have it ready by the time she left for Washington. Digging deep into her reserves, Rachel dressed and was driven in the carriage to Nashville.

The fittings were long and exhausting, for Sarah was determined that her gowns should reflect credit on Tennessee. When they were finished, Rachel said:

"Sarah, when my boy comes for me, please tell him I will be at the Nashville Inn; I'll rest there till it's time to go home."

She walked a block down the street, entered the inn, found the back parlor deserted at this hour, and with a sigh of relief sank into a comfortable chair in a hidden corner.

She had fallen into a half sleep when fragments of conversation from the next parlor awakened her. Two women were talking, discussing the election and the imminent departure of the Jacksons. The one with the deeper voice asked what would become of the country now that the lowest and most ignorant class of society had come into power, with a drinking, gambling bully and murderer sitting in the White House. The higher voice said she shuddered to think what Washington's international society would make of this dumpy, illiterate backwoodswoman who was now to become First Lady of the Land.

"Lady?" exclaimed the first. "How can you call her a lady? It's just as the newspapers kept asking: shall there be a *whore* in the White House?"

She was totally unprepared. A sharp, knifelike stab of almost unendurable pain went through her heart and down her left arm. She sagged. Had she thought it was over, now that Andrew had reached the top? It would never, never be over!

To her lips came a prayer:

No, no, dear God, not here . . . in a strange hotel parlor. Please let me get home to my own roof . . . my own bed.

With an intense effort she dragged herself to her feet, walked stiffly to the entrance.

Her carriage was waiting. The boy helped her in. She leaned back against the cushions. Her left arm felt useless . . . paralyzed. Her head was heavy, her thoughts cloudy. There was only one determination remaining: to hold on until she got back to the Hermitage.

ANDREW was completely distraught. He sat by her bed clasping her hand in his, unable to speak. The local doctor bled her at once, saying to Andrew: "Spasmodic affection . . . irregular action of heart. . . ." The family doctor found that the first bleeding had not caused an abatement of the symptoms, and bled her again. At night he bled her a third time, and now all her pain seemed to vanish. Andrew placed a pillow behind her and raised her a little in the bed, then seated himself in a chair beside her.

She did not know how much time passed; at least twice it was night, then twice it was day. Andrew never left her side. Dimly she heard the doctors telling him that he must get some sleep or he would collapse: there was the celebration banquet in Nashville the next day which he absolutely must attend.

She raised herself slightly and managed a little smile. She felt no pain; in fact she could not feel her body at all.

"Andrew, you must prepare to go to Washington without me. I'll follow in a few weeks, as soon as I am strong enough."

"No! I won't go without you! I can wait. I have time to wait. We've endured so much: we can conquer this, too. I'll not set foot out of this house until you are able to stand by my side. . . ."

She took his thin, seamed face in her hands, remembering the first time she had seen him, when he had knocked on the door of the Donelson stockade and she had stood smiling as she gazed at the bushy red hair, the piercing blue eyes. His hair was snow-white now, his lips taut, his brow and cheeks deeply furrowed. But how richly his life had been fulfilled; and in the doing, how richly it had fulfilled hers!

She kissed him on the forehead, murmured:

"Everything's all right. I'm better now. Lift me into the chair by the fire and then you go to bed and get some sleep."

He tucked her in the chair, blankets and all, and kissed her good night. She watched him go out the door, across the hall to the guest bedroom.

She sat watching the flames light up the fireplace and the room for a time . . . then suddenly felt herself slipping. . . .

She fell. In the distance she heard the sound of running feet. Someone picked her up. Was it . . . ? Yes, it was Andrew.

That was good. That was the way it should be.

With the last of her consciousness she felt herself put back into bed. She felt Andrew's tearstained cheek on hers, heard him say over and over:

"I love you, I love you."

Somewhere within herself, at a great receding distance, she smiled. And then she knew nothing more.

HE WALKED up Pennsylvania Avenue to the Capitol. Cannons boomed, the thousands of people lining the avenue cheered lustily; he heard neither. He made his way to a roped-off portico where Chief Justice Marshall administered the oath while the enormous assemblage roared its approval. His mind was back at the Hermitage; he had told Rachel she would be by his side when he took this oath of office, but she lay buried in her beloved garden in the Cumberland Valley. The Reverend Hume, at the funeral service, had said, "The righteous shall be in everlasting remembrance." And so it would be.

He mounted his horse and rode to the White House. Long tables had been set up in the East Room, laden with orange punch, ice cream and cakes. This was to be his first reception; yet he hated the thought of it.

Protocol had dictated who might be invited: the highest-ranking members of Washington society—the friends of John Quincy Adams and Henry Clay, who had branded him an ignoramus, a bully, a liar, a revolutionist who would destroy the Republic. The White House and the East Room would be filled with the bejeweled women and the socially and politically important men who had despised his wife, who had ended by murdering his beloved Rachel. These were the people he must receive!

But he had reckoned without the mob of his followers who had come to Washington from every part of the Union to witness his inauguration. They poured down Pennsylvania Avenue, streamed through the gates of the White House, fought their way into the East Room, devoured the ice cream and cakes and orange punch. They climbed on the furniture to catch a glimpse of Andrew, soiling the damask chairs with their muddy boots, staining the carpets, breaking glasses and china, shouting and surging and pushing, all thousands of them, wanting to reach Andrew, to embrace him.

He stood at the back of the room, imprisoned, yet feeling the first glint of happiness since Rachel's death. These were the people; they had stood by him. They had loved Rachel; they had vindicated her. For that, he loved them, and would fight for them the rest of his days.

A Word from the Author

The President's Lady is a biographical novel; it differs from a historical novel in that it does not introduce fictional characters against a background of history, but instead tells the story through the actual people who lived it. The history found within its pages is as authentic and documented as several years of intensive research can make it. Some hundred and fifty volumes, including old and rare books from all over America, were actually used in the construction of this novel.

The interpretations of character are of course my own, and much of the dialogue had to be re-created. But every effort was made to create it on the basis of recorded conversations. The language of the day was more flowery than our own; I have attempted to tell the story in a simpler English, but I have striven constantly to make certain that the difference is one of words, and never of thought, feeling or meaning.

—Irving Stone

ABOUT THE AUTHOR

Irving Stone had been an economics instructor at universities in his native California for several years when, in 1926, his desire to become a writer eclipsed his interest in obtaining a doctorate. He left for Paris to write plays while supporting himself with penny-a-word detective stories.

Ultimately Stone adopted detective-like methods to forge his own new genre, the biographical novel. His *Lust for Life*, a portrait of Vincent van Gogh, appeared in 1934 to great acclaim. Many best sellers followed, among them *The Agony and the Ecstasy*, about Michelangelo. As the Los Angeles *Times* has said, Stone's meticulously researched works succeed in "vividly restoring not only the era and the scene but most of all the person."

ACKNOWLEDGMENTS

Page 4: Margaret Bourke-White, *Life* magazine © Time Inc.

Page 5, 186: illustrations by Sheilah Beckett.

Page 71: The Keystone Collection, London.

Pages 111 (top), 112 (bottom): The Bettmann Archive.

Pages 111 (bottom), 113 (bottom): The Government of India.

Page 112 (top): The Press Association Limited, London.

Page 113 (top): AP/Wide World Photos.

Page 155: Werner Bischof/Magnum Photos, New York.

Pages 188–189, 209, 226, 251, 264, 277, 360, 379, 396–397, 417, 436–437, 454, 473: illustrations by Lealand L. Gustavson.

ABOUT THE PUBLISHER

Reader's Digest Fund for the Blind, Inc., is a New York not-for-profit corporation established in 1955 by DeWitt Wallace, co-founder of Reader's Digest. Its primary purpose is to publish easy-to-read material of excellent quality for the visually impaired. Its publications include the Large-Type Edition of *Reader's Digest*, the Large-Type Reader, Reader's Digest Great Biographies in Large Type, and the Large-Type Bible. If you would like more information about the fund, write to: Reader's Digest Fund for the Blind, Inc., Pleasantville, New York 10570.